A Contemporary Introduction to Thomistic Metaphysics

A Contemporary Introduction to Thomistic Metaphysics

Michael Gorman

The Catholic University of America Press
Washington, D.C.

Copyright © 2024
The Catholic University of America Press
All rights reserved

The paper used in this publication meets the minimum requirements of American National Standards for Information Science—Permanence of Paper for Printed Library Materials, ANSI Z39.48-1992.

∞

Cataloging-in-Publication Data is available from the Library of Congress

ISBN: 978-0-8132-3733-6
eISBN: 978-0-8132-3734-3

This book is dedicated to the memory of
Dom Luke Patton, OSB

Contents

List of Tables and Figures x

Prefatory Remarks for Readers of Various Kinds xi

Acknowledgments xiii

Introduction 1
   0.1 An Introduction to This *Introduction* 1
   0.2 What Is Philosophy? 5
   0.3 What Is Metaphysics? 8
   0.4 A Substance-Centered Metaphysics 14
   0.5 Coming Attractions 15

1 Basic Beings and Their Features 19
   1.1 First Look at Substance 19
   1.2 Essential and Accidental Features of Substances 24
   1.3 Additional Thoughts on Features; Some Remarks
         on Language 28
   1.4 The Uniqueness of Essence 31
   1.5 The Partial Normativity of (Some?) Essences 33
   1.6 Substance-Centeredness vs. Substance-Exclusiveness . . . 35
   1.7 Analogy 38

2 Change 41
   2.1 Change as a Topic in Metaphysics 41
   2.2 Wholes through Time or Temporal Parts? 41
   2.3 Accidental and Substantial Change 44
   2.4 Change and Identity 47
   2.5 Form, Matter, Subject, Privation, Actualization 50
   2.6 A Bit More on Change and Succession 54

3 Parts 57
   3.1 Kinds of Parts 57
   3.2 Physical Parts 57
   3.3 Features and Substrates as Parts 69

	3.3.1 Four Big Theories	71
	3.3.2 Problems with the Four Big Theories	74
	3.3.3 A More Thomistic Way of Thinking about Features and Feature-Bearers	81
3.4	Form and Matter as Parts	89
3.5	Essence and Existence as Parts	92
3.6	Some Summary Thoughts on Parts of Substances	94

4 Causes 97
    4.1 Causes in Cinematic and Snapshot Perspective 97
    4.2 Which Items Make Things Happen? 98
    4.3 Some Inadequate Understandings of the Movie Version . 98
    4.4 A Better Way of Talking about Movie Causation 101
    4.5 Onward to Snapshot Causation 108
    4.6 Summary 110

5 Universals and Particulars 113
    5.1 Universals and the One over Many Problem 113
    5.2 Universals and a Linguistic Argument 127
    5.3 A Hybrid Position Worth Considering 130
    5.4 The Problem(s) of Individuation 131
    5.5 Could Aquinas Be a Nominalist? 133
    5.6 A Tentative Conclusion 135

6 The Way Things Might Have Been 137
    6.1 Introduction to the Idea of Possible Worlds 137
    6.2 What Are Possible Worlds? 146
    6.3 Modality without Possible Worlds 152
    6.4 From Possibility to God 155

7 Thoughts about Everything 159
    7.1 Introduction 159
    7.2 Categories 159
        7.2.1 What Metaphysical Categories Are 160
        7.2.2 Why Being Is Not a Category or Genus 163
        7.2.3 So Which Are the Categories? 167
        7.2.4 A Brief Digression on Relations 173
        7.2.5 A Brief Remark on Categories and Universals .. 175
        7.2.6 De-Reifying Categories 176

    7.3   Transcendentals 176
          7.3.1   The Multiplicity of the Transcendentals 178
          7.3.2   A List of Transcendentals 179
          7.3.3   Goodness (and Beauty) 182
    7.4   Final Remarks on Categories and Transcendentals 186

8 To the Edge of Metaphysics ... and Beyond! 187
    8.1   God and Metaphysics 187
    8.2   Arguments for God's Existence 188
    8.3   Why Sourced Beings Can't Be the Whole Story 191
    8.4   From Small Conclusions to the Start of Something Big . 193
    8.5   God's Essence and Existence 195
    8.6   God's Perfection 197
    8.7   God's Uniqueness 198
    8.8   God's Perfections and How Creatures Participate
          in Them 198
    8.9   God's Ubiquity 202
    8.10 Relations between God and the World 204
    8.11 Talking and Thinking about God 204
    8.12 A Few Final Thoughts on God and Metaphysics 210

9 Metaphysics outside Normal Operating Conditions 213
    9.1   Initial Thoughts on Metaphysics and Theology 213
    9.2   Incarnation 216
    9.3   Transubstantiation 224
    9.4   Comparisons between the Assumed Human Nature
          and the Orphaned Accidents 226
    9.5   Summary Thoughts on Metaphysics and Theology 227

10 Not the Conclusion 231

Recommended Readings 233

Bibliography 235

Index 241

List of Tables and Figures

Table 2-1	Types of Change	47
Table 3-1	Four Theories of Substance	73
Table 5-1	Theories of Universals	124
Figure 6-1	First Way of Laying Out the Modal Distinctions	142
Table 6-1	Second Way of Laying Out the Modal Distinctions	142
Figure 6-2	Third Way of Laying Out the Modal Distinctions	143
Table 6-2	Fourth Way of Laying Out the Modal Distinctions	143
Table 7-1	Table of Classes	160
Table 7-2	Broader Table of Classes	162
Table 7-3	Ten Aristotelian Categories	172

Prefatory Remarks for Readers of Various Kinds

IN THIS LITTLE PREFACE, I would like to say a few words to different kinds of reader: to instructors who might be thinking of assigning this book to students, but first, to everyone else.

If you are fairly new to philosophy, this book has been written with you in mind. I do not assume that you know anything about metaphysics, or even that you know anything about philosophy at all. I try to explain even the most basic points, and I try to do so in non-technical language; when I do use technical language, I try to explain it. In numerous places, I deliberately avoid going into a lot of detail, on the theory that sometimes, an elaborate account is less helpful than a simple one (especially for beginners).

If it's the first philosophy book you read, I certainly hope it won't be the last. I hope it leads you on to reading books that go into more depth. So start here, but don't stop here.

Beginners are not the only readers I have in mind. More advanced readers, even if they already know a lot of what is in here, might find it interesting to see how I organize the material and formulate familiar concepts. And I do take stands on controversial issues (even if I do not always defend my stands in detail, in the way I would if writing a regular professional monograph). To give a sneak preview for such readers: this book presents a Thomistically-inspired account of central themes in metaphysics, one that strives (perhaps more than Thomists usually do) to put the notion of substance front and center, and thereby to give anti-reifying and even deflationary accounts of, for example, the internal principles of substances, of universals, and of possible worlds.

Now let me say a few things to professional colleagues who may be considering this book as something to assign to students.

Because the book is at pains to prioritize the notion of substance, it is not organized in the way that standard metaphysics textbooks these days usually are. I have, however, written the various chapters in such a way as to allow for other orders of presentation: The chapters themselves are meant to be relatively self-standing, and ample cross-references are provided when what is said in one place has implications for things said elsewhere. In short, although the book is presumably most easily understood when read from front to back, this is by no means the only fruitful way to read it (or assign it). Using the book in a course doesn't require that the course be organized in the way the book is organized.

Another point worth mentioning is this. The text is meant to be readable by beginners without much explication from an instructor, in a way that should make it suitable for use as complementary material in a course focused on primary texts. So, for example, a course unit on universals could assign various classic readings but then also chapter five, in such a way that less class time would need to be spent on setting up the issues, with the result that more class time could be spent investigating the primary sources in detail.

Acknowledgments

FOR THE PAST DECADE OR SO, I have been teaching an honors metaphysics course at The Catholic University of America in Washington, DC. This book grows out of that experience. I assigned a preliminary draft as course reading in the Spring 2020 semester, and a preliminary draft of a much different version in the Spring 2021 semester. I am grateful to my students for their cheerful encouragement and feedback.

Some of the topics discussed here have come up in graduate courses I have taught over the years, and I am grateful to the students in those courses, especially when they pushed back against various ideas I was trying out. Some can now say, "At last, he's come around!" Even those who have not (yet) convinced me of their views at least have helped me get my thoughts in better order.

Part of the difficulty of writing a book like this is finding a balance between saying something mainstream, which is important for a textbook, and saying something interesting, at risk of being merely idiosyncratic. I'm grateful to Patrick Toner and Andrew Jaeger for encouragement not to shrink from the path that seemed best to me.

After generously reading the whole manuscript as it existed in the Fall of 2021, and sending me excellent and extensive comments, W. Matthews Grant gave it a test-drive in a course he taught at the University of St. Thomas in St. Paul in the spring semester of 2022 and sent along even more comments. I have made many changes, both small and large, in response. If I have failed to learn enough from what he said, it isn't through lack of gratitude.

After incorporating Grant's comments, I submitted the book to the Press, whereupon it was handed over to a pair of anonymous referees, who made extensive comments which have saved me from not a few glitches and even embarrassments. After handing in their reports, they revealed their identities to me, and so I would like to thank Timothy Pawl and Patrick Toner for their generous and excellent work.

In the spring semester of 2023, Timothy Pawl test-drove an expanded version of the text in a class he was teaching at the University of St. Thomas in St. Paul. I am grateful to the students for their feedback, both in writing and during a very fun online session at the end of the semester.

I spent a decade trying to make up my mind about virtual presence, and then it all fell together during a half-hour conversation with Anselm Mueller in Chicago. I am grateful to him both for his generosity and for his pressure.

I would like to thank Matthew Advent, my graduate assistant in 2019–2020, and Miriam Pritschet, my graduate assistant in 2020–2021, for various forms of assistance, including comments on a number of chapters. I would like to thank Daniel Siciliano, my graduate assistant in 2022–2023, for his careful work on readying the final version of the manuscript. I would like to thank Matthew McShurley, my graduate assistant in 2023–2024, for his extensive and invaluable help in preparing the index.

Some of the material in chapter nine appeared first in "The Interaction of Philosophy and Theology in Aquinas's Christology," *New Blackfriars* 104, no. 1109 (2023): 23–38. My reuse of it here falls under the journal's general permission guidelines, but that's no reason not to express my thanks.

I am grateful to The Catholic University of America for granting me sabbatical leave in the spring semester of 2022, which made it much easier to actually get the thing done.

I would also like, more particularly, to express my gratitude to my colleagues in the School of Philosophy at The Catholic University of America. Their intellectual seriousness and collegiality make academic life worthwhile. While our scholarly fellowship really is a whole with emergent properties, I must here single out Greg Doolan for calling me at home on a Friday morning at 8:15 to help me through a crisis over the problem of whether being is a genus.

I would like to thank everyone at The Catholic University of America Press for their creative hard work, patience, and tolerance.

I would like to thank my wife and children for constituting the best family a professional academic could want. I would go on, but that would be gloating.

This book is dedicated to the memory of Dom Luke Patton, OSB, who got it all started by rashly asking me to make a presentation on Descartes in a tenth-grade history class.

Introduction

0.1 An Introduction to This *Introduction*

THIS BOOK IS AN INTRODUCTION to metaphysics. An *intro-duction* is supposed to *lead you into* the subject and give you enough knowledge of the territory that you can begin to explore it on your own. But there are a number of different ways to give an introduction to metaphysics.

One kind of introduction presents things almost exclusively from a single point of view, without much discussion of competing ways of thinking about the issues; if competing viewpoints come up for discussion, the discussion doesn't last long, because the competing views are not treated in depth. A good book of this type is Joseph Owens's *An Elementary Christian Metaphysics*.[1]

Very different is the sort of introduction that presents many views more or less as equals. Even if at times we can guess the author's preferences, overall what we get is a variety of different viewpoints, and that's all. A good book of this type is Loux and Crisp's *Metaphysics: A Contemporary Introduction*.[2]

Both of these kinds of book can be valuable, but each comes with a certain disadvantage. The first can give the impression that philosophy is easier than it really is. It can give the impression that all philosophical theories but one can be dismissed with little analysis, as if the truth in philosophy were quite easy to find. The second kind of introduction can give the impression that philosophy isn't really a quest for knowledge, but instead a kind of comparative playing with ideas, intellectual window-shopping, web-surfing without serious intent. If the first kind of introduction seems to arrive at its conclusions too easily, the second kind seems never to arrive anywhere at all.

---

1. Joseph Owens, *An Elementary Christian Metaphysics* (Houston: Center for Thomistic Studies, 1985).

2. Michael J. Loux and Thomas M. Crisp, *Metaphysics: A Contemporary Introduction*, Fourth edition (London; New York: Routledge, Taylor & Francis, 2017).

There's a third kind of introduction, which we can call an "opinionated" one, after the title of a good book by David Armstrong: *Universals: An Opinionated Introduction*.³ In contrast with the first kind of introduction, a book like this gives more detailed discussion of a wide range of views; in contrast with the second kind of introduction, it makes clear which views it thinks are best. A book like this, done well, can do justice both to the complexity of philosophy and to the search not just for interesting ideas, but for truth. The book you are reading right now aims to fit into the third class. It aims, that is, to allow the reader to grapple with a range of views, while also making clear which views it thinks best.

The views that it will be endorsing fit, roughly, into the Thomistic tradition. By that, I mean that its views are significantly inspired by the thought of St. Thomas Aquinas (d. 1274). Aquinas was one of many medieval philosophers who worked in a university setting—that is, a school setting, as opposed to a monastic setting—which is why we call him a "scholastic" thinker. And like many other medieval scholastics, he drew heavily on the work of Aristotle (d. 322 BC) as well as on the work of Aristotelians such as the great Islamic philosophers Avicenna (d. 1037) and Averroes (d. 1198). So, when the "opinionated" aspect of this book is coming out most strongly, it will often be, roughly, a Thomistic kind of opinionatedness: the views will be approximately those espoused by Aristotle and many scholastics, but especially Aquinas.

At the end of each chapter, I will list a few places where Aquinas discusses the main points made in that chapter. The places that I mention, however, may sometimes leave you a bit frustrated. Aquinas tends to state things very compactly. What's more, most of his works are theological, with the result that many of his philosophical remarks appear almost in passing, as he makes his way on to whatever it is that he is most eager to talk about. In the end, reading Aquinas for yourself can't be a matter of reading a few key texts here and there. You will need, in the long run, to read lots of him. Over time, it will become clearer how he approaches things.

I say that my viewpoint is "roughly" Thomistic to give myself some wiggle room; philosophy doesn't flourish when people feel obliged to

---

3. D. M. Armstrong, *Universals: An Opinionated Introduction* (London; New York: Routledge, 1989).

stick to a party line. Even among philosophers who most definitely identify themselves as Thomistic, there can be significant amounts of dispute. While agreeing on their general approach, they disagree, sometimes strongly, on the specifics. Thomism, like Scholasticism and Aristotelianism more generally, is a place of agreement, but it is a place of agreement within which interesting disagreements can be formulated.[4] I believe that the positions I advocate will fall recognizably within the Thomistic camp, but I fully anticipate that many philosophers who consider themselves members of this same camp will object to some of them.

Why take a (roughly) Thomistic view? Here's the best reason: because you think it's correct! Many years of thinking about metaphysics have led me—at times somewhat foot-draggingly—to the conclusion that this approach to philosophy, for all its limitations, is largely on the right track.

For one thing, Aristotle is basically on the right track. To put it a bit jokingly, let me say that Aristotle got seventy percent of philosophy seventy percent right. He was a genius, and very energetic, and he arrived at just the right time: There was a lot of sophisticated intellectual activity in the Greece of his day, and, in particular, he was able to stand on the shoulders of another genius, his teacher Plato. At the same time, philosophy was still enough in its infancy that there was a lot of opportunity to be the first person to see certain things. He got in on the ground floor, so to speak.

I said, somewhat jokingly, that Aristotle got seventy percent of philosophy seventy percent right. If you do the math, that means that he got almost half of philosophy right. That's an enormous contribution for just one person. But there is still a lot of philosophy left to do after that. Later philosophers did some of it, and in my view, Aquinas was particularly helpful. Like Aristotle, he was a genius, and very energetic. And he arrived at just the right time: he lived after the works of Aristotle had largely been rediscovered in Western Europe, but before phi-

---

4. See Joseph Owens, *An Interpretation of Existence* (Milwaukee: Bruce Publishing Company, 1968; repr., Houston: Center for Thomistic Studies, 1985), 27n6: "Thomism seems to be different in every one of its proponents who is thinking authentically on the philosophical level," as quoted in Kevin White, "Act and Fact: On a Disputed Question in Recent Thomistic Metaphysics," *The Review of Metaphysics* 68, no. 2 (2014): 287.

losophy got so very technical and specialized that the trees were obscuring the forest.

So there's something privileged about Aquinas's work. At the same time, there are many other great philosophers in this tradition, such as John Duns Scotus (d. 1308), Francisco Suarez (d. 1617), and many, many others, down to the present. Philosophy is not yet done, and it never will be. Indeed, philosophy is still going on right now, today. That is why I call this book not just an introduction, but a "contemporary" introduction. When I propose a Thomistic viewpoint, I aim to do so in dialogue with, and sometimes in debate with, various views held by philosophers in the last seventy years or so.

I should clarify right away, however, that I don't try to interact with all contemporary metaphysics, but only contemporary metaphysics that comes from the so-called analytic strand of philosophy. It's not actually very easy to say what "analytic" philosophy is. There are no views that all "analytic" philosophers accept, and there are no methods they all use. More than anything, it's a historical sequence of authors who are responding to one another, including figures like Ludwig Wittgenstein (d. 1951), Bertrand Russell (d. 1970), W. V. O. Quine (d. 2000), Elizabeth Anscombe (d. 2001), Peter Strawson (d. 2006), and many others still living and working. These authors write mostly in English, and they work mostly in the UK or its former colonies. (If you think that's not really enough homogeneity to make "analytic philosophy" into a legitimate philosophical school, then I agree with you a hundred percent. I think people worry too much about what is or isn't analytic philosophy, and about whether "it" is a good thing or a bad thing. There are so few true generalizations to be made about it that this is not a good use of one's time.)

Back to being "contemporary": One reason why philosophy needs to be contemporary is so that it has a chance to take new insights into consideration. More importantly, however, it needs to be contemporary because otherwise it's dead. Even if no one had had any good philosophical ideas in hundreds of years, we would still need to do philosophy afresh. You can't learn philosophy just by reading it. To learn philosophy, you must do philosophy, and, in a sense, rediscover it for yourself. You can't just read the writings, you have to think the thoughts. Having access to classical works by philosophers like Aristotle and Aquinas gives us an advantage, but still there's a sense in which philosophy begins anew with each person. That means you and me! To learn about metaphysics, we must do it. So let's jump in.

To make a good jump, however, it's often necessary to take a few steps back so as to have a running start. With that in mind, let's ask two questions. First, what is metaphysics? This is not an altogether easy question to answer, for reasons that I will explain soon enough. But even before that, we have to ask an even more basic question: What is philosophy?

0.2 What Is Philosophy?

Philosophy is the use of natural reason to ask and answer foundational questions. When I say that it is the use of "natural reason," I mean that philosophy does not rely on divine revelation. That's how it's different from theology. To be sure, theologians use reason too—everyone does—but they do so under the guidance of what they consider revelation, revelation from God. Philosophy does not rely on such aids but instead contents itself with what can be learned by natural human thinking powers alone.

When I say that philosophy asks and answers "fundamental" questions, I mean that it asks questions that concern what is most basic or foundational. It's probably best to explain this by means of an example.

Suppose you ask me how I got up on top of a rock, and I want to tell you that I did so by jumping. Unfortunately, I'm not quite certain about the correct verb form to use, so I ask: "Should I say I *jumped* onto the rock, or should I say I *jamp* onto the rock"? If you are a native English speaker, this question might sound foolish, but it isn't, at least not to someone who is learning English as a second language. After all, we don't say that we *swimmed* across the lake, but rather that we *swam* across the lake.

Later, reflecting on all this, I might come up with a more basic question: Why is it that in English, some verbs form their past tense by adding "-ed" (jump, jumped) while others change the vowel (swim, swam)?

Or I might have an even more basic question: Just what makes verbs special, as distinct from other words? (In elementary school, they tell you that a verb is an action word, but "is" is a verb, and it's hard to see how "the wagon is red" describes an action.)

Or I might ask a question that is more basic still: Why are some sounds words, while others are not?

If actual people had an actual conversation that wandered from "Is it 'jump' or is it 'jamp'?" all the way to "Why are some sounds words, while others are not?," at some point someone might say, "Wow, we're getting pretty philosophical here!" The person who said that would be right. A conversation that progresses in this way has indeed been getting increasingly "philosophical," because it has been getting increasingly basic. I mean basic in the sense that it has been getting down to basics. The conversation began by asking about a particular linguistic point, but it eventually got to where it was asking about the foundational nature of language.

There is probably no sharp dividing line between questions that are philosophical and questions that are not. As we just saw, questions that are linguistic can lead to questions in the philosophy of language. Or, to take another example, ordinary questions in history—for example, how old is this document?—can lead to deeper questions—for example, what is the correct way to decide how old a document is?—and eventually to very basic questions about the nature of historical processes and our knowledge of them. Questions in history can lead to questions in the philosophy of history. And likewise for chemistry, literature, sociology, medicine, and so on.

So philosophical questions are the most basic or foundational questions of all. It would be a mistake to think that this statement is just a case of philosophers trying to make themselves seem important. The fact that a question is basic or foundational is what *makes* it a philosophical question. If it turned out that the topics that philosophers are usually interested in weren't really fundamental, that wouldn't prove that philosophy wasn't foundational after all, it would prove only that philosophers had been doing philosophy badly. What's more, the person making this claim would be doing philosophy! So it's not that philosophers think about certain things and then arrogantly proclaim that the things *they* think about are fundamental. Rather, whichever questions really *are* most fundamental are the philosophical ones.

Philosophical questions lie at the roots of every discipline. Think, for instance, of the way in which economists sometimes give the impression that human rationality is only a tool for figuring out the most efficient way to satisfy one's desires, as if rationality had nothing to say about what it would be good or bad to desire. Sophisticated economists are, of course, more sophisticated than that, but to the extent that they are, they are edging toward thinking philosophically—for example, by thinking about how economic thinking is related to other kinds of thinking. Or think of the way in which physical scientists sometimes give the impression that matter and energy are all there is. If that is meant as a serious proposal, it's definitely a philosophical proposal, and far from obviously true. Perhaps the best way of understanding the physical world is one that leaves room for interaction with the non-physical; or perhaps that isn't the best way; but either way, the question cannot be answered, or even asked, in the language of physics. Merely to pose the question is to go deeper than physics. So, even if it were true that nothing non-physical existed and that physics was the best way of describing physical things, philosophy would still be more basic than physics.[5]

Understanding philosophy is important no matter what you study, because answers to philosophical questions are presupposed by every field of study. If your main field of study is not philosophy, you should still study philosophy, because that will help you to be aware of the questions at the basis of your field, and to be aware of how others are already answering them. If you don't study philosophy, you will be unaware of the questions at the basis of your field, and you will be unaware of how others are answering them. But the questions and the answers will still be there, steering the discussion in ways that you won't understand. You'll be at the mercy of intellectual forces that are operating beyond your range of vision. Philosophy is not just for philosophers. It's not just another part of the turf—the part that philosophers defend in academic turf-battles. Instead, philosophy is the soil that lies under the turf, and not under only one part of it, but under all of it. And yet, of course, philosophy alone is not enough: without philosophy, there's nowhere for the grass to grow, but if philosophy is all we have, the result is not a lawn but just a muddy field.

The fact that philosophy is the asking and answering of fundamental questions helps, by the way, to show why philosophy is so difficult, and why it is so hard to make progress and find definitive solutions. If

---

5. The question of how physics and the other natural sciences are related to philosophy, and more particularly, to metaphysics, is a tricky one. It will return from time to time, especially in §3.2. But a thoroughgoing treatment of the topic cannot be provided in this book.

you are trying to solve a problem in engineering, you can dig down one level, to physics or chemistry or whatever, to look for insight. But when you get to the bottom-most level, there's no way to dig deeper. Precisely because you are at the bottom, there are no principles to rely on, or appeal to, that are more basic than the ones you are trying to understand. Think of trying to renovate a shed: you can work on it while standing outside of it, and if necessary, you can more or less entirely take it apart. Now compare that with trying to renovate a ship at sea: You can't leave the ship, and even more so, you can't take it apart. You have to rebuild it while sailing it. And that's hard.[6]

0.3 What Is Metaphysics?

So much for our account of the nature of philosophy. It is, again, the use of natural reason to ask and answer fundamental questions. Then what is metaphysics? This question is not as easy to answer as it should be, because the word "metaphysics" has not always been used to name the same field of study.

Perhaps that sounds surprising. After all, everyone knows that in philosophy, it's important to be careful and rigorous in the use of words. And you'd think that being careful and rigorous would go hand-in-hand with using words in a consistent way. Think, for example, of terminology in physics. In ordinary speech, "force" and "work" sound pretty similar: We can say "it took a lot of work to push that rock over the edge of the cliff," and that's pretty much the same thing as saying "it took a lot of force to push that rock over the edge of the cliff." But in the technical language of physics, force and work are distinct concepts. If you are in the classroom or the lab, you have to know which one to use; otherwise, you may end up talking nonsense.

In philosophy, the precise meanings of words are also very important. You have to pay close attention to the words you use, and you have to pay close attention to the words others use. But unlike in physics, there's a lot of variation in how philosophers use terms, even standard and central terms. Words like "cause" and "person" and "substance" and "nominalism" get used in a variety of ways. This can be extremely frus-

---

6. This famous image comes from the Austrian philosopher Otto Neurath. See Otto Neurath, "Anti-Spengler," in *Empiricism and Sociology*, ed. Marie Neurath and Robert Cohen (Dordrecht: D. Reidel, 1973), 199.

INTRODUCTION

trating, but it has to do with nature of philosophy itself. Since philosophy asks the most basic questions, pretty nearly everything can be called into question, with the result that the meanings of standard words are always liable to rethinking.

Unfortunately, then, I can't just tell you how the word "metaphysics" gets used, because there's no one way in which it gets used. But what I can do is tell you (briefly) the history of its use, and then, relying on that, I can indicate which way I will be using it, and why.

Although there are definitely metaphysical explorations going on in the works of Plato, the first philosopher who tried to develop metaphysics as an organized field of study—a "science," in the old-fashioned use of that term—was Aristotle. He did this in the work that we now call the *Metaphysics*. But that was not his name for that work. In fact, many scholars believe that there was not really anything for Aristotle to name, in the sense that what we call the *Metaphysics* wasn't one work that Aristotle wrote. Instead, they think, it was a later bringing-together of a number of different things he wrote on more or less the same topic. When someone set out to collect all of Aristotle's writings in one place, this collection was listed after (*meta*) the set of works that are on physical topics: *Meta-physics*. If Aristotle himself had a name for the science discussed in this book, it would be "first philosophy" or "wisdom" or perhaps even (for reasons we'll see later) "theology."

Before discussing any of that, however, let me make a brief remark about the word "science." Nowadays, in contemporary English, this word primarily indicates the "hard" sciences, like physics and chemistry, along with biology. Secondarily—depending on who you ask, *very* secondarily—it indicates "social sciences" such as sociology and psychology. The picture here is clear enough: the more something is like physics, the more it counts as a "real science." But this presupposes a fairly narrow understanding of what science is. The word comes from the Latin word *scientia*, which means knowledge, and so in a way, any organized field of study ought to count as a science. Indeed, the German word *Wissenschaft* actually is neutral between the hard sciences (*Naturwissenschaften*) and humanities or social sciences (*Geisteswissenschaften*). The story of how the English word "science" got attached to certain disciplines in a way that made philosophy and the rest seem "unscientific" would be an interesting one to tell, but for our purposes here, it doesn't matter. I do need to say, however, that sometimes it will be convenient to use the word in its more traditional, broader sense, and doing so will also have the advantage of keeping us in touch with traditional terminology. So if I talk about the science of metaphysics in this book, please do not think that I am imagining laboratories and such. I simply mean to indicate metaphysics as a rigorous and organized field of study.

Back to Aristotle's understanding of metaphysics: the goal of this science, Aristotle makes clear early on, is to get to the very first principles, to the factors or truths or principles or realities that explain all others and that do not themselves get explained in terms of things more basic than they. It's the science that tries to get to where the buck stops, to where the last questions are asked and, hopefully, answered. If this sounds a bit like how I described philosophy in general, then that's correct. In a way, metaphysics is the philosophy within philosophy: if philosophy of human nature tries to get to the most basic principles of human nature, and philosophy of knowledge tries to get to the most basic principles of knowledge, metaphysics tries to get to the most basic principles of everything. You could call those principles the ultimate principles, or you could call them the first principles: they are ultimate in the sense that they are the last ones you come to, starting from everyday experience, but they are first in the sense that they are the ones that all others originate from.

If you had a knowledge of this first philosophy, you would, in a way, know the principles that governed everything. Because the principles would put constraints on what can legitimately be said in less fundamental fields of study—because those other fields could not rightly contradict these principles—knowing them would give you a kind of authority over other fields. You would, in short, have a kind of wisdom. But at the same time, it should be added that your knowledge would be very general and very abstract. As Aristotle puts it, the wise man knows all things, but not in detail.[7]

Metaphysics thinks about things in a very general way, then, but I hasten to add that the things it thinks about in this very general way are ordinary things. It does not, most of the time, think about extraordinary things. It may do so, from time to time—see chapter eight of this

---

7. Many of the things I have been saying in this paragraph are, in fact, drawn from the first two chapters of Book I of Aristotle's *Metaphysics*.

book for the strongest example—but mostly it does not. It thinks about cats and cars and colors, but in a way that abstracts from the details that belong to the study of cats, cars, and colors. Apart from a few special cases, then, metaphysicians think about the things that everyone else thinks about—they just do so in a special way. (And to pick up on a point from the previous section: This means that metaphysicians think about the things that physicists think about, just in a different and more abstract way.)

Having a grip on this can help us understand the relationship between metaphysics and the rest of philosophy, and the relationship between philosophy and the rest of knowledge. Metaphysics knows principles that govern the philosophy of science, for example, but just because you know metaphysics doesn't mean you know everything that needs to be known in the philosophy of science. The philosophy of science, in turn, knows principles that govern chemistry, but just because you know the philosophy of science doesn't mean you know everything that needs to be known in chemistry. The philosophy of science doesn't tell you what ionic bonds are, and still less does metaphysics tell you that! On the other hand, chemical theory is ultimately subordinate to metaphysics in the sense that chemical theory, like everything else, presupposes certain fundamental principles.

These sorts of tensions can reveal themselves in odd ways. At parties, philosophers sometimes intervene to straighten out what they take to be the shoddy thinking of sociologists or economists or physicists or whatever. This happens pretty often, actually. (A theologian colleague once said to me, "You philosophers think you can do everyone else's thinking for them.") Sometimes, the philosopher is in the right: the others are being too superficial, and they are failing to see how their claims come into conflict with deeper and broader principles. Sometimes, however, the philosopher is being ridiculous: he is forgetting that knowledge of particular sciences requires not only philosophical insight, but also knowledge of specific and sometimes quite technical matters. If specialists in particular sciences sometimes think that their technical expertise (in mathematics or languages or whatever) means they know everything, philosophers, and probably metaphysicians most of all, sometimes think that their insight into first principles means *they* know everything. Again, the wise man knows all things, but not in detail. To get a lawn, you need both soil and grass.

These remarks about how philosophy is related to other fields of inquiry raise a different but related question—namely, a question about how philosophy is related to the everyday commonsense beliefs that people have before they start philosophizing. The truth is that philosophy grows out of such beliefs, and while it involves the attempt to refine them, and even sometimes to correct them, it should never try to undermine them wholesale. Precisely because philosophy grows out of our pre-philosophical awareness of the world, it cannot reject that awareness entirely. Doing so would amount to rejecting its own basis. It would be a case of sawing off the branch one is sitting on.

Having made these remarks about the relationship between metaphysics and other things, let us return to metaphysics itself. For Aristotle, metaphysics is the first science—the ultimate, or highest, or most foundational science. Explaining the nature of this science in the *Metaphysics*, he says that it is the science of being. It gives us the first principles that govern everything that exists. That explains why it is universal: outside of being, there just isn't anything at all. (It's not as if "nothing" is a special kind of thing!) Pick anything you like, and whatever else it is, what it is *first* is a being. Of course, I don't mean "first" in the sense that it's a being at five o'clock, and then it's a cat at 5:15. "First" here means "most basically" or "most fundamentally." Being is first in fundamentality, not first in time.[8]

Aristotle specifies further that this science is the science of "being *qua* being," meaning being *as* being or being *insofar as* it is being. If you are studying anything at all, then in a sense you are studying being: studying a cat means studying being. But there are different ways to study cats. You can think of a cat while focusing on its cat nature, or you can take a step back and think about it not insofar as it is a cat, but more generically, insofar as it is a mammal. And that process can be continued: you can think about the cat as a vertebrate, as an animal, as a living organism, as a physical object—or just as something that exists, as a being. It is this maximally high-level viewpoint that metaphysics takes. It studies all of reality, all of being, and it does so in a way that

---

8. Sometimes people say "ontology" instead of "metaphysics." "Ontology" is a pretty good word here, because it's just Greek for the science of being. But other people make a distinction between ontology and metaphysics. In this book, I'm just going to say "metaphysics."

abstracts, as far as possible, from the immense multiplicity of types of being. It looks beyond the differences between cats and rabbits, or cats and square roots. It tries to figure out what all beings have in common. (These maximally common features of being are sometimes called the "transcendental properties of being.")

Not that metaphysics has no concern for the sub-divisions of being. Just as the science of cats might explore not only what all cats have in common, but also the most basic types of cats, so too the science of being explains not only what all beings have in common, but also the basic divisions of being. These basic divisions are often called "categories," and there is even a work by Aristotle which we call the *Categories*. As will become clear soon enough, differences among categories are very important in metaphysics, and in this book. My overall approach involves distinguishing categories of being and showing how one of them is the key to the others.

So far, I have been talking about metaphysics as it has been understood in the Aristotelian tradition. I have tried to bring out the ways in which it is the study of being, its properties, and its main categories, and how such a study gives us first and universal principles. But perhaps you have noticed that I have not yet said anything about one of the names for this science that I mentioned at the beginning—namely, "theology." This, in fact, has been a source of controversy among philosophers in the Aristotelian tradition. On one way of thinking about it, God or the gods ought to count as one of the things that metaphysics studies. If anything counts as a being, you might think, surely God does; indeed, what could be a better example of a being than that? On another way of thinking about it, however, God is so very different from all other beings that it's highly misleading to think of him as "a being" at all. Instead, one might say, he should be thought of as quite distinct from everything else, and utterly beyond it. God, you might suppose, is not a part of what metaphysics studies, but the cause of what metaphysics studies. I'll touch on these questions in chapter eight.

So much, then, for the traditional, Aristotelian understanding of metaphysics, an understanding that remained tolerably constant—with variations, of course—throughout medieval scholastic philosophy. I have left out a lot of details, but that is enough at this point. Let us switch over to discussing a more modern notion of metaphysics.

The word "modern" means different things in different contexts. Modern music probably starts in 1913, while modern philosophy starts in the 1600s. Anyway, sometime after the dawn of modern philosophy, the word "metaphysics" began to take on a somewhat different meaning. It's not that the traditional questions became irrelevant. It's that additional questions, like the nature of the soul or the problem of free will, started getting labeled "metaphysical" as well. I think it's understandable why someone might be tempted to call these questions "metaphysical": These questions are about the natures of things, about what they are like, about the kind of reality or being that these things have, and not, say, about how we know about those things. So, for example, there is an important difference between asking what an electron is and asking how we know about electrons. The latter concerns our knowledge of electrons and is therefore an epistemic question (from the Greek word *episteme*, knowledge), whereas the former concerns the very nature or being of the electron and is, thus, in a sense, a metaphysical question.

I do not mean to begrudge others this use of the word "metaphysics." I even use it that way myself at times.[9] However, there is a problem when we habitually use the noun "metaphysics" in this very broad way. The problem is that the core topics—being itself, its categories, and transcendental properties—risk getting crowded out by the more particular topics.[10] In this book, I focus on the core, traditional questions of metaphysics. At the same time, however, I do think it is important to see how they relate to questions that lie outside that traditional core, and for that reason, I will discuss some of those others as well. For example, in chapters two and three, I will discuss a number of topics that traditionally belong to the philosophy of nature, and in chapter nine, I will discuss some topics at the intersection of metaphysics and theology.

0.4 A Substance-Centered Metaphysics

I will, then, largely be discussing metaphysics in the traditional Aristotelian-Thomistic sense, metaphysics as the study of what is common

---

9. For example, in the following book title: *Aquinas on the Metaphysics of the Hypostatic Union* (Cambridge: Cambridge University Press, 2017).

10. See, for example, the table of contents of Peter van Inwagen's *Metaphysics*, 4th Edition (Boulder: Westview Press, 2015).

to all of being, along with the main divisions of being. My discussion will be traditional in another way as well: it will be centered around the notion of *substance*. I will have a lot to say about this, especially in chapter one, so for now I will keep things brief.

First, to give a quick initial look at the idea of substance, we can say that a substance is an independent unified thing, like a cat. A cat is independent, meaning that it is not dependent on anything else in the particular way that, for example, the cat's weight is dependent on the cat, and unable to exist apart from it. And a cat is unified, meaning that it is not a mere collection, like a pile of trash, but instead a single tight unity.

In the Aristotelian-Thomistic approach to metaphysics put forward in this book, substance is central. Substance is the central kind or category of being. It is the primary sort of being, and others are secondary, meaning that they exist only in relation to substance, and cannot properly be understood except as related to substance. The claim is not that substances are the only kinds of being. There are indeed other kinds of being, such as weights and colors. But substance is primary and foundational. As we will see in what follows, there are many ways to deviate from this thought, and these deviations (in my view) lead to serious problems. But avoiding the deviations is difficult; it requires us to think accurately about beings that aren't substances, which is something that humans are not very good at.

If all this seems absurdly abstract at this point, do not fear. It will become clearer in later chapters, as it gets spelled out more concretely. For now, it is enough to keep in mind that the question of substance, and of how substances are related to other sorts of beings, will be very important for us.

0.5 Coming Attractions

Explaining metaphysics is a bit like explaining baseball: no matter where you start, you wish you had started somewhere else, because it seems as if everything presupposes everything else. But obviously this book must start somewhere and proceed in some order.

Chapter one concerns the central category of being: substance. I explain what a substance is, and I explain (and weigh in on) a dispute about the crucial distinction between the essential and the accidental features of substances. After discussing a few further complications, I make some remarks about the relationship between substances and other kinds of beings.

Chapter two is about change: how substances change, and what change is, and the different types of change that there are. Looking into all this will require us to ask interesting questions about the nature of time. It will also lead us to a discussion of concepts that belong more properly to the philosophy of nature, like form and matter. What's more, it will, through a discussion of concepts like identity and potentiality, set us up for later discussions in chapters five and six.

Chapter three concerns the parts of substances. Metaphysicians use the language of "parts" in a variety of ways, and this chapter will therefore explore a wide variety of issues, many of them growing out of sharp disagreements about what substances are made out of. The question of the relationship between substances and beings that are not substances will receive a thorough airing in this chapter, in part because some of these disputes are precisely disputes about whether the parts of substances are themselves substances.

Chapter four is about causes. We will distinguish two ways of thinking about causation: one which focuses on causes as explanations of things coming to be in a certain way, and one which focuses on causes as explanations of things being the way they are, without reference to their coming to be that way. All this will involve contrasting the Aristotelian-Thomistic approach to some other approaches, and it will tie back to some points made in chapter three.

Chapter five is about universality and particularity. Substances, and their parts, are particulars: Socrates is one individual being, not a kind or type, like humanity. But is humanity, the type or kind to which Socrates belongs, a being? If humanity is a being, is it a substance, or something else? If humanity is not a being, then how can it be true to say that Socrates and Plato both "share in humanity"? As we will discuss, philosophers have proposed many different ways of thinking about these topics; the one I will eventually propose attempts (among other things) to preserve the centrality of individual substances. But my proposal will, perhaps, seem incomplete, and I will address that in chapter eight.

Chapter six is about possibility, necessity, and related concepts. There are possible ways for reality to be. Of those possible ways, some of them are, in addition, ways that reality actually is, and some are ways in which reality cannot fail to be. It's possible for me to be typing, and, as a matter of fact, I am typing; but I don't have to be. By contrast, the number three has to be greater than the number two. How are these different modes of being related to one another, and what are they rooted in? Thinking about these topics has led some philosophers to believe in rather extravagant metaphysical theories. After discussing some of them, I will propose a way of eliminating the extravagance by thinking about the issues simply in terms of substances and facts about substances. But this proposal may, like the proposal at the end of chapter five, seem incomplete; that, too, will be taken up in chapter eight.

Chapter seven involves a shift of focus, toward an attempt to speak not of this or that aspect of reality, but about all of it at once. In one sense, this turns out to be impossible: to the extent that talking about things means talking about the categories they belong to, it is not possible to talk about everything at once, because there is no category that everything belongs to. In another sense, however, it is possible to talk about everything at once, because (as mentioned earlier) it is possible to identify transcendental properties, properties that all beings possess, even if these do not correspond to a category that all beings belong to.

Chapter eight introduces another shift, a more dramatic one. It talks about God. As mentioned already, metaphysicians have debated about whether God (if he exists) is part of what metaphysics studies. It seems best to say that God is not strictly a part of what metaphysics studies; instead, he is the cause of what metaphysics studies. In this way, he plays an indirect but extremely important role in metaphysical inquiry. If God exists and is the creator of all, then God will be at least part of the deepest explanation of why things are the way they are. In fact, as I will propose, some problems in metaphysics—problems discussed in chapters five and six—are best solved by bringing God into the picture.

Chapter nine shifts once again, going beyond philosophy in the strict sense to engage two topics in traditional Catholic theology: Christ's status as one person with two natures (divine and human), and the nature of the Eucharist. These are theological issues, rather than philosophical ones, but they require heavy doses of metaphysical thinking, and for that reason, they can be of interest even to people who don't accept the theology that gives rise to them.

By way of rounding out this discussion of what the book will contain, I'd like to mention two topics that could be discussed in an introduction to metaphysics but that will not be discussed in this one. To begin with, I will not be worrying about objections to the very possibility of doing metaphysics. Many philosophers, often philosophers of an empiricist stripe, such as David Hume (d. 1776), have raised deep doubts about whether metaphysics is something that can be done at all. This is an important debate to have, but in this book, I'm not going to get into it.[11]

Another thing I'm not going to discuss is the interesting question of how our minds can get hold of the core subject of metaphysics, namely, being. This question can take many forms, and here I will mention just one. Some Thomists have held that you cannot grasp being as being until you have first proved that reality includes not only physical objects, but also non-physical objects (like God or angels or the soul). Before you have done this, they say, you can't be sure that your thoughts apply to being as such; maybe they really apply only to physical being. Until you know that there really are non-physical beings, you can't do the science of being *qua* being. Other Thomists, however, hold that this isn't necessary. For them, all that's necessary is grasping the truth that being doesn't *have* to be physical; if you have the insight that being *could* be non-physical, whether or not it actually *is* non-physical, then that is enough to allow you to think about being as such. As mentioned, the question has been debated among Thomists, but again, I'm not going to get into it here.[12]

I have been talking about things I won't talk about. This is as good a place as any to say that even when I do talk about something, I will not talk about it in all its fullness. I will not go into every detail, or every objection, or every aspect. I'm not saying this merely because, after all, no book could ever discuss any topic completely. It's a deliberate part of my strategy not to go into too many details. Getting too far into the weeds would pull us away from the main path and result in the reader understanding less, not more. That said, I will try, in footnotes, to point out which issues I am skipping over, and sometimes I will give some clues about how to dig deeper if you want to.

That's enough for the introduction to this introduction.

---

11. I will say something relevant, very briefly, when Hume comes up in §4.3.

12. For some discussion, see John F. Wippel, *The Metaphysical Thought of Thomas Aquinas: From Finite Being to Uncreated Being* (Washington, DC: The Catholic University of America Press, 2000), chapter 2.

CHAPTER 1

Basic Beings and Their Features

1.1 First Look at Substance

IN THE INTRODUCTION, I said that explaining metaphysics was difficult in the way that explaining baseball is difficult: when many issues are so closely interrelated, you don't know where to start. Perhaps the best way to solve the baseball problem in metaphysics is by starting with the concept of substance. In ordinary English, we use the word "substance" for things like glue or plastic, but this is not very closely related to the technical, philosophical use of the word. Philosophers use "substance" as a technical word for a certain category of being. And substance, in this sense, is the magic key to metaphysics. Substances are basic beings. They are the beings that other beings are based on, and the best way to understand non-substances is by seeing how they are related to substances. Substance is the category of being that allows us to understand the other categories of being.

First, then, here is a short list of central or paradigm cases of "substance" in the philosophical sense: a cat, a tree, you, and I. (Throughout the book I will be using examples of cats, so let me name two of them right away: Rusty and Mickey.)

Second, because contrasts are so useful when explaining ideas, here are some things that are definitely not substances. Rusty's redness and Mickey's agility are definitely not substances. Also not substances are a pile of sand or a pair of shoes. Finally, the universal nature felinity, catness, is also not a substance. But having something negative in common—in this case, being non-substances—doesn't automatically mean these non-substances have much positive content in common. Rusty's redness and Mickey's agility are non-substances for a different reason than the pile of sand or pair of shoes are non-substances, and the universal natures felinity and redness are non-substances for still another reason.

Rusty's redness and Mickey's agility are non-substances because they are dependent entities: Rusty's redness depends on Rusty, and Mickey's agility depends on Mickey. The pile of sand and the pair of shoes are non-substances for a very different reason—namely, that they are not unified: a pair of shoes is not one thing but two things, and a pile of sand is not one thing but thousands. Finally, redness and felinity are non-substances because they are universals rather than individuals. Flipping these remarks on their head, we have the following provisional account of substance: a substance is an *individual* that is *independent* and *unified*. Each of these deserves a bit of explication.

"Individuals" (or "particulars") have to be understood through a contrast with "universals." A universal is something general or shareable, a kind or type or species, like felinity or humanity. It's something that there are examples or instances of: Mickey is an instance of felinity, and so is Rusty. Put differently, there's something that Mickey and Rusty both share in (or have, or exemplify), and that's felinity. It's something in virtue of which they are alike. It's something they have in common.

An individual, by contrast, is not common or shareable in this way. An individual is not something there can be an instance of; instead, it is itself an instance. Mickey is not felinity, but an instance of felinity. He's not cat-in-general, he's this particular cat. Individuals or particulars are instances of universals, but nothing is ever an instance of a particular: some other cat can be like Mickey, but nothing can be an instance of Mickey.[1]

What about independence? Substances are independent, but that doesn't mean that they don't depend on anything in any way. Living substances like cats depend on many things, such as oxygen and food. Some kinds of dependence, then, are consistent with being a substance. When we say that substances are independent, we don't mean that they are utterly independent, but only that they have a special kind of independence, the kind for which the technical name "subsistence" is often used. Something is subsistent if it lacks the kind of dependence char-

---

[1]. This book's main discussion of the distinction between universals and individuals can be found in §5.1.

acteristic of a feature: it is not the sort of thing that must, by its very nature, belong to something else in the way that a feature does.[2] Rusty's redness must, by its very nature, belong to Rusty; to use a technical term, it must "inhere" in him.[3] Rusty himself, by contrast, is not related in that way to anything: he may belong to a team (a mouse-trapping team), but he can easily exist without being part of that team. Putting the point more positively, Rusty exists "on his own," or "through himself" (*per se*, in Latin).[4]

Now, finally, let us talk about the unity of substance. Think of a pile of sand. Each grain of sand is a substance, but is the pile a substance? The answer is no, because the pile isn't unified, or anyway it's not unified enough, not unified in the right way. Instead of being a substance, a pile of sand is many substances. Its parts don't add up to one thing, and so "it," the pile, isn't really a thing, but a bunch of things. But Rusty, it seems safe to say, is not like that. He has parts, to be sure, but they are unified much more tightly than the grains of sand in a sandpile are unified, unified in such a way that he, Rusty, is one thing.

Intuitively, this seems pretty reasonable, but you might wonder if we can develop the intuition by adding some deeper conceptual insight. Here's a thought along those lines. Think about that pile of sand again, and suppose it's on top of a frisbee. We might say that the pile of sand blocks our view of the frisbee, but really what is happening is that each individual grain of sand is blocking our view of one tiny part of the frisbee. There are enough grains that all the parts of the frisbee get blocked, but it's not really as if "the pile" is acting as one single agent that performs one action of view-blocking. Contrast this with the case

---

2. Cf. Patrick Toner, "On Substance," *American Catholic Philosophical Quarterly* 84, no. 1 (2010): 25–48. See also Michael Gorman, "Independence and Substance," *International Philosophical Quarterly* 46, no. 2 (2006): 147–59.

By the way, I will use "feature," and sometimes "property," as catch-all words to indicate any quality or attribute (or whatever) that belongs to a thing. If those words suggest to you some particular type of attribute (or whatever), please try to disregard that. Everyone needs a catch-all word or two; these are mine.

3. Some readers may wonder whether this is consistent with, or can be made consistent with, the theological doctrine of transubstantiation, or whether instead it might need rephrasing in a theological context. See §9.3.

4. If God exists, and if Rusty depends on God, does that mean Rusty is not subsistent? In a word, no, but fuller discussion of substantial independence will not begin until the end of §1.2, and it will not be complete until §3.5.

of Mickey pouncing on a mouse. It isn't right to say that his left front paw does one thing, his right front paw another, and so on, with the result that a mouse gets pounced upon. No, Mickey is acting as one single agent. Generalizing now, the point is that we have one substance when we have one agent.[5]

To be sure, it may not always be clear how to decide when we have a case of multiple things acting at the same time and when we have a case of a whole acting as a whole. Presumably we will usually need information from some of the more specific sciences, like biology. But getting into those details is not part of metaphysics.

Having spelled out the basic idea of substance, I would like now to say a few things about the word "substance" itself. One obvious way of using that word is in a sentence like this one: "Excuse me, but I'm afraid there's a sticky green substance on the cuff of your pants; it looks like colored glue." But as you already know, that is not how philosophers use the word. As typically used by philosophers nowadays, the English word "substance" is an excruciatingly literal translation of the Latin word *substantia*. A substance in that sense is a "sub-stance": something that sub-stands or stands under something else. Think of Rusty and his redness: because his redness depends on him—because it leans on him, so to speak—he might be said to support it, to "stand under" it. Substances are what features or properties exist in and depend on.[6]

The philosophical word "substance" has a long and complicated history. The way I am using it here is one of the two main ways philosophers have used it historically. The other main way is as a word for essence, or nature, or kind. Think of how we sometimes say that a question or remark is "substantive" rather than procedural, meaning that it bears on the real nature of whatever is under discussion. (This meaning is also reflected in the slightly archaic way in which some translations of some Christian creeds say that the Son is "consubstantial" with the

---

5. Recent philosophers who have (in different ways) placed emphasis on unity of action include Trenton Merricks, *Objects and Persons* (Oxford: Clarendon Press, 2006); Patrick Toner, "On Substance"; and Peter van Inwagen, *Material Beings* (Ithaca, NY: Cornell University Press, 1995). The question of unity will come back, in more than one form, in chapter three.

6. We will examine the difficult question of what it really means for features to exist in and depend on substances in §3.3, and especially in §3.3.3.

Father, meaning that the Son shares a nature with the Father or is of the same kind as the Father.)

A third meaning lies beneath these two: the word "substance" seems to mean, at the most primordial level, *whatever is most basic*. It's hard to avoid the thought that *something* must be most basic and, for that reason, not dependent on other things. If that is right, then the idea that substances are independent is more or less true by definition: if substances are basic beings, and if "basic" things are independent of others, then substances are independent. But why think that substances are unified and individual? Why think, in other words, that whatever is most basic is not only independent but also unified and individual? Why think that substance in the sense of what is most basic is also substance in the sense of independent, unified, and individual?

If you want to know what *a* basic being is, you have to be asking about *a* being, and therefore you have to be talking about something unified. If a being isn't unified, then it's not *a* being, but instead merely a collection of beings. Aggregates or collections presuppose units, not the other way around. That is why basic beings need to be unified.

Individuality is perhaps more controversial. Some philosophers say that the most basic beings of all are not individuals but universals: not Rusty or Mickey, but the catness they instantiate. For now, I will simply assert that in the Aristotelian-Thomistic tradition, this is not how substance is understood. But the question of universals will return in chapter five.

Another thing that's controversial is this. Even if you agree that substances are independent, unified, and individual, you still have a right to ask *which* beings are that way. You have a right to ask which beings are independent, unified, and individual. More specifically, and more pointedly, you might wonder whether we have really been right this whole time in taking it for granted that organisms like Mickey are substances.

In response, I first want to say that of all the things that we encounter in ordinary experience, organisms seem best suited to fit our description of substances: they stand out as independent, unified individuals. And philosophy has no choice but to start out from ordinary experience. If we were to completely deny the truth of ordinary experience, we would be unable to do philosophy at all. For that reason, it seems right to start with the presumption that organisms count as substances. Second, however, this presumption needs to face up to doubts and objections, such as the thought that an organism is not a unified substance but really just a collection of atoms. Without thinking through objections like these, philosophy will not advance beyond common sense. In the chapters that follow—above all chapters three and five—I will develop a number of considerations that confirm the commonsensical intuition that Mickey and the like are true substances.

1.2 Essential and Accidental Features of Substances

If all there was to say about Mickey was that he is an independent and unified individual, then he would be a pretty paltry sort of thing. In fact, of course, there is much more to say about him. Mickey has many features beyond being unified, independent, and individual. He is, for example, gray, agile, feline, purring, fifteen pounds in weight, and blocking the doorway.[7]

One of these is not like the others: his felinity is a special or privileged kind of feature for him. Suppose you and a friend are walking along in the fog. You spot a shape in the distance, and you ask, "What is that?" If your friend says, "It's something agile," you would not accept this as a proper answer to your question. You want to know *what* the thing you've spotted *is*, and that means you want to know what *kind* of thing it is. You want to know *what it is* in the most central or deep-down sense. You want to know what its *essence* or *nature* is. Grayness and agility belong to Mickey, no doubt about it, but they are relatively unimportant or superficial aspects of him. They are what he's like, not what he is. They are not his nature or essence. His essence is his catness, his felinity.

To say all this seems to fit with a pre-philosophical intuition that we have: Some features are the not-so-important ones, the ones that don't tell us what things are; other features are the very important ones, the ones that do tell us what things are. Using traditional philosophical terminology, let's say that the not-so-important features are "accidental," while the important ones are "essential." When we need nouns, we can call essential features "essences," and we can call accidental features "accidents."

---

7. The question of whether there actually are any paltry substances of this sort will be taken up in §§3.3.1–3.3.2.

Two clarifications are now in order. First, to say that an accident is "not so important" is not to say that it is unimportant. Whether you are a very wicked person is, metaphysically speaking, not as important as whether you are a human being, and it is an accident; but whether you are a very wicked person is obviously very important!

Second, the adjective "accidental" and the noun "accident" should not be taken to suggest random misfortune. Many of the things that metaphysicians call accidents are not random misfortunes at all, but perfectly non-random non-misfortunes, like color. Conversely, however, it is true enough that random misfortunes are accidental in the philosophical sense. It's not essential to driving down the highway that there be a crash, which is why a crash on the highway is called an accident.[8]

It's probably the case that most of the time, we can go with our gut instincts about which features count as essential and which as accidental. But there may be borderline or disputable cases, and even if there aren't, philosophy can't be satisfied with gut instincts. What would it look like to have a philosophical theory of the essential-accidental distinction?

In most metaphysical discussions in the analytic tradition, the distinction is understood in the following way. If Mickey has a feature, but he can exist without having that feature, then the feature is accidental to him; if Mickey has a feature, but he cannot exist without that feature, then it is essential to him. Mickey is agile, but he doesn't have to be: he could change from agile to clumsy while remaining himself, so his agility is accidental to him. But he can't change from feline to canine while remaining himself: if he changed from feline to canine, the "he" at the end of the process would not be Mickey but something else, and therefore his felinity is essential to him. The same point can also be made without thinking in terms of change. Even if, for some strange reason, Mickey can't now *change* from agile to clumsy, he *might have been* clumsy if the universe had unfolded in a different way. By contrast, Mickey *couldn't have been* a dog. It wasn't possible for the universe to unfold in such a way that Mickey was a dog. True, it was pos-

---

8. Interestingly, not all crashes are accidents: the collisions in a demolition derby are not accidents but are, instead, essential to it and indeed pretty much the whole point of it. Of course, to say this is to use these notions in an extended way. A demolition derby is not a basic being, but more like what you get when a number of them interact in various ways. A bit more light will be shed on this in §3.2.

sible for the universe to unfold in such a way that it contained some dog instead of Mickey, but that's completely different.

This theory of essence and accident—according to which an accident is whatever can change about a thing or, at least, whatever *could* have been different about it—is called the "modal" theory.[9] It is far from foolish. In fact, it gets things right most of the time. That said, it's interesting to note how untraditional it is. No Aristotelian would accept it. Aristotelians think that it's possible for a substance to have an accidental feature which it, the substance, can't exist without. The classic example is a human's feature of being able to laugh: no human can exist without being able to laugh (even if that capacity is well-hidden by a sour disposition, or quite dramatically blocked by brain damage). Despite the fact that this is a feature without which a human cannot exist, the traditional approach would count it as accidental, not as essential. In this book I will call such accidents "necessary accidents": because the substance cannot lack them, they are "necessary," but they are not essential, so they are "accidents."[10] (Accidents that are not necessary accidents are "contingent" accidents.)

Of course, an advocate of the modal theory would say that these features that cannot be lacked are essential and not accidental. So why, from the Aristotelian perspective, are they understood to be accidental? It's because they are not good answers to the question, "What is it?" If I ask, pointing to some human being, "What is that?" it's not a good answer to say that it's "something that can laugh." However important and even irreplaceable that feature might be, it's not *what* a human is. It's not the core of what a human is.

Noticing that the modal theory wrongly counts certain features as essential is enough to show that the modal theory does not give us a satisfactory account of essence. But this is not enough. If possible, we need to find a better theory of essence to replace the modal theory.

---

9. Why "modal"? Because necessity—the way things have to be—is a "mode" of truth. Some things are not just true, but necessarily true. This will receive much more attention in chapter six.

10. In the Thomistic tradition, the word "property," or *proprium*, is sometimes reserved for necessary accidents, or for a subset of them. But I will in this book be a bit more casual and use "property" and "feature" interchangeably, as catch-all terms to refer to, well, the features or properties of things—whether essential or accidental, necessary or contingent.

Here is a way to formulate the more traditional Aristotelian approach. Let's choose Socrates as our example, and let's label one of his features "F." We want to know whether F is essential to Socrates or not. If Socrates has some other feature—call it G—such that Socrates has F *because* he has G, then F is accidental to him and not essential. So, for example, suppose that F is the ability to laugh. The reason why this is not essential to Socrates, but accidental instead, is that there is some other feature of Socrates *because of which* he is able to laugh. (This other feature is his rationality. It's because Socrates is rational that he can get the joke.)[11] But Socrates's humanity is not like that. He's not human *because* of any other features that he has. Being human is his bottom-level or fundamental or foundational feature. Think of his features as being arranged like the stories of a house. Essential features are like the house's foundation: if it rests on anything at all, it rests on something external to the house. It is the house's foundational level. Accidental features are like upper stories. They rest on lower parts of the house.[12]

We can call this the foundationality theory of essence. It says that a substance's essence does not rest on any prior feature of the substance and constitutes the substance at the most basic level. Being feline is what makes Rusty what he is; indeed, it is, in a sense, what makes him be there in the first place. His other, accidental features ride piggyback on this one.

When we say that accidental features ride piggyback on essence—that the substance has its accidental features "because" of its essential features—this need not mean that the essential features are *sufficient* for the accidental ones. Having one's essential features is not enough, on its own, for having one's accidental features. Socrates's being human allows him to get a sunburn, but it's not sufficient for that; he must also spend time in the sun.

---

11. Maybe it's not just his rationality, but his rational animality. Angels can get jokes, presumably, but since they don't have bodies, they can't laugh. They just nod and say, "Ah, yes, that's a good one."
 Actually, you're right. If they don't have bodies, they can't nod, either.
12. For more on this approach to essence, see my "Essentiality as Foundationality," in *Neo-Aristotelian Perspectives in Metaphysics*, ed. Daniel Novotný and Lukáš Novák (New York; London: Routledge, 2014), 119–37 and also my "The Essential and the Accidental," *Ratio* 18, no. 3 (2005): 276–89.

Earlier in this chapter, I asked why, if Rusty depends on God, that doesn't make him non-subsistent. We now have the tools to start answering that question. On the modal view, Rusty's dependence on God is essential: it's something that Rusty can't exist without. On the foundational view, however, one can say that dependence on God isn't actually essential, but only a necessary accident. True, Rusty cannot exist without depending on God; however, that dependence is not an element of his nature, but rather something that belongs to him on account of his nature, or as a result of his nature; therefore, it's not essential but instead a necessary accident.

If that's right, then we can offer a refinement of the idea that substances are independent. It's not that they don't depend on other things, but that they don't *essentially* depend on other things; their dependence is accidental to them, rather than essential. (By contrast, accidents are essentially dependent on something; even if, like a substance, an accident's dependence on God is non-essential, its dependence on the substance to which it belongs is essential to it.[13]) Even though Rusty cannot but depend on God, his dependence, being non-essential, is of the sort that doesn't interfere with his being a substance.

The foundational view of essence distinguishes necessary features from essential features, and that has created room for saying that dependence on God, while necessary for a substance, still lies outside that substance's nature or essence. But I haven't yet given any reason for saying that dependence on God actually does lie outside a substance's essence. In a nice illustration of the above-mentioned baseball problem, that will have to wait until §3.5.

1.3 Additional Thoughts on Features; Some Remarks on Language

Up until now, we have been speaking naively about the features of substances, as if it's easy to know what is and what isn't a feature. But it turns out that this is more complicated than it might sound.

To begin with, just because there is a word that we can attach to something doesn't necessarily mean there's a feature expressed by that

---

13. Or at least that's how we'll put it for present purposes. As noted earlier, we will have to revisit this topic in §9.3.

word. For example, think of the sentence "Taylor Swift is popular." As of this writing, that sentence is certainly true, just as these sentences are certainly true: "Taylor Swift is blonde" and "Taylor Swift is musical." But should we really say that here we have three features that belong to Taylor Swift—namely, musicality, blondeness, and popularity? The first two certainly seem like features of hers, but is *being popular* a feature of hers? What I mean is: Is it a feature of *hers*?

The answer is "no." *Being popular* is not a feature of Taylor Swift; instead, *liking Taylor Swift* is a feature of many music-listeners. Even though we attach the word "popular" to Swift, the reality that this word points to belongs not to her, but to her fans. It's not that Swift has a popularity-feature; rather, her fans have a liking-feature. Her popularity resides not in her, but in them. The facts that make it true to say that she is popular are not facts about Swift, but facts about Swifties. The proof of this is that she could become unpopular without changing at all. All that has to happen is for her fans to change.

The point is not to get anyone to stop using sentences like "Taylor Swift is popular." There's nothing wrong with that sentence. It is a perfectly legitimate way of indicating that many people like Taylor Swift. The point instead is to realize that sentences like "Taylor Swift is popular" can mislead us when we are doing metaphysics. A sentence like "Taylor Swift is musical" suggests, rightly, that there is a feature, musicality, that belongs to Taylor Swift. A sentence like "Taylor Swift is popular" is grammatically parallel to that, but it would be a mistake to infer from this grammatical parallelism that there is a parallelism in the reality that the words are meant to express.[14] In particular, not every *predicate* that is truly applicable to a substance necessarily corresponds to a *property* or *feature* that belongs to that substance as one of its parts.[15] We have to be careful. As Ludwig Wittgenstein (d. 1951) put it, we must not allow our intelligence to be bewitched by language.[16]

---

14. The classic discussion here is Gilbert Ryle, "Systematically Misleading Expressions," *Proceedings of the Aristotelian Society, New Series* 32, no. 1 (1932): 139–70.

15. For a helpful and much-discussed discussion of this distinction, see David Lewis on the question of whether properties are sparse or abundant in his book *On the Plurality of Worlds* (Malden, MA: Blackwell Publishers, 2001), 59–69.

16. Ludwig Wittgenstein, *Philosophical Investigations*, ed. P. M. S. Hacker and Joachim Schulte, trans. G. E. M. Anscombe, P. M. S. Hacker, and Joachim Schulte, rev. 4th ed. (Malden, MA: Wiley-Blackwell, 2009), §109.

30   CHAPTER 1

Now let us consider another and more particular point about predicates and properties, one that can be brought up in the context of an objection to the foundationality theory. Someone might say that the foundationality theory of essence must be false, on the grounds that it implies something false.[17] The objection looks like this:

> Socrates is human—a rational animal—*because* he's an animal. Therefore, according to the foundationality theory, his being human is nonfoundational; and therefore it's accidental, not essential. But it's false to say that being human is accidental to Socrates. Therefore, the foundationality theory must be false.

This objection is based on the erroneous idea that animality and rationality are two distinct features, features that give rise to a third feature, namely, humanity. Instead of being features in their own right, animality and rationality are aspects of the feature humanity. Socrates is not rational, and also animal, and also human, as if these were three different features. Socrates is human, which means that he's rational in an animal way, and animal in a rational way.

In giving this response to the objection, I am committing myself to a claim that can be expressed using the language of "determinate" and "determinable." Let's first apply that language to predicates, like "scarlet" and "colored." The word "colored" does not name any specific, determinate, definite color. It can be made definite, but it is not itself already definite. It is determinable, but it is not determinate. The word "scarlet," by contrast, names a specific, determinate color. Interestingly, however, nothing is ever just generically colored; anything that is colored always has some specific, determinate color. (Similarly, nothing is ever just a generic animal: it's got to be an Eastern Gray Squirrel or a Northern Cardinal or whatever. Or for still another example, nothing is ever just a generic polygon: it's got to be a triangle or a pentagon or whatever.)

Equipped with the distinction between determinates and determinables, we can claim, as a general principle, that while there certainly are both determinate predicates and determinable predicates, there are no true determinable properties. There are only determinate properties, and

---

17. This is an example of a perfectly general rule: if what you say logically implies something false, then what you said in the first place was false. There is never a logical path from truth to falsehood.

therefore any predicate that is determinable—for example, "animal"—is therefore not really the name of a true property or feature. Instead, it is a predicate we use when we want to draw attention to only part of a true (determinate) property. "Animal" does not name some property that an Eastern Gray Squirrel has in addition to having the property of being an Eastern Gray Squirrel. Instead, when used to talk about an Eastern Gray Squirrel, it names that squirrel's nature, but in such a way that we focus only on part of what of what goes into being an Eastern Gray Squirrel—on, say, having the powers of sensation and appetite.

What was just said about "animal," as applied to an Eastern Gray Squirrel, works just as well when "animal" is applied to a human, like Socrates. And this provides a way to respond to the objection against the foundational theory of essence. Being animal is not a property separate from the property of being human, but instead just an aspect of it. It follows that there is no need to worry that being human is not fundamental on the grounds that Socrates is human *because* he is an animal. For that to be a good objection, the property of being an animal would have to be a property distinct from the property of being human.[18]

We have seen some points about language and how attention to language can help us avoid misunderstandings about features. We have also used these points to answer an objection to the foundationality theory of essence. Now let us go on to consider essence in more detail.

1.4 The Uniqueness of Essence

I have been switching back and forth between talking about a substance's essential features, in the plural, and its essence, in the singular. Should we say that one thing can have multiple essential features? Or should we say, rather, that each thing can have only one essential feature, its one and only essence? The question is a difficult one.

---

18. For another use of the argument I make here, see Michael Gorman, "Two Types of Features: An Aristotelian Approach," *Ratio* 27, no. 2 (2014): 140–54. It's only fair to note that many philosophers think that there are determinable properties or features. For a general discussion of some of the issues, see Jessica Wilson, "Determinables and Determinates," in *The Stanford Encyclopedia of Philosophy*, ed. Edward Zalta and Uri Nodelman (Stanford University, 1997–), article first published February 7, 2017, substantive revision January 18, 2023, https://plato.stanford.edu/archives/spr2023/entries/determinate-determinables/.

If you adopt the foundationality approach over the modal approach, the number of essential features certainly gets much smaller, because many of the features that the modal approach says are essential are counted as accidental on the foundationality approach. For example, on the modal view, it is essential to Socrates not only that he be human, but also that he be able to laugh. But being able to laugh does not count as essential on the foundationality view, so adopting the foundationality view brings us closer to the idea that each thing has only one essence.

If you further accept the idea that there are no determinable properties, then the number of essential features gets even smaller. Before accepting that idea, we might have been tempted to say that Socrates has both the essential property of being human and the essential property of being animal; or, to take another example, to say that he has the essential property of being animal and the essential property of being rational. Once we accept it, however, those temptations disappear.

All this is nudging us toward the view that perhaps each thing has only one essential property or feature—just one essence. But a nudge is not an argument, or anyway it's not much of one.

Consider once again the thought that essential features are foundational. The first story of a house builds on and adds to the foundation of the house; the first story is an addition to, and enhancement of, a house that is already there (at least in a rudimentary way). A house's foundation, by contrast, does not build on or add to a house in any way; until the foundation is there, there's no house at all.[19] Foundational features are like foundations. A foundational feature does not build on a deeper-level feature and add to it; a foundational feature constitutes an object in the first place. When a foundational feature comes to be, that's not because an object that is already in existence comes to possess that feature, but instead because the object itself comes to exist, for the very first time, as a thing having that feature. And if a foundational feature is thus responsible for a thing's very existence, then it seems hard to understand how a thing could have more than one such feature. If Rusty had more than one foundational-level, absolutely-constituting principle, then he would be more than one

---

19. Don't overthink the metaphor. Don't worry, for example, about whether the house has a basement.

thing! For this reason, then, I think it best to say, in the end, that each thing has only one essence.[20]

1.5 The Partial Normativity of (Some?) Essences

Because the metaphysician knows all things, but not in detail, it is not the metaphysician's job to state the essence of a cat, or an electron, or anything else like that. On the other hand, it seems that the metaphysician should be able to provide at least some concrete examples of his theory, if only to check that the theory is not leading us away from the truth. Doing so leads to an important objection, an objection that is best faced by refining our way of thinking about some essences.

Think of Mickey. His essence is to be feline, to be a cat. But what is a cat? This is not quite as easy to say as we might like. But let's note at least this much: to be a cat involves having four legs. Obviously, there's much more to cats than that—to say that they have four legs isn't even enough to distinguish them from dogs—but to say even this much is already to run into an important problem. The problem is that there could be a cat that is missing a leg.

Suppose Mickey were like that. What then would we say? Would we insist that having four legs is part of the definition of cat, and therefore that Mickey is not really a cat at all? Or would we say that since Mickey obviously is a cat, therefore having four legs is not part of the essence of cat? Each of those seems problematic. The first one seems wrong because Mickey obviously is a cat. The second one seems wrong because having four legs is obviously an important part of what a cat is.

The issue would arise in just the same way if I mentioned other apparently-essential features of cats, like the feline genetic code, or having whiskers. Whatever genome belongs to the essence of cats, some cats will have genetic defects; and some cats have lost their whiskers. In fact, the more features we mention, the worse the problem seems, because each feature will be just another way for a cat to fail to

---

20. The idea that foundational features constitute the very existence of an object will return, above all in §3.3.3. In §9.2 we will discuss a possible exception to the rule that each thing has only one essential feature, namely, the Christian doctrine of the incarnation, according to which Christ has two natures, humanity and divinity.

live up to the definition of cat. If we try to fix the problem by eliminating all those aspects from the definition, then we end up in an intolerable situation: we end up saying that having legs isn't necessary for being a cat, and also that having a certain genome isn't necessary, and so on. Pretty soon, hardly anything will be left in the definition of a cat.

There is a way out. It involves refining how we define essences. The refinement does not involve eliminating things from the essence, but rethinking precisely how we formulate them. Instead of saying, for example, that it's essential to cats that they have four legs, we can say that it's essential to cats that they *should* have four legs. It's essential to cats that they be the kinds of things that *ought* to have four legs. Or, to put it somewhat differently, it's essential to a cat that it be the sort of thing that, if it does not have four legs, something has gone wrong. Cats are the sort of thing for which not having four legs is a defect or deficiency.

It's important to notice that not having legs is a defect for only some types of being. Snakes do not have legs, but this is not a defect for them. Imagine a snake together with a cat that has no legs: In one way, they are alike, namely, they have no legs. But in another way, they are very different: having no legs is not a problem for the snake, whereas obviously it is a very big problem for the cat. We would not say that the legless snake *lacks* legs, but we would say that the legless cat lacks legs.

Just to be clear: I said that a cat is the sort of thing that should have legs or that ought to have legs, but this should not be interpreted as if the "should" or the "ought" were a kind of moral requirement. Lacking legs is not a sin on the part of the cat!

There is a lot more to say about this topic.[21] For now, I just want to point out that when we talk about *what things are*, we are, often enough, talking about *what they ought to be*, about what counts as the *best and most fulfilled* versions of those things. Understanding what would count as perfection for that thing is an important part of understanding what that thing's essence is. In other words, often enough, essences need to be understood in a way that involves norms. The essence of something is not so much what it *is* as what it *ought to be*. To

---

21. I say some of it in my "Personhood, Potentiality, and Normativity," *American Catholic Philosophical Quarterly* 85, no. 3 (2011): 483–98 and my "Categories and Normativity" in *Categories*, ed. Michael Gorman and Jonathan J. Sanford (Washington, DC: The Catholic University of America Press, 2004), 151–70.

state the essence of something is to state the norms that it is supposed to live up to.

In the preceding paragraph, I included the qualification "often enough." That's because normativity might not apply to all essences, but only to living essences. A cat can fall short of the norms governing cat-kind by lacking the right number of legs, but can an electron fall short of the norms governing electrons? Are there electrons that are underweight or over-charged? The point will not be pursued further here, but I do want to at least raise the question.

To add one more complication, perhaps an essence could involve normative and non-normative elements. For example, while it seems inessential to cats that they actually have whiskers, it does seem essential that they actually have bodies; if a cat lost its whole body, it, the cat, would just pass out of existence.[22]

1.6 Substance-Centeredness vs. Substance-Exclusiveness

This chapter has given an account of substance that goes beyond the brief look that was given in the introduction, and it has gone into a fair amount of detail on the difference between essential and accidental features of substances. It has also made some points about the language we use in talking about the features of substances, and it has brought up the question of normativity and essence. Now I want to return to the question of what it means to have a substance-centered metaphysics.

Substances are the basic beings, and if substances are as I have described them, then the basic beings are individual, unified, and independent beings. But not every being fits that description. To be a being is not the same as to be a substance. Instead, to be a being is either (a) to be a substance or (b) to be related to a substance in some way. Already in this chapter we have gotten a first look at non-basic beings, beings that are not substances: We have, for example, seen that substances have accidental features (accidents). Mickey is a being, but so is his grayness. His feature of being gray is a being, but in a rather differ-

---

22. If this applies to humans too, then when a human being dies, he ceases to exist, even if his soul keeps on existing. But perhaps having a body is, at least in the case of humans, to be understood normatively. See Gorman, "Personhood, Potentiality, and Normativity"; Allison Krile Thornton, "Disembodied Animals," *American Philosophical Quarterly* 56, no. 2 (2019): 203–17.

ent sense from the sense in which he himself is a being, because it, his grayness, is not a substance.[23]

In theory, perhaps, this should not give rise to any difficulties, but in practice, it does. As will become clear in some of the chapters to follow, philosophers can end up treating all beings as if they were substances. Some deny the existence of non-substances.[24] Others treat non-substances as if they were substances—mini-substances, to be sure, weak-substances, second-tier substances, but substances nonetheless.

For example, to anticipate an important topic from chapter three, philosophers sometimes speak as if features are there, like parts from the auto parts store, waiting to be assembled into full-blown substances. Even when they know better, and state clearly that features are not substances, they fall into thinking of the features as being more substance-like than they really are. It isn't just features that are occasionally treated as substance-like: to anticipate an example from chapter six, philosophers who want to talk about what is possible—who want to talk, for example, about the fact that it is possible for me to stand up and do some jumping-jacks—sometimes end up treating *possibilities* as if they were things, substances or anyway substance-like.

There is, I believe, a reason why this happens. It grows out of a deep human tendency. Whenever we think about something, we are tempted to reify it: to treat it as if it were a thing, even when it isn't.[25] That very sentence exhibits the tendency in question: in warning against excessive use of thing-language, I used the word "something"! It's a very hard temptation to resist, but resist it we must. In Jonathan Lowe's amusing formulation, "Not everything is a thing."[26]

Let's avoid verbal tangles by swearing off words like "thing" and "everything," at least for this one paragraph. Not every being is a substance, but there is a strong tendency to think about all beings as if they

---

23. Is it just random that I chose an accidental feature here, and not an essential one? It is not. See §3.3.3.

24. Robert Pasnau seems to attribute such a view to Aquinas in his "On What There Is in Aquinas," in *Aquinas's* Summa Theologiae: *A Critical Guide*, ed. Jeffrey Hause (Cambridge: Cambridge University Press, 2018) 10–28.

25. The Latin word *res* means thing, so to reify means to thingify.

26. E. J. Lowe, "Identity, Individuality, and Unity," *Philosophy* 78, no. 3 (2003): 321–36, at 328.

were substances, either by literally treating them as substances, or else by treating them as if they were nearly substances.[27]

One possible explanation of this tendency is the nature of our language: we use sentences with subjects and predicates, and in the most natural examples of such sentences, the subjects do indeed name substances. In "Mickey is gray," the subject-term, "Mickey," names a substance. But then we use the same kind of sentence when we talk about non-substances. We say, "Mickey's color is pleasing to the eye," almost as if his color were a kind of substance. Again, we need to work hard, lest our intelligence be bewitched by language.

Relatedly, perhaps, substances are probably what we are best at thinking about. They are certainly what is most familiar to us, and words for substances (like "Mama") are among our very first words. Like the guy who looks for his keys under the lamppost because that's where the light is, we tend to assimilate non-substances to substances, even when this makes it harder to grasp what they really are.[28]

In the chapters that follow, this is a theme that will return a number of times. We need to keep substance at the center of metaphysics—to keep basic beings as our reference point. But saying that substances are at the center goes hand-in-hand with saying that there's a periphery, and that there are things that belong to that periphery: beings that are real, without being substances. Temptations lie in wait for us at every turn. It's hard not to think of the features of substances as little mini-substances, or quasi-substances. It's hard not to think of the natures of substances as special eternal substances that ordinary substances share in. It's hard not to think of possibilities as special ethereal substances that can be de-etherealized and thereby become actual. Philosophy is hard.

---

27. Fighting this tendency is very hard. In editing the paragraph that this footnote is attached to, I had to eliminate two uses of thing-words that had crept in against my firm resolve.

28. Thomas Nagel, "What is it Like to Be a Bat?" *The Philosophical Review* 83, no. 4 (1974): 435–50, at 435: "[P]hilosophers share the general human weakness for explanations of what is incomprehensible in terms suited for what is familiar and well understood, though entirely different."

1.7 Analogy

To say that not all beings are substances leads us to an important topic in the Aristotelian-Thomistic tradition, namely, *analogy*. There are many details and disputes here. Some of them will be discussed in chapters seven and eight. For now, a brief look will be sufficient.

To use an example from Aristotle, the word "healthy" can be used in different ways.[29] We can say that a cat is healthy, and we can say that a certain food is healthy, and we can say that a urine sample is healthy. Now a bit of reflection will show that the word is not being used in exactly the same way in these three cases. To say that a cat is healthy is, roughly, to say that all its physiological systems are functioning as they should: the cat's internal temperature is in the right range, its heartbeat is neither too fast nor too slow, and its blood pressure is neither too high nor too low. But that's not what we mean when we say that the food in a can of cat food is "healthy." We are not saying that the cat food has an appropriate blood pressure! When we say that the cat food is healthy, we mean that it contributes to health—to the health of the cat. And notice that this second sense of "healthy" is a secondary sense, a sense parasitic upon the primary sense. You can't understand what it means to say that cat food is healthy unless you understand what it means to say that a cat is healthy; to be healthy cat food is to be related in the right way to the health of a cat. Similar remarks apply to a "healthy" urine sample: it is called healthy because it is a sign of health—of the cat's health.

If these three uses of "healthy" were exactly the same, we would call them "univocal" uses. If they were utterly different and unrelated—think of how we use the word "bat" both for a small flying mammal and for what we hit baseballs with—then we would call them "equivocal" uses. But "healthy" is not like that. It has various uses that are at once different and related. For this reason, philosophers say that the word gets used "analogously."

Philosophical language is often used analogously. For example, the words we use about God, like "wise" or "powerful," are often, and perhaps always, meant analogously. What we mean by them is different from, but related to, what we mean when we apply them to creatures.[30]

---

29. See, for instance, *Metaphysics* IV.2, 1003a35–37.
30. See §8.11.

But quite apart from the question of God, the very word "being" can be used analogously. A substance is a being, and so is an accident, but they are beings in different (related) senses. A substance is a being in the primary sense, and an accident is a being in a secondary sense (we will leave open for now how many non-primary senses there are). The primary sense stands on its own, while the secondary sense or senses are what they are only by relation to the primary sense. Resisting the temptation to reify goes together with being sensitive to the analogous nature of the language of being. And sensitivity to analogy in language goes hand-in-hand with sensitivity to analogy in reality.[31]

So much for this first chapter, on substances and their features. Now we must change topics—by turning to the topic of change.

➤ To get started on reading Aquinas himself on the ideas developed in this chapter, begin with *On Being and Essence* and *On the Principles of Nature*.

---

31. This sort of point will return a number of times throughout this book, but it will be especially important in §7.2.2 and §8.11.

CHAPTER 2

Change

2.1 Change as a Topic in Metaphysics

IN CHAPTER ONE, we looked at substances as they are understood in the Thomistic way of thinking: individual, unified, independent beings. We also saw that standard examples of substances are ordinary living objects like cats.

On that basis, you won't be surprised to hear that substances change: they meow, for example, or they stretch and then nap. Understanding substance, therefore, requires understanding what change is all about, and for that reason, the topic of change fits well into this book. There is another reason to discuss change, as well: doing so puts us in a better position to bring up other topics later, such as the sense in which substances have parts (chapter three) and the nature of potentiality and its actualization (chapter six).

2.2 Wholes through Time or Temporal Parts?

Change is temporal, in the sense that every change takes at least a little bit of time. "A little bit" might be a *very* little bit: as little as a nanosecond (a billionth of a second), or a billionth of a nanosecond, or any amount you choose, as long as it's not strictly speaking no time at all. It simply makes no sense to think of change without thinking of it taking place through time.

But what is time? St. Augustine (d. 430) famously said that as long as no one asks him what time is, he knows, but as soon as someone asks him, then he doesn't.[1] Time is a very, very difficult philosophical topic. Some philosophers think that time is really something that belongs to

---

1. Augustine, *Confessions* XI, 14.17.

our minds, rather than to reality outside of our minds. Of philosophers who think that time belongs to reality outside of our minds, some think that it's there on its own, providing a context for change, while others think that change is more basic, with time being parasitic upon change.

I won't try to work out a philosophy of time here. But I do need to say just a little bit. I will explain the difference between "three-dimensional" theories of change and "four-dimensional" theories of change, and I will make clear which approach I will be following.

Things exist through time: they "persist." They exist now, on Monday, and they still exist on Tuesday. It's not just that *you* exist on Monday and *someone similar to you* exists on Tuesday: it is *you* who exist on both Monday and Tuesday. But what does this mean?

The three-dimensional theory of time says that when an object persists, the whole object persists. It's you, the whole you, who exists on Monday, through to Tuesday, and onward for the rest of the week. This view is called "three-dimensional" because it acknowledges space as having three dimensions while not thinking of time as a fourth dimension.

The four-dimensional theory of time does not agree. Think of a movie, consisting of a bunch of individual images—frames—scooting by at twenty-four frames per second. To make things simple, however, suppose the movie goes by ridiculously slowly: not 24 frames per second but one frame per day. And suppose the movie is a movie of you. The first frame is a picture of Monday-you, the second frame is a picture of Tuesday-you, and so on. The Monday-frame is not the whole movie, and neither is the Tuesday-frame. Only all the frames together are the whole movie.

Four-dimensionalism does not, of course, literally say that you are a film, made up of frames, but it does say that you are a *whole* made up of *temporal parts*: your Monday part, your Tuesday part, and so on. Being a whole made up of temporal parts is analogous to being a whole made up of spatial parts. Your spatial parts, let's say, are items like these: your left foot, your right foot, your left calf, and so on. Your temporal parts are items like these: Monday-you; Tuesday-you; and so on. The four-dimensionalist thinks that temporal parts are sufficiently similar to spatial parts that we can speak of time as a fourth dimension.

Now we have to add a complication. I initially presented the four-dimensionalist theory using one temporal part per day because that makes it easier to explain, but in reality the parts have to be much smaller. The frames have to go by much more quickly. In fact, it probably makes the most sense to say that there are infinitely many frames, each of them infinitely short—not just a billion frames per second, but infinitely many.[2]

For the three-dimensionalist, "existing through time" means being a whole that exists, as a whole, at different times. This mode of existing through time is often called "enduring," and three-dimensionalism is thus often called "endurantism." For the four-dimensionalist, by contrast, "existing through time" means being a whole whose *parts* exist at different times. You have many temporal parts, and they (not the whole you) are what exist at each individual time. You exist through time only indirectly, by being a whole made up of parts existing at different times. This mode of existing through time is often called "perduring," and four-dimensionalism is thus often called "perdurantism."

Four-dimensionalism is interesting, but it seems to deviate pretty far from common sense. Intuitively, it is I who exist today, not just a part of me. So why would anyone accept four-dimensionalism? One important reason is this: it might seem that three-dimensionalism cannot give us a good understanding of change. Suppose that yesterday you had black hair, but today you have blue hair. If you-yesterday and you-today are the same person, then one and the same person is both black-haired and blue-haired—and that sounds like a contradiction![3] A four-dimensionalist can respond that no single entity has both blue hair and black hair: the yesterday-you had black hair, and the today-you has blue hair, and when we say that "you" once had black hair and now have blue hair, we mean, ultimately, that you are a whole consisting of a black-haired part (yesterday-you) and a blue-haired part (today-you).[4]

There are multiple versions of both three- and four-dimensionalism, and the debates are very complex. It would be a fine thing to work through it all, giving the various views the attention they deserve. But that would lead us too far afield and interfere with the plan of this

---

2. If you worry that these infinities might lead to problems, I hear you. The issue lies beyond the scope of this book, although it does come up very briefly in §6.3.

3. To clarify: the idea is that yesterday your hair was entirely black, and today it's entirely blue. After all, it's not contradictory to have partly black hair and partly blue hair.

4. See the discussion of "temporary intrinsics" in Lewis, *On the Plurality of Worlds*, 202–4.

book.[5] For our purposes, I will do only two things. First, I will say that because three-dimensionalism is more commonsensical, we should stick with it if we can. It's *you* who have the properties you have today, and it will be *you* who have the properties you have tomorrow. And by *you* I mean the same whole you in both cases. Second, I will, in the next two sections, propose a way to make this work, in other words, a way to think about change without resorting to temporal parts.

2.3 Accidental and Substantial Change

Let's consider a garden-variety example of change: Mickey changes from lying down to standing up. There are three things to notice here.

First, when Mickey stands up, something "comes into being," and something "passes out of being": his lying-down posture passes away, and his standing-up posture comes to be. Or, to put this using a somewhat more technical and perhaps more dramatic-sounding terminology, his lying-down posture is "destroyed," and his standing posture is "generated."

Second, while something comes to be and something else passes away, some third item persists: Mickey himself. The process of change exhibits both discontinuity (lying down before, standing up after) and continuity (Mickey before, Mickey after).

Third, what changes in this case is something accidental, and what stays the same is a substance. Mickey loses one accident and gains another, but he remains throughout as a cat. There is no change in essential features, only a change in accidental features.[6]

This kind of change is called an "accidental change." A substance persists throughout, but not all of its accidents persist; one of them goes away and is replaced by another. The substance changes, but only in an accidental way.

But there is another and deeper kind of change. Mickey came into being when his parents mated. A cat ovum and cat sperm were joined, and Mickey was the result. The wrong way to think of this is as follows: the cat sperm and cat ovum still exist, only now they are a cat. The right way to think of it is this: the sperm and ovum passed out of existence,

---

5. If you are interested in this, your next step might involve looking at chapter eight of Loux and Crisp, *Metaphysics*.

6. Notice how we are making use of the essential-accidental distinction from §1.2.

and they were replaced by a cat (a very small, one-celled, zygotic cat). In this case, we don't have one substance remaining in existence while changing its accidents; instead, we have a new substance coming into being, and some old substances passing out of being. We have the destruction of the old substances, and the generation of a new one. This is called a "substantial change."

One might be slightly suspicious of the idea that sperm and egg are substances, although if they aren't substances, it's hard to say what they are. But never mind: we are metaphysicians, so we aren't responsible for such details. We can simply switch examples. Think of poor Mickey dying. At first, there is a cat. Later, there is no cat at all, but instead mere "feline remains"—in other words, what's left behind when a cat goes out of existence, which is basically just a pile of chemical substances (many, many chemical substances).

As in accidental change, so too in substantial change: something comes to be, and something passes away. But in substantial change, this happens on the level of essence and substance. Mickey comes to be while those gametes pass away, or chemicals come to be while Mickey passes away.[7] A new substance comes to be, an old substance passes away, and there is a change of essence: sperm and ovum are not cats, and a cat is not chemicals.

In talking about substantial changes involving Mickey, I said two things, corresponding to the first and third things I said about Mickey's accidental change from lying down to standing up: I mentioned that there is both coming-to-be and passing-away, and I mentioned the level that this happens on (accidental in one case, substantial in the other). But what should we say about the second of the three points? What stays the same through substantial change?

An answer that comes naturally to mind to us, in the twenty-first century, is this: there are a bunch of atoms involved, and those atoms are what persist through the change. Certain atoms used to make up a sperm and ovum, and later they made up zygotic Mickey; certain atoms used to make up adult Mickey, and now they make up a pile of chemicals. The atoms stay the same, and what changes is only how they are related to one another.

---

7. Did I really just say that chemicals come to be when Mickey passes away? Weren't they there already? See §3.2.

However natural this might sound to us, it can't be the right answer to the question of what stays the same through substantial change. That's because thinking of conception and death as rearrangements of atoms means thinking of conception and death not as substantial changes but instead as accidental changes! Cats, on this way of thinking, are not substances, but accidental arrangements of atoms; the true substances, the true basic beings, are the atoms, which undergo accidental changes (changes in location and how they are bonded to one another) that add up to the phenomena we call conception and death.

In short, if this is the right way of thinking about conception and death, then they aren't examples of substantial change, and we haven't made any progress in exploring that topic. We still have the problem of what stays the same through substantial change. And we also have a second problem: we now have concrete doubts, beyond the rather abstract doubt raised near the end of §1.1, about whether organisms like cats are basic beings.

Neither of these problems can be solved until chapter three. The second one will not even be addressed in this chapter: for present purposes, we will simply forge ahead, continuing (at our peril) to use Mickey and Rusty as examples of substances. As for the first problem, let me make some brief initial remarks, remarks that do not presuppose any particular answer to the question of which beings are the basic ones.

Whether or not cats are basic beings, still, something has to be! If cats are merely accidental groupings of atoms, well, maybe atoms are true substances; or, if atoms are merely accidental groupings of quarks and electrons, then maybe quarks and electrons are true substances; at some point, it seems, we have to come to beings that aren't made up of smaller substances, but just are what they are. Those will be the basic beings. And if they can undergo substantial change, then we can ask what stays the same through the substantial changes that those basic beings undergo.

In the Thomistic tradition, the way to answer this question is to say that what persists through substantial change is "prime matter," with prime matter understood to be an internal principle or explanatory factor that does not, in and of itself, have to exist in any particular way at all. It's a pure potentiality for being, a potentiality that can be actualized as sperm and egg, or as cat, or as chemical remains, but that does not, in itself, have any inclination or tendency toward any of these. In itself, it's indifferent to being actualized in this or that way, and that's what allows it to exist both before and after a substantial change.

If this sounds a bit mysterious, that's because it is. I will try to dispel at least some of the mystery in chapter three. For now, let us keep moving by setting out the distinctions made so far in Table 2-1.

Table 2-1 Types of Change

	accidental	substantial
coming-to-be	Mickey standing up	Mickey being generated
passing-away	Mickey ceasing to be standing up	Mickey dying

Accidental changes appear in the first column, and substantial changes appear in the second; generations appear in the first row, and destructions appear in the second row. What persists through the changes in the first column, through the accidental changes, is a substance. What persists through the changes in the second column, through the substantial changes, is less clear; we have spoken of prime matter, but we have not yet said much about it.

2.4 Change and Identity

Change is related to what philosophers call "identity." Identity is the state of being the same: two things are identical if they are the same. But "being the same" can mean different things, as illustrated by the following story. Once, in high school, at a formal dance, my date and I were sitting at a table, and I was surprised to see her looking around the room in a suspicious way. I asked what was wrong, and she said, "I'm looking to see whether anyone else is wearing my dress." Now obviously, in one sense, there was nothing to worry about: no one but she was wearing the particular dress that she was wearing! And yet, in another sense, it was possible that someone else was wearing "the same dress" that she was. Some other girl might have been wearing a dress of exactly the same design and color.

This difference can be set out more generally as follows. Let us treat 'A' and 'B' as names of objects (dresses, cats, whatever), and when we use these names, let's not make any assumptions about whether they refer to the same object or not. So when someone talks about A, and then talks about B, he might be talking about two different objects, but he might be talking about the same object under two different names.

If A and B are not the same individual object, then they are said to be "numerically distinct": counting (one, two) reveals them as distinct individuals. If they are the same individual, then they are said to be "numerically the same" or "numerically one": if counting makes sense here at all, we would count to one and then stop. Mickey and Rusty are numerically distinct from each other. Mickey is numerically the same as himself.[8]

But numerical identity is not the only kind of identity. If A and B are both agile, or both cats, or whatever, then they are said to be "the same in kind" or "specifically the same" or "generically the same."[9] If they differ—if one is agile and the other clumsy, or one is a cat and the other a squirrel—then they are "different in kind" or "not the same in kind" or "not specifically (generically) the same." And notice that being the same in kind is not all or nothing: A and B could be the same in kind with regard to color, but not the same in kind with regard to shape.

Back to the dress story: My date was wondering whether some other girl was wearing "the same dress" in the sense of "the same in kind." The humor in the story comes from the fact that the very same words—"Is someone else wearing my dress?"—could also express the absurd question as to whether someone else was wearing numerically the same dress.

Now if we think about identity (or difference) in kind or in number, and if we think about it as holding at just one time, then it seems clear how different types of identity fit together. At any one time—let's say, 2:10 p.m. on Tuesday—Mickey is numerically the same as himself, and he's numerically distinct from everything else. (If this sounds obvious and trivial, that's because it is.) Furthermore, Mickey is specifically the same as himself; at that time, he has all the properties that he has at that

---

8. Of course, no one would ever have any practical reason to say that something was numerically the same *as itself*. But someone might have a practical reason to say something like "Mickey is numerically the same as the cat that left the dead mouse on our doorstep this morning."

9. It's unfortunate that words like "kind" and "species" and "genus" get used for this: they suggest essence, while the sort of sameness or difference at issue includes both essential and accidental sameness or difference. Also unfortunate is the fact that words like "species" and "genus" sometimes indicate not just kinds in general, but higher or lower degrees of similarity (see §7.2). Be careful! Don't be misled!

time. (If this sounds obvious and trivial, that's because it is.) Finally, he is specifically different from some other things, at least in some respects, and he is specifically the same as some other things, at least in some respects. (Those last points may be obvious, but they are not trivial. It is possible to imagine a universe in which everything is specifically the same in every respect—in other words, everything is just alike. And it *might* be possible to imagine a universe in which no two things were specifically the same in any way—but see §7.3.)

But when we talk about different times, matters get more complicated. For our purposes here, the thing to focus on is the following: if we assume that we are dealing with Mickey both on Monday and on Tuesday, then obviously, on that assumption, Mickey on Monday is numerically identical to Mickey on Tuesday. But what if we don't know this in advance? If you see a cat while waiting for the bus on Monday, and if you see a cat while waiting for the bus on Tuesday, you might not be sure whether the cat you saw on Monday was numerically identical to the cat you saw on Tuesday.

On one way of thinking about it, they can't be numerically the same, at different times, unless they are completely specifically the same—unless they have all the same properties. On this way of thinking, numerical identity across time requires complete identity of kind, and so nothing can change and yet still remain the individual that it was before. By contrast, on the way of thinking I wish to put forward here, that's not so. Numerical sameness across time does not require complete specific sameness across time. The cat yesterday and the cat today could be numerically the same cat even if they are different in color (the cat is going gray) or size (the cat ate a lot overnight). And this, by the way, is how to handle the problem that has led some philosophers to accept four-dimensionalism. On the assumption that numerical identity over time requires complete specific sameness, it really is true that you-on-Monday can't be the same as you-on-Tuesday if you-on-Monday has a different hair color from you-on-Tuesday. But it's not necessary to accept that assumption, and if complete specific sameness isn't required, then dyeing your hair raises no metaphysical problem at all.

To say that numerical sameness across time does not require complete specific sameness isn't to deny that it requires *some* specific sameness across time. At the very least, the thing you saw yesterday can't be numerically identical to the thing you saw today unless they are *essen-*

tially the same in kind; if the thing you saw yesterday was a cat, then the thing you saw today must be a cat if it is the thing you saw yesterday.[10]

One last point about identity and change. I have said that numerical identity across time requires sameness of essence but not sameness of accident. But I want to repeat that sameness of essence is not enough. The mere fact that the cat on Monday and the cat on Tuesday are both cats doesn't mean they are the same individual cat. Sameness of essence is necessary, but it's not sufficient.

2.5 Form, Matter, Subject, Privation, Actualization

At this point I would like to introduce some traditional words that help us to talk about change. They come in sets. The first set is "form," "matter," and "subject." The second set—an overlapping one—is "form," "matter," and "privation." The third set is "potentiality" and "actuality."

"Form" and "matter" are concepts that appear in various contexts and with various analogous meanings. Sometimes what they mean is rather clear. If we have a bronze statue, its matter is the bronze it is made out of—that is, its material. Its form is its shape; it's literally the way it is formed. But Aristotle and his followers found ways to extend these concepts in a number of analogous ways. For example, Aristotle says the form of a human being is the soul, and the matter is the body.[11] The idea that a human's matter is his body seems rather similar to the idea that a statue's matter is its bronze, but it's not entirely the same: the bronze is bronze regardless of how it is shaped, but a body without a soul is not a true body.[12] As for the idea that a human's form is the soul, here the notion of "form" has clearly changed, because whatever a soul is, it's certainly not merely a shape! And for still a third example, it's standard in Catholic theology to talk about the form and the matter of a sacrament: in baptism, for example, cleansing with water is the

---

10. The idea that numerical identity across time requires retaining all the same properties is often associated with the philosopher Gottfried Leibniz (d. 1716). For a very helpful discussion of how Aquinas differs from Leibniz on this point, see Eleonore Stump, *Aquinas* (New York: Routledge, 2003), 44–46.

11. For the record, Aristotle—and pretty much all Aristotelians, including Aquinas—think that the form of *any* living thing is a soul, even cats, fish, and plants. As long as you add that only human souls are *rational* souls, it actually makes a lot of sense. But we can't get into it.

12. This will come up again in §3.2.

matter, and the words of baptism are the form. Here we are very far from the simple idea of stuff and shape.

Without trying to do justice to all these various meanings, let me say that we use the language of form when we want to talk about a property that a substance has, and we use the language of matter when we want to talk about a substance's potentiality for having a property. This enables us to use the notions of form and matter to talk about change. Think of Mickey lying down. We can think of his lying-down shape as a form, an accidental form, while the matter that corresponds to this form is Mickey himself. His posture is related to him in a way that's analogous to (but not exactly the same as) the way in which the shape of a statue is related to the bronze of a statue. His posture is the property that he has, and he himself is where (so to speak) the potentiality for having the property resides. We can, that is, say that an accident is a form, while the substance bearing that accident is matter. And then we can describe change in the following way: we have change when one form in a substance is replaced by another. Change involves a succession of forms in matter.

But not all forms are alike. Above I mentioned the idea that, in an expanded sense of "form," the soul of a human is the form of that human, while the body is the matter. At the same time, I noted that there is an important difference between this case and the case of the statue. Bronze is bronze, regardless of form: the form changes the shape of the bronze, but it doesn't have any effect on its fundamental, essential character as bronze. The accidental form affects it in a merely superficial way. But soul is different, and deeper. A form like soul doesn't take a substance that already exists and modify it, superficially, to make it exist in a somewhat different way. A form like this causes there to be a new substance in the first place: in this case, a human being.

Perhaps you can see how this is related to the distinction between substantial and accidental change. I said, in a generic way, that change is a succession of forms in matter: the matter persists, while the forms change. When the forms are accidental forms, the change is an accidental change, and the matter that persists throughout is the substance. But the kind of form that gives rise to a new substance is not accidental. It's called *substantial* form, and succession of substantial forms gives rise to a substantial change. Substantial change puts a lot of strain on our language and thought. Just above, I spoke of a substance's "potentiality for having a property," but in a case of substantial change, we are dealing with a substance's potentiality for being replaced by another substance, with another essence. The ovum and sperm have become a cat, you might say, but not in such a way that the ovum and sperm are themselves now a cat!

Sometimes, to highlight this difference, Aquinas brings in the word "subject." When he does this, he says that what bears accidental forms, and persists through a succession of accidental forms, is a "subject," and then he reserves the word "matter" for what persists through a substantial change. To some extent, this is a merely terminological affair. We could decide to use the word "matter" in both cases and say that sometimes matter is a substance underlying accidental change, while other times it's whatever it is ("prime matter") that underlies substantial change. Or, we could decide to use the word "matter" only for the latter of these, and the word "subject" for the former. Insofar as it's a terminological affair, nothing vital is at stake. However, there is a substantive issue lying beneath the terminological issue: however we choose to talk about it, there is an important difference between substantial and accidental change, and corresponding to this difference, there is an important difference between the matter that persists through substantial change and the matter that persists through accidental change. More will be said about this in chapter three; meanwhile, watch the terminology carefully!

Now let's talk about a different set of terms: "matter," "form," and "privation." Think of Mickey again, and ask yourself whether he can stand up. A number of things might be required for this to be possible, but for present purposes, the one to notice is this: he can't already be standing. You can't become what you already are; to change into something that is standing, you must first lack the property of standing. A word that is sometimes used to indicate such a lack is "privation." In addition to the matter or subject—namely, Mickey—and the form of standing that Mickey comes to have, there must also be, before the change, a privation of the form of standing. Change, then, requires form, matter, and privation.

This leads us to the last set of words I want to introduce—namely, "potentiality" and "actuality." I said that a cat that is already standing can't stand up. Another way to put this is that such a cat lacks the potentiality to stand up. Change presupposes a potentiality for change: before something happens, it must be possible for it to happen. And when it does happen, that happening is the actualization of the potentiality. When Mickey stands, he actualizes his potentiality to be standing.

The distinction between actuality and potentiality is related to the question of privation in the following way. If you are actually in a certain state—if, let's say, you are standing up—then you do not have the privation of that state. But as we saw, change requires privation. If you don't have the privation of a state, you can't come to be in that state; to put it a bit differently, if you don't have the privation of a state, you can't acquire the actualization of that state. So the potentiality for coming to be in a certain state requires the privation of actually being in that state; actually being in a state excludes the potentiality of coming to exist in that state. Again, you can't become what you already are.

If actually being in a state excludes the potentiality of *coming to be* in that state, does it also exclude the potentiality of *being* in that state? Should we say, that is, that if you are *actually* standing, you don't have the *potentiality* to be standing? This strikes me as a verbal matter. If by "potentiality" we mean "*unactualized* potentiality," then it's clear that having a certain property excludes the potentiality for having that property. But if by "potentiality" we mean "either actualized or unactualized potentiality," then having a property doesn't exclude having the potentiality for it. You still have the potentiality, but now it's an actualized potentiality rather than an unactualized potentiality.

To repeat, I think we can treat this as a verbal matter: it's merely a matter of deciding which way one will use the word "potentiality." (Context will sometimes determine which one sounds more natural. If I said to you that I have the potential to be a philosophy professor, you might scrunch up your face and say, "But I thought you *were* a philosophy professor!" On the other hand, if someone said that philosophy professors can't make beer, I might say, "Well, obviously they *can*, because I *do*." However you responded to that, it wouldn't be by saying that if I actually do make beer, then obviously I don't have the potentiality to do so!) Anyway, often enough it's just a matter of being careful to make one's own meaning clear, and of being alert to how other people are using the words they choose.

Here's something else about potentiality and actuality. Potentiality is never the bottom line: whenever there's a potentiality, it's always based on some more fundamental actuality. Think of a gallon of water in a bucket. The water is not actually jumping, but neither is it potentially jumping: water isn't the sort of thing that can jump at all. A potentiality is a kind of power or ability, but it is rooted in the essence of what has the power. Cats have the power to jump, but water doesn't, and that's because cats are different in kind from water. It's a good general principle that potentiality always piggybacks on some prior actuality. (In fact, Aquinas says that the powers or potentialities of a thing are necessary accidents that flow from the essence of that thing.)[13]

So when we think of change, we should think not merely of succession of forms, but also of the actualization of potentiality: the arrival of the new form is the actualization of a potentiality for having that form. More will be said about actuality and potentiality in chapter six.

This is a good time to recall the danger of reification that I warned against in the introduction. It's very easy to think of form and matter, or any of those others, as parts, and of taking this too literally: for example, to think that when a substance goes from having a lying-down form to having a standing-up form, this is like a car getting a new and different oil pump. But a posture (lying down, standing up) is not very thing-like. Ways of avoiding this error will be proposed in chapter three.

2.6 A Bit More on Change and Succession

I have described change as a succession of forms: one form comes, and another goes. I would like first to clarify that idea, and then to point out a kind of change that doesn't involve succession.

When we say that change involves a succession of forms, the idea is not merely that one form goes away while another takes its place, as if those were two events that just so happened to occur in succession. The coming-to-be of the new form and the passing-away of the old form are far more intimately related than that. Think of Mickey standing up. It's not a mere coincidence that when he stands up, he ceases to lie down. His standing up is very closely linked to his ceasing to lie down. His standing up drives out his lying down. Or think of Socrates getting a sunburn: his getting a sunburn drives out his being pale.

All this applies in what we might call the usual case, but now I want to mention another sort of change. Think of learning a new word:

---

13. See Aquinas, *Summa Theologiae* I, q. 77, a. 1, ad 5.

think, for example, of learning that *Hund* is the German word for dog. Once you've learned it, you have a certain accidental form; but did acquiring that new form drive out some previous form? It seems that it did not. It's not as if *not-knowing-what-Hund-means* is a form or property; it's merely the lack of a property. Here, then, is a case of change without succession: a new form comes to be without some previous form departing. And the reverse can happen as well. If you forget what *Hund* means, then you no longer have a certain form, but it's not as if that form was replaced by some special kind of *used-to-know-what-Hund-means* property; you just now lack a bit of knowledge. Lack of knowledge is a merely negative reality, or rather, it's not a reality at all, but a lack of one.[14] A form has departed, but no other form has come to take its place.

Although change often involves succession, it doesn't always. If I were in a fussy mood, I might (as Aquinas sometimes does) reserve the term "change" for the kind of thing that involves succession and say that so-called change without succession isn't really change at all, but merely becoming. We won't usually need to be this fussy.[15]

We have talked a lot about change: above all, about the distinction between substantial and accidental change, about identity and difference, and about what's needed to make sense of change, namely, form, matter, and the like. We have answered certain questions, but raised many more. Some of them involve asking whether the elements of change, for example, form and matter, are *parts* of the substances that change. And that leads us to the next chapter.

▶ To get started on reading Aquinas himself on the ideas developed in this chapter, begin with *On the Principles of Nature*.

---

14. "Lacks knowledge of *Hund*" is a nice example of a predicate that doesn't correspond to a property. Don't be bewitched!

15. Aquinas thinks that change with succession is characteristic of the material world, whereas change without succession is characteristic of immaterial processes like knowledge. There are deep issues that we can't get into here; if you want to know more, see David Cory, "Agency and Materiality in Aquinas's Soul Theory" (PhD diss., The Catholic University of America, 2018).

CHAPTER 3

Parts

3.1 Kinds of Parts

EVERY SUBSTANCE HAS PARTS or constituents: things that go to make it up or constitute it.[1] But there are different kinds of parts.

You could say that Mickey is made up of legs, tail, and so forth, and maybe atoms, too. Those would seem to be parts of his. But there's a very different way to talk about what makes up Mickey. You can think of him as being made up of his features: his size, his color, his agility, and so on. Insofar as these go together to make him what he is, it is tempting to use the language of "parts" for them as well; but if we do, we shall certainly have to add that features are parts in a sense very different from the sense in which, say, legs and tail are parts.

In this chapter, I will be talking about a number of ways in which substances are made up of parts. But because these "parts" are so different from one another, we shall in fact have to engage in multiple discussions. They won't all fit into one way of thinking.

3.2 Physical Parts

The most obvious kinds of parts are the ones that we might naturally call "physical parts." Examples include parts mentioned in the preceding section: legs, tail, atoms. But physical parts can be divided into three basic types.

The first type is the strangest, and I bring it up only to set it aside. Parts of this sort are sometimes called "arbitrary" physical parts. They are arbitrary in the sense that they don't correspond to any natural divisions; instead, where one part ends and the next one begins is

---

1. Maybe "every" takes it too far. Does God have parts? Then again, is God a substance? See §8.5 and §8.8.

entirely a matter of choice. Here is an example of an arbitrary part: the last three inches of Mickey's tail. Here is another: the last four inches of Mickey's tail. Here is a third: the last two-fifths of Mickey's tail. I'm not a felinologist, but I feel confident that there's nothing special about these divisions. They don't correspond to anything important about the anatomy or physiology of cats. And that's the point: they are completely arbitrary divisions.

I won't be talking about arbitrary parts in this book, precisely because they are arbitrary. Metaphysics is about how the world is, not about how we choose (for no reality-based reason) to slice the world up. Just as there are verbal predicates that correspond to no real properties, so too there are verbal formulations that correspond to no real parts.[2]

But not all physical parts are arbitrary. Think of Mickey's legs, his tail, his liver, and so on; and then think of the particles that seem to make up Mickey, whether they are molecules, atoms, or sub-atomic particles like quarks and electrons. Legs and livers, or particles, are not arbitrary, not a matter of human convention. They have a structure and nature of their own, one that's "out there" for us to discover.

These non-arbitrary physical parts fall into two main classes, as my way of phrasing things in the previous paragraph was meant to suggest. Those two classes give us the second and third main types of physical part. The second class contains parts like legs, and the third class contain parts like atoms. But what exactly is the difference between them?

To grasp what is at stake, let us take a bit of a side route and think again about the sand pile mentioned in §1.1. Note how each grain of sand is what it is—a grain of sand—quite independently of whether it belongs to the pile. It's not crucial to the nature or identity of the grains that they belong to the pile. The grains can exist, as themselves, with or without the pile. Or, using a concept that we met in §1.2, it's a non-necessary, contingent accident of each grain that it belongs to the pile.

By contrast, think of Rusty's legs, his tail, and so on. Belonging to him is essential to them. To be a cat leg is, in part, to belong to a cat; to be Rusty's leg is, in part, to belong to Rusty. If someone asked you to explain what a leg was, you couldn't really do it without also explaining what an animal was. The very idea of leg (or tail or liver)

---

2. See Peter van Inwagen, "The Doctrine of Arbitrary Undetached Parts," *Pacific Philosophical Quarterly* 62, no. 2 (1981): 123–37.

depends on the idea of a whole animal; the very idea of cat leg (or cat tail or cat liver) depends on the idea of a whole cat. A leg's being a leg depends on its having a role in the animal overall. It's essential to the leg that it belong to the animal. It's not merely a leg, but a leg *of an animal*. The "of an animal" part is essential to the leg.

It's interesting to notice how this conflicts with the conceit of Mary Shelley's *Frankenstein*, in which Dr. Frankenstein starts with body parts and somehow assembles them into a living being. It's fine for a story, but that's not how it works in real life. Organisms are not built up out of pre-existing organs. Instead, organs come from organisms; organisms develop organs. The organism, as a unified being, is prior to all its parts, and the parts are what they are only insofar as they belong to the organism.[3]

I will call parts like legs and tails "whole-dependent parts," because they depend on their wholes. They need those wholes so that they, the parts, can be themselves. If they are separated from their wholes, then they, the parts, are no longer what they were. They pass out of existence and become mere clumps of chemicals or whatever. What we call an amputated or detached leg is not really a leg at all, even if it will, for a short time, look like one. (To say this is analogous to saying that these parts undergo substantial change, but it's only analogous, because such parts are not substances.)

Parts like grains of sand, by contrast, are "whole-independent parts." They are what they are independently of whether they belong to the whole. A grain of sand is a whole-independent part of a sandpile, and a person is a whole-independent part of a team or company.[4]

It's clear that substances like Mickey have whole-dependent parts, and it's also clear that non-substances like sand piles have whole-independent parts. But do substances have whole-independent parts? It seems that Mickey includes atoms as parts. It also seems that if he does have atoms as parts, they are whole-independent parts. Indeed, we say things like, "This carbon atom was part of the cat food, and then Mickey

---

3. See *Metaphysics* VII.10, 1035b14–25, where Aristotle says that the whole is prior to bodily parts, and that if you separate an eye or a hand from the whole, then it's not really an eye or a hand at all.

4. I am adopting this distinction from Patrick Toner, and much of his use of it, but not his terminology. He calls whole-dependent parts "inseparable parts" and whole-independent parts "separable parts." See Toner, "On Substance."

digested the food, at which point the carbon atom became part of him; later it will cease to be part of him and become part of something else." But as we saw in §2.3, thinking of cats as made up of parts in this way gives rise to a serious difficulty: if a cat is made of atoms, why think of it, the cat, as anything more than a pile or collection? Such a difficulty cannot be brushed aside in an introduction to Thomistic metaphysics; as we saw in §1.1, it's part of that approach to metaphysics to think of ordinary organisms like Mickey as paradigmatic examples of substances. We need to confront this problem squarely, and now is the time.

Let's think more about sand piles. In a sand pile, each grain can exist apart from the pile; relatedly, the pile seems to be little more than the grains themselves, all hanging out in the same spot. The pile is just a pile, a mere heap. There's not much to it, above and beyond the grains themselves. The grains do have to be related to one another in a certain way: they must be bunched closely together and heaped up in a roughly rounded shape. But really this is just to say that the pile of sand is what you get when the many grains undergo the right accidental changes: they change their locations, and they acquire certain accidents such as *being on top of* and *being underneath* and *being crammed in next to*. What you get, in this case, doesn't seem to be much of a thing at all. It's not tightly unified, and this is why we don't think of it as a substance.

The point of this reflection on the sand pile can be expressed much more generally. If you bring together a bunch of things whose identity and essence is independent of their being together, the result—a whole whose parts are all whole-independent parts—appears to be little more than a heap or pile. If Mickey is made up of particles, then "he" is nothing more than merely what you get when a bunch of particles undergo the right accidental changes. The particles interact for a while, like a crowd or a dance troupe, and then they go their separate ways. I don't wish to exaggerate. The parts do have to be interrelated in some way, and those interrelations can be very complex. A dance troupe's movements can be very complicated. But in the end, all these interrelations are accidental. If this is the right way to think about Mickey, then although he is obviously more complicated than a pile of sand or a dance troupe, in the end he is no more a substance than they are.

Let's relate this to a three-way distinction some recent philosophers have made. They start with the assumption that what's most basic in reality is elementary particles: electrons and quarks, or whatever it turns out to be. Then they add the idea that other things, if they exist at all, are built up from these particles. (This is the vision of *Frankenstein*, but with elementary particles playing the role of pseudo-limbs snatched from corpses.)[5] From this starting point, there are three options: nihilism, universalism, and something in between.[6]

Nihilism says that no matter how the particles are combined, they *never* make up a larger whole: all larger wholes are illusory, and the only things that exist are the particles. Probably you would agree that no whole is made up of the following three parts: your left shoe, the fish closest to the mouth of the Mississippi, and the Eiffel Tower. We can put these three into one verbal formulation—I just did so—but they don't constitute any real, non-arbitrary whole. Well, says, the nihilist, the same goes for *any* collection, including the collection of particles that make up the fish closest to the mouth of the Mississippi. The particles exist, but the fish does not. Neither do the shoe, the tower, the sand pile, nor, in fact, any of the individual sand grains.

Universalism, at the opposite extreme, says that no matter how particles are combined, they *always* make up a larger whole. Any and every possible combination makes an existing thing. Each grain of sand is an existing thing, and so is the whole sand pile. The same applies to the left two-fifths of the sand pile, or the bottom seven-elevenths. Your left shoe is an existing thing, the fish closest to the mouth of the Mississippi is an existing thing, the Eiffel Tower is an existing thing, and so is the combination of that shoe, that fish, and that tower. Admittedly, some of those are pretty weird objects, but for the universalist that's no objection: to repeat, the universalist holds that *any* grouping of however many particles constitutes a thing. A shoe-fish-tower may not be the sort of object we refer to in ordinary speech, but that doesn't make it any less real.

This second view, universalism, sounds truly crazy to me. If any combination of particles makes up a substance, then there's really no point in talking about substances at all. Nihilism seems crazy, too: Mickey does really seem like a whole, and so do you and I. A middle-of-the-road theory seems to be needed. But the problem is that it's hard

---

5. I say "pseudo-limbs" because limbs are whole-dependent parts, meaning (as noted earlier) that a severed limb isn't really a limb at all.

6. See van Inwagen, *Material Beings*, esp. 72–80.

to come up with one—a fact that explains why people sometimes opt for nihilism or universalism.

In §1.1, I mentioned the idea that a substance requires the sort of unity that allows it to act as a unified agent, a thing that acts. Can we arrive at the desired in-between view by saying that we have a substance when the particles make up a unified agent? This may well be true, but it's not really the right kind of answer. It tells us *when* particles make something up: it says that when they make up a unified agent, then that agent is a substance. But it doesn't explain, or even begin to explain, what it is about the particles, or how they interact, that yields this very special result. We have been given no answer to the question of why one combination of particles results in a unified agent while another combination does not.[7]

What would an answer look like? Some philosophers might propose that the particles interact in such a way that a new level of being "emerges" from them: the existence of the particles, and their interacting as they do, guarantees the existence of the higher level, and the higher level could not exist without the lower.

Things are complicated, however. It is not enough for there just to be *some* sense—some technical sense perhaps—in which the operation of the whole substance is "new," and distinct from the operations of the particles. The substance needs to have operations that are robustly irreducible to those of the particles. If the new level is wholly caused by, and reducible to, the level of the physical particles, in such a way that the higher level doesn't account for anything that is not already accounted for by the particles, then I see no reason to think that we really have a higher unified agent, and therefore no reason to think we have a true substance. In the end, the particles are just doing what they were going to do anyway. If, on the other hand, the new level really is new, and the substance acts in ways that go beyond what is already there in the particles' natures, then it's hard to understand the claim that the higher level has emerged from the lower level in the sense of being necessitated by it.[8]

---

7. Van Inwagen puts emphasis on this sort of point while also emphasizing that he does not know what the right answer is; see *Material Beings*, 38–51.

8. For a detailed discussion of emergence, see Timothy O'Connor, "Emergent Properties," *The Stanford Encyclopedia of Philosophy*, ed. Edward Zalta (Stanford University, 1997–), August 10, 2020, https://plato.stanford.edu/archives/win2021/entries/properties-emergent/.

One way to proceed would be to go beyond emergence and say that the particles are only *part* of what necessitates the higher level. Something else is required as well. For example, one might propose that, in addition to particles, Mickey has an immaterial part that gets the particles to act in ways that they wouldn't act on their own. If you call this a form, with particles playing the role of matter, it even sounds Aristotelian.[9] However, it is problematic to say that Mickey's form gets his particles to act in ways that they wouldn't act on their own. It is problematic to say that his form gets his particles to act in ways that are inconsistent with their own proper natures. It is problematic, in other words, to say that Mickey is (partly) made up of particles like carbon atoms, while also holding that the laws of physics and chemistry do not really apply to those particles because how they act is ultimately controlled by Mickey's form.

In the face of these difficulties, you might feel obliged to say, however reluctantly, that perhaps nihilism is right after all. Perhaps even Mickey isn't an existing substance; perhaps "he" is just a temporary grouping of particles, less fleeting than a snowball but more fleeting than a hill. But let's not give up just yet. It turns out that there is a different approach, one built on some of Aquinas's ideas. It may seem entirely insane at first, but be patient.

The core idea is that Mickey has *no* non-feline parts. His "parts list" includes neither elementary particles, like quarks, nor larger-scale particles, like carbon atoms. *All* his parts are cat parts. True, if his cat food contains carbon atoms, then carbon atoms enter into his body when he eats; but when he digests his food, the carbon atoms pass out of existence, and we end up with new cat-parts. He is made *from* carbon atoms, but he isn't made *of* them. Digestion brings about something like a substantial change, as a result of which the atoms no longer exist: they have been replaced by feline parts.[10] On this way of thinking, Mickey is not a substance made up of smaller substances, whether carbon atoms or quarks, because there cannot be a substance made up of smaller substances: substances only make up collections, so any true unified substance must be made of non-substances. On this way of

---

9. This is, perhaps, the outlook found in Leon Kass, *The Hungry Soul: Eating and the Perfecting of Our Nature* (Chicago: University of Chicago Press, 1999), 40–44.

10. For the distinction between substantial and accidental change, see §2.3.

thinking, then, all of Mickey's parts are whole-dependent cat parts, like legs. There is no problem of how they make up Mickey, and that's because there's nothing else they could possibly do: to be them just is to be cat-parts. Belonging to him is essential to them. It's not that non-feline things get together and make him up. It's that he exists as a substance with feline parts, a substance that (through digestion) transforms non-feline things (for example, carbon atoms or quarks) into more of himself. He is more basic than his parts, and his parts get their nature from him, not the other way around.

The parts of Mickey that seem to be whole-independent parts are, when understood in this way, just more examples of whole-dependent parts. We saw earlier that Mickey's legs are whole-dependent parts of him. Being part of him is essential to them: they are feline legs. If you subdivide his legs into smaller parts—for example, bones and muscles and the like—you will still be dealing with feline parts (smaller ones, of course). On the view I'm presenting now, it doesn't matter how far you go: you can divide the muscles into cells, and the cells into organelles, and so on, but you will never get to a point where the parts are whole-independent parts. You will never arrive at parts that are what they are regardless of their role in a cat. You will never arrive at little substances. Even at what we think of as the atomic and sub-atomic levels, we will still be dealing with (very small) cat parts.

The view just described is in conflict with something that seems true to many people nowadays. People nowadays are inclined to think along the following lines. A cat's legs may well be essentially cat legs, and those legs may well be made of muscles that are essentially cat muscles, and those muscles may well be made of cells that are essentially cat cells, and so on. But even if this is granted, people will say, eventually we will arrive at some sub-cellular level at which the parts are not essentially feline. For example, maybe it will turn out that while specifically feline cells are made of specifically feline molecules, those molecules are ultimately made of components that are not specifically feline but that are instead, for instance, carbon atoms. In other words, even if some of the higher-level parts of the cat are whole-dependent, the lowest level of parts are not: instead, those lowest and smallest parts are whole-independent parts.

The Thomistic view I am proposing says that this is not the correct picture. Even at the lowest possible level, we will still have parts that are specifically feline, with the result that it's whole-dependent parts all the way down. There are, in short, no carbon atoms in a cat! There are, instead, tiny cat pieces that look and act like carbon atoms in certain ways.

Let us go over this again, with an emphasis on the idea that a substance has the sort of unity that is revealed by unitary action: to be a substance, something has to be able to act as a whole. It's very hard to understand how a substance could be made up of particles: these parts, because they are whole-independent, have their own essences, independent of the whole substance, and for this reason, they would by nature tend to "do their own thing," instead of acting in concert. On my Thomistic proposal, by contrast, there simply aren't any whole-independent parts that need to be cajoled into acting together. There are parts, but they are all whole-dependent: they all share in the nature of the substance they belong to. If Mickey's parts are not feline, then we will have trouble understanding why they reliably take part in distinctively feline action. But if we deny that they are whole-independent in the first place, then the problem of why they act in concert will not arise. Of course they all contribute to feline activity: they're all feline!

To be sure, these tiny cat parts do act very much like carbon atoms (or iron atoms, or whatever). The cat parts, in other words, exercise powers very much like those of carbon atoms. Some philosophers, picking up on an expression of Aquinas's, describe this by saying that carbon atoms are "virtually present" in the cat, meaning that the powers (*virtutes*) of the carbon atoms are now possessed by certain parts of the cat, or more carefully perhaps, that certain parts of the cat possess powers that are similar to those of the carbon atoms.

To me, this type of language of "virtual presence" is very misleading. Suppose I tell you that I own a Lamborghini. You might be very impressed; at any rate, you will certainly be surprised. But then suppose I clarify by saying that I own a *potential* Lamborghini. That would be silly. To say that I "have a potential Lamborghini" is not to say that I have a special kind of Lamborghini—the potential kind—but rather that I don't have a Lamborghini but could have one (if I sold my house). Talking about a "potential Lamborghini" is misleading, because it seems like a way of talking about a kind of Lamborghini, when really it's a way of talking about something else. Similarly, talking about virtual carbon atoms, or carbon atoms that are virtually present, is misleading: to say that a carbon atom is virtually present is to say that it's *not* present, but that something else is, something that has powers like those of a carbon atom.[11]

In §2.5, we met the idea of form and matter, and we also met the idea that a substance is, in some sense, a combination of form and matter; but we didn't say much about what that really means. Given what's been said in this section, one thing it doesn't mean is this: that matter is a multitude of whole-independent parts, little substances governed by a substantial form. But then what does it mean? Thomistically speaking, substantial form doesn't arrange or organize whole-independent parts, parts whose essences are established apart from the substantial form. Instead, substantial form is responsible for the material parts having the essences or natures that they do. Mickey's muscles, and even his microscopic parts, are what they are because of Mickey's substantial form. In short, form doesn't just arrange or govern matter, it makes it be what it is. Mickey's matter is the kind of matter it is—feline matter—because of Mickey's feline form.

The flip side of this claim is that apart from his substantial form, a cat's matter does not and cannot constitute a feline body. What we call a "dead cat," a cat corpse, is not a cat, or even merely a cat's body, but instead non-feline chemicals left behind when the cat dies; in short, the cat's remains are not feline. On this picture, all the actuality in Mickey comes from his substantial form; his matter (his prime matter) is simply a principle of potentiality, a potentiality that was actualized as feline.[12]

The Thomistic approach, as presented here, has one very clear advantage. It solves the problem of how the non-cat particles make up a cat. It solves it by denying the existence of the non-cat particles. No particles, no problem! Instead of wondering why whole-independent

---

11. For some discussions of this difficult topic, including discussions that would say that I minimize virtual presence a bit too much, see Patrick Toner, "St. Thomas Aquinas on Mixture and the Gappy Existence of the Elements," *History of Philosophy and Logical Analysis* 18, no. 1 (2015): 255–68; Christopher Decaen, "Elemental Virtual Presence in St. Thomas," *The Thomist* 64, no. 2 (2000): 271–300; Joseph Bobik and Thomas Aquinas, *Aquinas on Matter and Form and the Elements: A Translation and Interpretation of the De Principiis Naturae and the De Mixtione Elementorum of St. Thomas Aquinas* (Notre Dame, IN: University of Notre Dame Press, 1998).

12. I will say more in §3.4.

parts make up a whole in this case but not in the case of a sand pile, we simply say that there aren't any whole-independent parts at all, and instead that all the parts are cat-parts. If they are all cat-parts, then their unity is exactly what we should expect.

On the other hand, there's a disadvantage as well, one noted already: it sounds insane. It sounds insane because it seems to involve rejecting science. Didn't we all learn in high school that cats are made up of atoms?

One possible way to respond is to say the following: Yes, the view is inconsistent with modern science, but so much the worse for modern science. If we have to choose between (a) denying that Mickey is a substance, and (b) affirming, against what modern science says, that Mickey has no whole-independent particles, then it actually makes sense to choose (b). That's because (a) makes Mickey not a substance but just an accidental arrangement of non-feline particles, and we know that's wrong. (If you are inclined to choose (a) in the case of Mickey, I'll change the example: Don't you think that *you* are a substance? Aren't *you* one unified whole? Or are you just a bunch of non-human particles?) In short, maybe this is a situation where we should go with what metaphysics says, even if that means going against science. After all, metaphysics is the highest science. It sits in authority over the others. Even if we are not scientists and don't know what the correct scientific account should be, maybe we can rightly conclude, in a situation like this, that what scientists are currently saying just can't be right.

That's a pretty radical response. But it's altogether possible that less radical responses will turn out to be right. Here are two other possible responses that don't involve a clash between metaphysics and natural science.

First, maybe adopting the Thomistic approach to physical parts of substances does not mean rejecting science, but only reinterpreting it somewhat. When chemists describe the actions of cat-particles by saying that the particles are carbon atoms, maybe their descriptions can be reinterpreted to mean that the particles are cat-particles that act a lot like carbon atoms. Everything that the chemist has said about how the particles behave can remain as before, and the only thing that will have to change is the claim that these particles are carbon atoms. We might even keep on calling them "carbon atoms"—in fact, we surely will—as long as we don't think of them that way, strictly speaking.

Second, even more optimistically, maybe the Thomistic approach doesn't require reinterpreting science, because maybe real science doesn't actually say that Mickey is made up of whole-independent atoms. Let's face it: for most of us, anyway, what we call "science" is merely what (we think) we were taught in high school: that particles are like little balls attached to one another by sticks, in ever-larger and more complicated patterns, like microscopic Tinker Toys. But in fact, sophisticated understandings of science give us a more subtle and complicated picture. When atoms enter into combinations to make molecules, they undergo very significant changes. Hydrogen tends to explode, and oxygen promotes burning, but water, which is what you get when you combine hydrogen and oxygen in the right way, has neither of those properties; indeed, water is a classic way to put a stop to burning. Maybe, then, when two hydrogens and one oxygen are joined, the result isn't literally a pair of hydrogen atoms linked to an oxygen atom, but, instead, well, a water molecule: a molecule that has parts that *resulted from* hydrogen and oxygen atoms but that are not actually and literally *themselves* hydrogen and oxygen atoms. These parts have powers that are, in some respects, similar to those of hydrogen and oxygen atoms, but very different in other respects. On this way of thinking, such parts are not truly hydrogen and oxygen, not truly whole-independent parts, but instead whole-dependent parts, water-parts, analogous to the way in which cat legs are cat-parts. Bringing this back to Mickey, maybe the idea that cats don't have whole-independent, non-feline parts is perfectly consistent with modern science rightly understood. Mickey's parts, on this way of thinking, are simply cat parts, even though of course they are derived from, and somewhat similar to, things like carbon atoms and the rest.

I have presented a Thomistic view of physical parts; I have talked about why one might want to adopt it; and I have discussed three different ways to respond to the objection that it conflicts with science and is therefore insane. Now I would like to turn briefly to one interesting question raised by the Thomistic view.

Can a man-made object, an "artifact," ever be a substance? It seems that at least some of them are not substances, because they contain whole-independent parts. A car, for instance, is made up of bits of metal and plastic, and these bits are what they are regardless of whether they are part of the car. It is difficult to say whether *all* artifacts are like this, or only some of them, but it seems clear enough that many artifacts are not substances, but merely collections of substances.[13]

This is as much as I will be saying on the question of substances and their physical parts. To sum up: (1) We should simply reject the idea of arbitrary physical parts. (2) Whole-dependent parts, like legs and tails, are legitimate parts of substances, and they pose no threat to a substance's unity; on the contrary, they presuppose it. (3) It seems best to endorse the idea that substances do not have whole-independent parts; this seems the best way to preserve the idea that they are unified things that act as unitary agents.

3.3 Features and Substrates as Parts

Having discussed physical parts in section 3.2, let's move on to consider another way in which philosophers have thought of substances as having parts: by thinking of features and "substrates" as parts. I'll explain what substrates are later; for now, let's focus on features, asking first why anyone might think of them as parts.

Consider Rusty and Mickey. Both are asleep, but Rusty is sprawled out while Mickey is curled up. They are the same in one way, but not in another. (Of course, by "the same" here, I mean specifically the same, not numerically the same.) This situation seems perfectly possible, but we can imagine someone objecting that it isn't possible after all. Such a person might say, "Rusty is the way he is, and Mickey is the way he is. Either those two 'ways'—the way Rusty is, and the way Mickey is—are the same, or they aren't. If they are the same, then Rusty and Mickey are alike. If they are not the same, then Rusty and Mickey are not alike. But it makes no sense to say that they are both alike and unalike."

There's pretty clearly something wrong with this objection. As I said above, it's pretty clearly possible for Rusty and Mickey to be both alike and unalike. But it's not very philosophical to say to the objector, "You're wrong," without also explaining how the objector has gone wrong.

---

13. For discussion of Aquinas's complicated approach to this question, see Michael Rota, "Substance and Artifact in Thomas Aquinas," *History of Philosophy Quarterly* 21, no. 3 (2004): 241–59. Toner holds that artifacts are not substances; see his "On Substance." For authors who argue that we should not believe in artifacts at all, but only in the parts they are made up of, see Merricks, *Objects and Persons*; van Inwagen, *Material Beings*.

How has the objector gone wrong? His mistake lies in thinking that we should just talk about *the way Mickey is* and *the way Rusty is* as if these were solid, undifferentiated, homogenous blocks. We need instead to think of *the way Mickey is* and *the way Rusty is* as being internally complex, as composed of multiple elements. Mickey (or Rusty) exists in multiple ways. These various ways, inasmuch as they go to make him up, can be seen as parts of him. We can say, for example, that Mickey has both an alertness part and a posture part. Their alertness parts are alike—each cat is asleep—but Rusty's posture part is "sprawled out" while Mickey's posture part is "curled up." Their alertness parts match—they are specifically the same—but their posture parts do not. This makes it possible to explain how they can be both alike and unalike: they are alike inasmuch as some of their feature-parts match, and they are unalike inasmuch as some of their feature-parts do not match. Putting things generally now: if A and B have no parts, then it looks like a contradiction to say that A and B are at once alike and unalike, but if A and B have parts, contradiction can be avoided. I think that this line of argument is persuasive, and that it therefore makes good sense to think of substances as having a multiplicity of parts, where those "parts" are their features.[14]

It might seem like an abuse of language to call features like agility "parts." It certainly is an unusual use of that word. Some philosophers add on a special label, for example, by speaking of "metaphysical" parts. This doesn't exactly explain anything, but on the other hand it does serve the important purpose of flagging the fact that something special is going on.

I think it's legitimate to use the word "part," but also legitimate to feel uncomfortable with it. Think about Mickey again. There's more to him than being feline. He's gray, too. And indeed, there's more to him than being feline and being gray: he's male, he's agile, and on and on. Each of those—feline, gray, male, etc.—gives us only a *partial* description of him. He is, as we say, gray *in part*. Anything that belongs to him while not taking up the *whole* of him can be said to be, well, *part*

---

14. This paragraph's reasoning is inspired by Armstrong, who distinguishes between "blob" theories of substance and "layer cake" theories of substance. Blob theories treat substances as if they have no parts, while layer cake theories treat them as having parts—one layer per feature, so to speak. See Armstrong, *Universals*, 38.

of him. That's why it makes sense to call these features parts. But maybe it still sort of bothers you; maybe the word "part" suggests to you something that takes up space. Or maybe it bothers you to use the word "part" both for physical parts (the ordinary use of the word) and for features. Whatever the reason, I think this discomfort is good. As we will see by the end of this chapter, features are very different from mini-things. The ways in which they are unlike ordinary parts is very important, and so discomfort with the word "part" is a good thing to feel. It's a prod to further thought.

So far, then, we have seen the value of thinking of substances as having multiple features, and also the value of thinking of those features as "parts" in a certain extended sense of that word. Now let us consider *how* features can serve as parts of substances. In what way do they contribute to making up the whole substance? And do they do so on their own, or only together with parts that are not features but instead something else?

3.3.1 Four Big Theories

Every ordinary substance has a large number of features. If we were to list all the features of a substance, would we have given a complete account of it? For example, if we listed Mickey's agility, his color, his weight, and so on, would that be the whole story? Or would this still just be a partial account of him? Would some "part" still be left out?

If you answer that only the features of a substance are its parts (its metaphysical parts), then you are committing yourself to what's usually called the "bundle theory." Bundle theory says that a substance is a bundle of features. The features are the substance's only parts. Mickey, say, is a bundle of felinity, agility, and so on. (The number of parts in such a bundle is very, very large. Mickey has a lot of features.)

The bundle theory has two versions, depending on what you think about the features in the bundle. One way of thinking about them is as universals, and the other way is as particulars. Because the universal-particular distinction is the topic of chapter five, I will here provide only a quick reminder of the quick look we took in §1.1.

A universal is a kind, type, or species, like felinity or humanity. There may be exceptions, but universals are typically shareable: both Micky and Rusty share in felinity. They share in it by both being instances of it. Felinity is a universal, something there can be an instance of, while Mickey is a particular, an instance of felinity.

Now, when explaining the notion of a particular, I just gave Mickey as my example, and Mickey is, of course, a substance. But many philosophers think that features too can be particulars. There's such a thing as *Mickey's agility*, which is an individual agility distinct from *Rusty's agility*. Mickey has his agility, and Rusty has his. To use some technical terminology, Mickey has one agility-"trope," and Rusty has a numerically distinct agility-trope.[15] The question then arises: When we think of Rusty's features, are we thinking of items like agility-in-general, or of items like the-particular-agility-that-Rusty-has? Are we thinking of universals or tropes?

This question gives rise to two different versions of bundle theory. If we say that Mickey is a bundle of features—agility, felinity, sleepiness, and so on—we can mean that he is a bundle of universal features, or that he is a bundle of individual features. We can mean, in other words, that Mickey is the bundle consisting of agility-in-general, sleepiness-in-general, grayness-in-general, and so on, while Rusty is the bundle consisting of agility-in-general, sleepiness-in-general, redness-in-general, and so on; or we can mean that Mickey is the bundle consisting of his personal agility, his personal sleepiness, his personal grayness, and so on, while Rusty is the bundle consisting of *his* personal agility, *his* personal sleepiness, *his* personal redness, and so on.

The idea that a substance is a bundle of features, whether universal or particular, faces a number of objections. For now, I want to mention just one of them, solely for the purpose of introducing the main alternative to the bundle approach. The objection states that the very concept of a feature requires that there be more to a substance than its features: it's intrinsic to the idea of a feature that there be something that the feature is a feature of. Agility isn't just there; it's always there as belonging to something that's agile, to some thing that has agility.

15. "Trope" is really a word from literary theory, so how did it end up here? Believe it or not, it all started out as a little joke made by D. C. Williams in his "On the Elements of Being: I," *The Review of Metaphysics* 7, no. 1 (1953): 3–18, at 7. One philosopher had used the word "trope" to mean "the essence of an occurrence," and Williams, apparently in a whimsical mood, used it to mean "the occurrence of an essence," that is, a single instance of a kind or essence (this individual catness, rather than catness in general). Weirdly, the term caught on and has become completely standard.

This sort of concern has led some philosophers to reject the bundle view. They have proposed that features are not, and cannot be, the only kind of parts that substances have. There needs to be something, within the substance, that the substance's features belong to and depend upon. We need, in addition to features, a "substrate" or "substratum" (I will use these words interchangeably). A substratum is a lower, underlying level. It's the bottom level of a substance. It's the part of the substance that does the substanding; it's what the features of the substance depend on, or rest on, or (to use a word introduced in §1.1) "inhere" in. It serves as a feature-bearer, by being what bears or carries the features.

That is what the substratum *does*: it serves as the independent item that the dependent features rely on. But you might want to know not just what it does, but what it's *like*. This question is not easy to answer. The substrate is a particular, not a universal. But beyond that, substrate theorists usually say that, in itself, the substrate has no features at all. Of course, it "has features" in the sense that features depend on it or inhere in it. After all, that's what it's there for! But in its own inner reality, it's featureless, or, to use a very common term, "bare."[16] The bare substrate, although it bears features, does not have any features in and of itself.

There are a lot of things to say about substrate views and bundle views. For now, however, the thing to do is to get clear on the menu of options. So far, we have seen two choices to make: bundle vs. substratum and universals vs. particulars. That gives us four possibilities, as indicated in Table 3-1.

TABLE 3-1 FOUR THEORIES OF SUBSTANCE

	Features are universal	Features are particular
Features with no substratum	Substances are bundles of universal features	Substances are bundles of particular features ("tropes")
Features + bare substratum	Substances are universal features together with a bare substratum	Substances are particular features ("tropes") together with a bare substratum

16. I know what you're thinking. If there is a bare substrate, can there also be a naked substrate? How about a nude substrate? And are there perhaps scantily clad substrates? And—to get to the real question—can I use one of these expressions for a catchy title to an academic article? Sorry, that lake has been fished out. Every dumb joke along these lines has already been thought of, and published, and groaned at.

The table sets out the four big theories mentioned in the title of this section. Most substance theories in twentieth- and twenty-first-century analytic metaphysics have fallen into one of these camps. Mickey is a bundle of universal features (felinity, grayness, agility, and so on), or he is a bundle of particular features (his felinity, his grayness, his agility, and so on), or he is made up of a bare substratum plus universal features, or he is made up of a bare substratum plus particular features.

3.3.2 Problems with the Four Big Theories

Now that we have seen these four theories, let us discuss them in some detail, with the goal of discovering whether they are satisfactory or not.[17]

It is convenient to begin with the bundle-of-universals view, together with a standard and very interesting objection to it. The objection starts from two plausible assumptions. The first is this: It's possible for two substances to be *exactly* alike, the same in kind in every respect. If one is red, the other is red; if one is spherical, the other is spherical; and so on.[18] Even if in practice this is extremely unlikely, even if it's almost always the case that two things are at least a little bit dissimilar, still it seems possible in principle.

The second assumption takes a little more setup. Let me talk for a bit about something that isn't a substance—namely, a pair of gloves. Suppose that Will and Tina each have a pair of gloves: Will has Pair 1, and Tina has Pair 2. Will's pair—Pair 1—consists of a right glove and a left glove, which we will name R1 and L1. Tina's pair—Pair 2—consists of a right glove and a left glove, which we will name R2 and L2. Now it makes sense that the gloves that make up Pair 1 are different from the gloves that make up Pair 2. But suppose that Tina loses her left glove, and Will agrees to allow Tina to borrow his left glove when he doesn't need gloves. Should we say that there are now two pairs of gloves, one pair consisting of R1 and L1, and the other pair consisting of R2 and L1? Frankly, I think this is a weird question, and I don't really have an answer to it. But I don't need to have one, because what I'm

---

17. For a different account of the theories and the various objections to them, see Loux and Crisp, *Metaphysics: A Contemporary Introduction*, chapter three.

18. You might object that it's not really possible for two things to have *all* the same properties on the grounds that they will, at the very least, be located in different places. I'll come back to this later.

really trying to get to is the following. Suppose that Tina goes on to lose her right glove as well, and that Will generously allows her to borrow his right glove. Should we say that there are two pairs of gloves in this situation? Should we say, that is, that we now have both Will's pair, consisting of R1 and L1, and Tina's pair, consisting of R1 and L1? Here, I think, the answer is clearly no. If the "first" pair consists of R1 and L1, and the "second" pair consists of R1 and L1, then the "first" pair and the "second" pair are really just the same pair. Whatever we want to say about the odd situation where there are (allegedly) two pairs that share a left glove but not a right glove, we certainly don't want to allow for a situation where there are two pairs that share *both* gloves. If the "two pairs" share both gloves, then there aren't two pairs.

The point of this discussion is not to contribute to Glove Science. The point is to set us up to understand the second plausible assumption: If "two" things share all the same parts, then they aren't two things, but really just one thing. It's meant to apply not just to pairs of gloves but to everything. No two things can share all the same parts. There can be conjoined twins joined at the hip, but there cannot be conjoined twins joined at the everything.

With these two assumptions in hand, let us turn to the bundle-of-universals theory. Think of Rusty and Mickey. According to the bundle-of-universals theory, Rusty and Mickey are both bundles of universals. Rusty is a bundle of felinity, redness, and so on, while Mickey is a bundle of felinity, grayness, and so on. That means that one of Rusty's parts, felinity, is also one of Mickey's parts. They share a part, but they don't share all parts. They are sort of like the weird glove pair consisting of R2 and L1. But now consider another case: Rusty and his identical twin Rufus. Rusty is a bundle of felinity, redness, and so on, while Rufus is a bundle of felinity, redness, and so on. Since they are identical twins, they are alike not just in being cats, but in every respect; they are the same in color, size, agility level, and so on.[19] This leads to a problem for bundle-of-universals theory. For bundle-of-universals theory, to have a feature is to have a universal as a part, so if two things are alike in terms of some feature, that means they have the very same

19. In reality, of course, identical twins are not perfectly identical in this way. Maybe it only happens when very simple entities are in question, like two electrons. But anyway, it doesn't matter; to repeat something noted earlier, all that's required to raise this metaphysical problem is for such a case of exact matching to be possible in principle.

universal as a part, with the result that they have a part in common. But if two substances have *all* the same features, then they have *all* the same parts as each other. That violates the principle that no two things can share all the same parts. It's like saying that there are two distinct pairs of gloves, both consisting of the very same gloves.

Here is where we are. Let's assume that the bundle-of-universals theory is true. If it's possible for two things to be just alike, then it's possible for two things to share all the same parts—but it's *not* possible for two things to share all the same parts. If, on the other hand, two things cannot share all the same parts, then it's not possible for two things to be just alike—but it *is* possible for two things to be just alike. The bundle-of-universals theory has put us in a bad spot. If we accept it, then we have to reject at least one of our plausible assumptions: that two things can be exactly alike, or that no two things can share all the same parts. Since the two assumptions are so plausible, however, what should be rejected instead is the bundle-of-universals theory.

It's worthwhile pausing to consider a reply that could be made by the advocate of the bundle-of-universals theory. He might say that it's not actually possible for two things to be completely alike: any two things will always, at a minimum, be unalike as far as their locations go. One of them will have the property of being located in this place, and the other the property of being located in that place, and therefore they won't have all the same properties.

But this reply is not as good as it looks. It misunderstands the nature of location. If there were only one substance in all of reality, it would not be here, or there, or anywhere—it would have no location at all. Locations arise only through relations between different substances. Rusty's location is ten feet to the north *of Mickey*, for example. But that means that differences in location, and hence differences in locational properties, can arise only if Rusty and Mickey are *already* distinct substances. We cannot, then, appeal to locational properties as being responsible for the distinctness of Rusty and Micky. That Rusty and Mickey are in different places does, it is true, *prove* that they are distinct, but it cannot *make* them distinct. That must be explained in some other way. Locational properties, then, cannot save the bundle-of-universals theory.[20]

---

20. See Loux and Crisp, *Metaphysics*, 97–99. If you are wondering what *does* make them distinct, see §5.4.

It seems we have good reason to abandon the bundle-of-universals theory. Can any of the other three theories serve as a superior alternative? To answer that question, it will be helpful to come up with a deeper understanding of why an alternative is needed. Our initial assumptions, again, were these. (i) It's possible for two distinct things to share all the same features, that is, for two numerically distinct things to be specifically the same in every respect. (ii) It's impossible for two numerically distinct things to share all the same parts. Both seem plausible, and the problem with the bundle-of-universals theory is that it blocks us from affirming both. But how does it do that? It does it by combining the view that features are universals with the view that features are the only parts. If features are universals, then substances that are specifically the same in some respect are substances that share a part, and substances that are specifically the same in every respect are substances that share all their parts.

If, however, at least some of the parts were not universal features, then this problem would go away. Now there are two ways for there to be metaphysical parts that are not universal features: there can be parts that are particular features, or there can be parts that aren't features at all. Either way, two substances could be alike in all their features without violating the rule against sharing all parts.

Let's consider the first option: the one that says that a substance is a bundle of features, but a bundle of particular features. If features are particulars, then Rusty and Rufus share no parts at all. Rusty's felinity is Rusty's felinity, while Rufus's is Rufus's; Rusty's agility is Rusty's agility, while Rufus's is Rufus's; and so on. They don't share any parts, so we certainly aren't violating the principle that no two things can share all their parts.

Just because this theory avoids this one objection doesn't mean it avoids all objections, however. In the previous section, when I was laying out the four theories in the first place, I mentioned the following objection to any bundle view: Features need to belong to something. Adding more features only makes the problem worse. A feature without a bearer is impossible, and a bundle of features without a bearer is, so to speak, even more impossible. I think that this objection is quite powerful: the very idea of a feature just does include the idea that it's a feature of something, and if you've got a hundred features, that just means you've got a hundred problems to solve. In my view, then, the bundle-of-particular-features view is not an acceptable alternative to the bundle-of-universals view. (I hope it's clear that this objection works against the bundle-of-universals view as well.)[21]

Now let's consider the second option, the one that involves saying that there are parts that aren't features at all. Universals-plus-substratum theory fits this description very well. If features are still universals, but Rusty has his own private substratum, and Rufus has *his* own private substratum, then they don't share all their parts: they do share most of their parts, but that's not a problem. So again, we aren't violating the principle that no two things can share all the same parts.

It's worth noticing that this is a different reason for believing in substrates than the one mentioned earlier. Earlier the point was to provide something for features to inhere in; now the point is to provide something that explains how two things that are completely alike in kind can be different in number. When substrates are introduced for this reason, they are often called not bare substrates but instead "bare particulars."

The universals-plus-substrate view does avoid the objection that created so much difficulty for the bundle-of-universals view, but that doesn't mean it has no difficulties. For example, some philosophers reject the existence of universals in the first place, for reasons we will see in chapter five. For another example, it is strange to say that individual substances can have parts that are not themselves individual. Even if you believe that there really are universal properties, like agility and felinity, still you might think it necessary for the parts of Rusty and Rufus to be not these universals, but particular instances of them: you might think that it's not agility-in-general that serves as a part of Rusty, but Rusty's personal agility-trope, which is an instance of agility-in-general. (Both of these concerns apply to the bundle-of-universals theory as well.)

Thinking like this pushes us toward the fourth theory, tropes-plus-substratum theory. It solves the problem that defeated the bundle-of-universals view twice over: it has particular features instead of universal

---

21. Some philosophers resist the idea that features need bearers at all—see Jody Azzouni, *Ontology without Borders* (Oxford: Oxford University Press, 2017). For an attempt to save the bundle theory while still accepting the idea that features need bearers, see Peter Simons, "Particulars in Particular Clothing: Three Trope Theories of Substance," *Philosophy and Phenomenological Research* 54, no. 3 (1994): 553–75. I will discuss Simons's theory in the next section.

features, and it has substrata. That might seem like overkill, but the theory is also meant to address other concerns that we have seen: it makes the parts of substances individuals, rather than universals, and it provides a substrate for features to inhere in.

This seems like progress! Still, this theory also has a problem, a problem that it shares with the universals-plus-substrate view. The very notion of a bare particular or bare substrate has seemed problematic to many philosophers. In a nutshell, it seems very strange to suppose that there are entities that have, in themselves, no features at all.

Perhaps it's unfair to attribute to the bare particularist the view that bare particulars have no features at all. At the very least, they are particular, and perhaps they are also independent and unified, making them mini-substances. But even if this is right, still, such entities are very strange. It is strange for there to be entities with such a minimal set of very abstract features. We should believe in them only if we have to.

So far, each of the four theories has problems, either problems unique to it or else problems shared with others. Nor, unfortunately, are we done with all this negativity, because there is a final pair of objections to consider.

Suppose Rusty is a bundle of features (whether particular or universal). What makes Rusty *this* bundle as opposed to some other? It seems that what makes him be *this* bundle is that he is made up of *these* features. If there were different features in the bundle, then it wouldn't be the same bundle, and therefore we wouldn't have Rusty anymore, but some other cat. Now suppose that Rusty starts going gray. He would have a different color, and therefore the bundle would be different. But Rusty *is* the bundle, according to this theory. So instead of saying that Rusty is now gray, we should say instead that Rusty no longer exists: he (that bundle) has been replaced by a different cat (a different bundle). The upshot of this line of reasoning is that Rusty cannot change at all. Either he stays exactly the same, down to the very last detail, or else he passes out of existence, to be replaced by a numerically distinct cat. (And note how this is true regardless of whether the features are taken to be universals or particulars.)

Bringing in the substrate seems to help. If Rusty includes a bare substratum among his parts, then when his features change, there's something that stays the same—the substratum—and as long as it remains the same, we can say that we still have the same old Rusty. However, we've really just gone out of the frying pan into the fire. If the bare substratum is what makes Rusty be Rusty, then Rusty can be Rusty no matter how his features change. He can change color, he can lose his agility, but he can also change from cat to dog and even to dandelion. In short, the bare substrate theory implies that any degree of change is possible. (And note how here again, it doesn't matter whether the features are taken to be universals or particulars.)

It seems false both that Rusty can't change at all and that he can change without limit while remaining himself. It seems obvious both that Rusty can change and that there are limits to how much he can change. But that means that all four of our theories are in trouble.

There's a related pair of problems based not on change, but on alternative possibilities. I'm sitting right now, but I could have been standing: what I mean is not that, starting from sitting, I could change to standing, but rather that I could have been standing in the first place. Standing is a way I might have been. Or, to pick another example, I am baptized, but I might not have been. This second example is particularly worthwhile for the following reason: Although I might have been unbaptized, meaning that having been unbaptized is an alternative possibility for me, it's not possible at this point for me to change from having been baptized to being unbaptized. It's too late for that. This proves that the question of change is distinct from the question of alternative possibilities: Even if standing is both something I could change to and an alternative possibility, not being baptized is not. Being unbaptized is an alternative possibility for me, but it isn't something I could change to.

For substances understood as bundles, there simply are no alternative possibilities. Being even slightly different would mean having a different set of features and therefore being a different substance altogether. Rusty has to be the way he is: there are no alternative ways for him to have been. For substances understood as bare substrata with features attached, there is no limit to alternative possibilities. Rusty's substratum makes him be Rusty, regardless of which features he has.[22]

---

22. I'm not sure who originated it, but the slogan is "Bertrand Russell could have been a poached egg."

But it is obvious both that substances might have been other than they are and that there are limits to this. It's possible that Rusty could have been a different color, but not that he could have been a dog. (To recall a point made in §1.2: We can say that although there's an alternative way for the world to be that includes a dog instead of Rusty, there's no alternative way for the world to be in which Rusty is a dog. Rusty is a substance that could have been different, but he couldn't have been a different substance.)

Things are looking bad for all four theories. They all have serious problems. Should we abandon the entire idea of substance altogether? Or could it be that there's something we have overlooked?

3.3.3 A More Thomistic Way of Thinking about Features and Feature-Bearers

There is a version of the bundle theory that is supposed to avoid the problems discussed in the previous section. It is the one proposed by Peter Simons.[23] It assumes that the features of things are tropes, and it proposes that each substance has two layers of features: the inner layer, or nucleus, consists of a number of tropes that cannot be separated from one another, and that therefore cannot be separated from the nucleus; the outer layer, or halo, consists of a number of tropes that can be separated from the nucleus. As long as the features in the nucleus stay the same, we have the same substance, but features from the halo can be present or absent without the substance losing its numerical identity. Rusty's changes or alternative possibilities involve there being different features in the halo; changes or alternative possibilities that would involve there being different features in the nucleus are not possible for him.

Leaving aside the problems with the modal theory, Simons's approach seems to be very promising in the following respect: by making some features indispensable to the substance while leaving others dispensable, it allows us to have change within limits: change of tropes in the halo is possible, while change of tropes in the nucleus cannot take place without destruction of the substance overall. The theory thus seems to do a good job of addressing concerns about change and alternative possibilities.

---

23. Simons, "Particulars in Particular Clothing."

However, there is a serious problem with Simons's view. His view is, as mentioned above, essentially a bundle view: objects are made up of tropes and of nothing else. Crucially, he thinks that tropes alone can make up something independent. For him, the fact that a single feature cannot exist on its own does not mean it needs *something other than a feature*. Instead, it just means that it needs *something*, and that something might well be another feature. In particular, if there are two features, each of which needs the other, then the features can meet each other's dependence needs, with the result that the two of them together make up something independent. Of course, the minimum needed might not be two: it might three, or three hundred.

Whatever the number, I do not think this works. Features need something to inhere in. Adding more features doesn't change that fact; again, if anything, it makes the problem worse. Even if some features can inhere in other features—even if, say, brightness inheres in color—those other features will still need something to inhere in, and so on. This can't go on forever: it needs to come to an end in something that doesn't inhere in anything.

Nor will it help to say that things move in a circle: to say, for example, that A inheres in B, and B inheres in C, and C inheres in A. That would mean, in the end, that A inhered in itself or, at any rate, gave support to itself, which makes no sense. (We sometimes say that someone is self-reliant, but this really means that he isn't reliant on anyone; such a person is not like a feature that inheres in itself, but instead like something that isn't a feature at all.)

Simons's theory, then, which seemed at first to be a good alternative to the four main theories, does not work out in the end. However, as hinted already, it contains an important part of the solution.

Let us approach this somewhat indirectly by returning once more to the four main theories. They all have problems understanding change and alternative possibilities. Now when there is a set of competing theories, and all of them seem to have interrelated problems, it can be very helpful to ask: What do all these theories have in common? They disagree, yes, but what do they agree on? If all of them have problems, problems that involve the same set of issues, it might be the case that their common problems are rooted in a common agreement.

Here is something that all four of the main theories have in common: they see all the features of a substance as being, so to speak, on the same footing. Every feature of a substance is related to the substance in the same way as every other feature of that substance. In particular, none of these four theories thinks that any feature of a substance has a privileged role or status within the substance.

In bundle theories, every feature is equally indispensable to the substance, and every feature belongs to the substance in the same way as the others do: by belonging to the bundle. In substrate theories, every feature is equally dispensable, and every feature belongs to the substance in the same way as the others do: by being borne by the substrate.

Simons's theory is different. It makes some features special: the ones that belong to the nucleus. If Simons's theory could be freed of the problem we noted above—namely, the problem that an independent, non-inherent being can't be constructed out of dependent, inherent beings—then we would be on our way to a solid alternative.

One thought might be to retain Simons's nucleus-halo distinction while adding a bare substrate. This would solve the problem of unborne features: All the features, instead of being unborne, would be borne by the substrate. They would inhere in it, and it would be the thing that doesn't inhere in other things. The substance as a whole, then, would consist of the features and the substrate they inhere in. This would be a substrate-plus-tropes view with the nucleus-halo distinction added on. However, the bareness of the bare substrate poses a problem. Remember that the whole point of the nucleus-halo distinction is that the features in the nucleus are indispensable, while the features in the halo are not. This requires that the features in the nucleus be related to the substrate—and thereby, to the substance as a whole—differently from the way in which the halo features are related to it. A bare substrate theory can't make sense of this. If the substrate is really bare, then there is nothing about it in virtue of which it requires *these* features rather than any others, *this* essence rather than any other. With nothing to ensure the necessary connection between the substrate and the nuclear features, we have no understanding of how the nucleus-halo distinction is to be maintained.

We need to reorient ourselves on a deeper level. Aquinas's approach allows us to do so, and I will present it now: but I will present it very differently from the way he does, because he wasn't aiming to contrast his approach with twentieth- and twenty-first-century analytic approaches.

Let us begin by endorsing the idea that a substance has a special or privileged feature, which we call its essence. But let us also think of this essential feature as being related to the substance very differently from the way in which accidental features are. The essence is not just another feature, which for some inexplicable reason happens to be more important than the others. Its way of belonging to the overall substance is radically different from the way in which the other features belong to it. The question then becomes: What is that radically different way? What is the special relation to the substance that only the essence has?

Think back to §1.2 and the foundational theory of essence. According to the foundational theory, each substance has a special feature that constitutes it at the most basic level. Felinity is not merely bundled up with Mickey's other features; if it were, it could not be more foundational than they. Nor, on the Thomistic way of thinking, is it added to a bare substrate. Mickey's felinity is not borne by anything. At Mickey's most basic level, there is no bare substrate on which felinity can be layered. The most basic layer of Mickey—if it even makes sense to talk that way—is the cat Mickey himself. Mickey himself, not some component of his, is what's most basic. He is himself a basic being. He, a cat, a full-blown substance of the feline sort, is what you start with. He is not some substrate to which felinity can be added; he is, in and of himself, something that's feline. Felinity makes him be the type of thing he is on the most basic level, and it's simultaneously what makes him be there at all. Nothing about him is more basic. And this is the answer to our question. The radically different and special way in which an essence is related to a substance is not by being bundled or borne, but by constituting the substance at its most fundamental level.

Non-essential features, by contrast, are indeed borne: not by nothing, as in the bundle view, and not by a bare substrate, but by the cat Mickey himself. In short, although Mickey's essence has no bearer, his accidents do. Their bearer is the substance that sub-stands them: it's Mickey himself, as constituted by his essential feature of felinity.

The picture this gives us is unlike all four of the main theories. Instead of seeing substances as made up of features only, or of features plus a bare bearer, this approach sees substances as (a) constituted by their essences or natures at the most basic, foundational, substantial level, and (b) further constituted by their accidents as existing in less fundamental, more superficial ways. It makes sense to think of Mickey's accidents as borne by a bearer, but that bearer is not something bare, it's Mickey himself. By contrast, it does not make sense to think of Mickey's essence as borne by anything. As we saw before, there's no Mickey at all prior to Mickey's being a cat. It's not as if he was there, and then he acquired felinity; his coming-to-be-feline is simultaneous with, and indeed identical to, his coming-to-be-at-all. This goes hand-in-hand with the thought that Mickey's coming-to-be is a substantial change.

Consider the following image: pin cushions and pins.[24] One way in which pin cushions differ from one another is in terms of which pins are stuck in them: Pin Cushion 1 has a red pin and two blue pins, while Pin Cushion 2 has a red pin and two yellow pins. Take this as a model for the substrate approach. The pins stand for features, and the pin cushion stands for the bearer. *All* features are pins, and the pin cushion is a *bare* substrate: all features (pins) are added to it from the outside. But suppose we take the model in a more Thomistic way, by noticing that pin cushions differ from one another not just by which pins they bear. Some are shaped like tomatoes, some are shaped like bananas, and so forth. This is a deeper kind of difference between pin cushions. The essence of a substance is like the pin cushion's type (tomato or banana or whatever): its essence is a feature that is not stuck into it, but that instead constitutes it initially and at the most basic level. The accidents of a substance, by contrast, are indeed like the pins: they are added to a pin cushion that is presupposed as already there.

Even more light can be shed on how essential and accidental features constitute substances by looking more carefully into something we've been taking for granted—namely, the very idea of features. Perhaps we know well enough what it means for Rusty to have redness: it means he has a disposition to reflect light of certain frequencies. But what, we might ask, is the feature of redness itself? What is *it*? First, we will ask what features in general are, and then we will ask about the difference between accidental and essential features and their roles in constituting substances.

---

24. Much of the material in this paragraph is inspired by P. V. Spade's "pin cushion model." See his "The Warp and Woof of Metaphysics: How to Get Started on Some Big Themes," www.Pvspade.Com/Logic/Docs/WarpWoof.Pdf, 1999.

Recent philosophical discussions have proposed the following two ways to think about what a feature is. First, you can think of a feature like redness as a metaphysical part that is itself red; a red substance is red because it has a red part. On this account, Rusty is red because one of his parts—namely, his redness feature—is itself red. Second, you can think of a feature like redness as a metaphysical part that is not itself red, but that has the power to make the things that have it be red. On this account, Rusty is red because one of his parts—namely, his redness feature—is a red-maker; in other words, it is something that is not itself red but that makes other things be red.[25]

I think that both these approaches have a problem inasmuch as they involve a lot of reification.[26] They do not perhaps treat features as if they were substances, but they do treat them as if they were, so to speak, thinglets—little things that belong to the big thing, the substance. This is a problem for a number of reasons, but here is one: if a feature is a mini-thing, then presumably it has features of its own. Let's look at the two approaches in the previous paragraph one by one. On the first approach, Rusty is red because he has a feature that is itself red. But what makes his red feature red? Does it have its own feature, a red feature belonging to the red feature that belongs to Rusty? On the second approach, Rusty is red because he has a feature that is not itself red but that is instead a red-maker. Why is this feature a red-maker? Does it have its own feature, a red-maker-maker that belongs to the red-maker that belongs to Rusty? If we say yes to these questions, we will land in an infinite regress: a feature will have features which have features which have features. . . . This is just kicking the can down the road. We wanted to know why Rusty was red, and the answer was that he had a feature, but that feature was understood in a way that invited the question: Why does that feature have the features that *it* does? This

---

25. See Robert K. Garcia, "Tropes as Character-Grounders," *Australasian Journal of Philosophy* 94, no. 3 (2016): 499–515; Robert K. Garcia, "Two Ways to Particularize a Property," *Journal of the American Philosophical Association* 1, no. 4 (2015): 635–52. See also Robert C. Koons, "Forms as Simple and Individual Grounds of Things' Natures" *Metaphysics* 1, no. 1 (2018): 1–11.

26. The material from here to the end of this section is explored in my "On the Ontological Statuses of Features," in *The Philosophical Legacy of Jorge J. E. Gracia*, ed. Robert A. Delfino, William Irwin, and Jonathan J. Sanford (Lanham, MD: Rowman & Littlefield, 2022), 133–42.

is what comes of treating the feature as a kind of mini-thing.

How did we get into this situation? We started out with the following thought: We know what it is for Rusty to be red, but we want to know something further: what that redness of his *is*. But this desire for "something further" is illusory. The redness just *is* "what it is for Rusty to be red." An example or two can make this clearer.

What is it for Rusty to be red? It is his disposition to reflect light of a certain frequency.[27] This, I am suggesting, is *what his redness is*. His redness is not something other than this disposition, something in virtue of which he has the disposition: his redness is this disposition itself. Or think of a spherical metal ball. What is it for it to be spherical? It's for all of the points on its surface to be equidistant from its center. There's no reason to think that the ball needs to have some special piece of metaphysical equipment in virtue of which its surface points are equidistant like that. Its surface points' being like that *is* its sphericality. It's not as if scientists who think about color, or geometers who think about shapes, need to ask the metaphysician for "the real reason" why things are colored or spherical. When metaphysicians talk about features like color or shape, they are talking about ordinary features, not about special entities that only metaphysicians know about.

This last point is related to something we saw in the introduction: The metaphysician knows all things, but not in detail. The point of metaphysics is not that it tells us about things that ordinary fields of inquiry have never even heard of, like "red-makers." Metaphysics *may* do that from time to time, but usually it doesn't. What metaphysics usually does is talk about ordinary realities in an extremely general fashion. It's not the metaphysician's job to weigh in on what sphericality is, or what redness is. He may use these as examples, of course, but his real goal is to arrive at something very general, like this: a feature of a substance is whatever it is about that substance in virtue of which it is true to say that it, the substance, is a certain way (red or agile or whatever). This doesn't mean discovering unfamiliar entities. It means fitting familiar entities into unfamiliar and extremely general categories.

Over the last several paragraphs, we have been looking into the

---

27. Truth to tell, color is really complicated, but I trust that this will serve well enough as an example.

question, "What is a feature?" Our real target, however, is not this, but the distinction between accidental and essential features, and how they work together to constitute substances. Let us see how our account of what features are takes on two different forms, one for accidental features and one for essential features.

An accidental feature is a way for a substance to exist that goes beyond its foundational, essential way of existing.[28] Such a way to exist presupposes a substance that is, so to speak, "already there on the scene" so that it can then exist in that additional, accidental way.[29] A redness, for example, can exist only if there is some substance there to be red; an agility can exist only if there is some substance there to be agile.[30] By contrast, an essential way to exist does not *presuppose* some substance; instead, it *constitutes* a substance on its fundamental level. An essence is a way for there to be a substance in the first place (a substance with that very essence). To say "something red exists" is to say that something bears the feature of redness, but to say "a cat exists" is not to say that something like a substrate bears the feature of felinity. Instead, it's to say that a fundamentally feline substance exists.

An accidental feature, then, is a way for a substance to be, while an essential feature is a way for there to be a substance. An accidental feature gives additional characterization to a substance that is already there; an essential feature constitutes a substance initially, establishing it as existing in the first place. Because an accidental feature characterizes an already-existing substance, it makes sense to think of the substance as the bearer of the accident. Because an essential feature constitutes a substance that wasn't already there, it doesn't make sense to think of that essential feature as having a bearer.[31] The coming-to-be of that substance is the original coming-to-be of a bearer—a bearer of

---

28. This language of "ways," and some of what he means by it, comes from D. M. Armstrong, *A World of States of Affairs*, Cambridge Studies in Philosophy (Cambridge: Cambridge University Press, 1997), 30–31.

29. To recall a point made in §0.2, such language must be interpreted in terms of fundamentality, not in terms of time.

30. If you are wondering whether this can, as stated, be squared with the doctrine of transubstantiation, see §9.3.

31. This is closely related to Aquinas's claim, in chapter one of *On the Principles of Nature*, that substantial natures have no subjects, or (in more contemporary language) bearers.

accidents. A substance, you might say, is an un-bare bearer of accidents.[32]

All of this can be re-expressed by relating features to potentialities. A feature is the actualization of a potentiality: in the essential case, a potentiality for there to be a substance of a certain sort, and in the accidental case, a potentiality for an already-existing substance to have a certain feature.

It can also be put in terms of change. The coming-to-be of an accident is an already-existing substance's coming to have an accident. The coming-to-be of an essence is the coming-to-be of a substance, not an already-existing substance's coming to have some allegedly essential feature.

In this section, after considering and rejecting some ideas about features and substrates found in analytic philosophy over the last several decades, I have advanced a more Thomistic way of thinking about such matters. On the view I have set out, accidents are borne by substances, while essences are not borne by substances but instead are constitutive of them. Crucial to the analysis was de-reifying both accidental and essential features, in other words, coming to think of them not as mini-things or mini-substances but as ways that substances are.

Now let us turn to a rather different way of thinking of substances as having parts.

3.4 Form and Matter as Parts

In §2.5, we met up with form and matter when thinking about change. Roughly speaking, matter was treated as what stays the same through change, and form was treated as what comes to be different through change. In the case of accidental change, what plays the role of matter is the substance itself, while in the case of substantial change, the role of matter is played by prime matter, which has no features of its own, but which is, instead, a pure potentiality for gaining and losing form. In §3.2, we met up with form and matter again, focusing on substantial form as the source of all actuality in a thing while understanding prime matter as a principle of potentiality alone.

32. For a view that is like this one is important ways—and different from it, too, also in important ways—see Jeffrey E. Brower, *Aquinas's Ontology of the Material World: Change, Hylomorphism, and Material Objects* (Oxford: Oxford University Press, 2014).

But what *are* form and matter? Should we think of them as parts of a substance? If so, in what sense? The language of parts—of form and matter as parts of substance—can lead us to imagine that form and matter are things, ethereal thinglets that work together to make up normal substances. That is not a path we should go down.

There is a way of avoiding it. Let us try thinking of matter and form less in terms of what does or doesn't stay the same in a process of change, and more in terms of potentiality and actuality.

Matter is that in virtue of which change is possible.[33] It's an internal factor, possessed by a substance, that allows that substance to cease being the way it is now in favor of something else. And we can think of this either in terms of the substance's having a potentiality to undergo accidental change, or in terms of its having a potentiality to undergo substantial change and be replaced by other substances.

Correspondingly, we can think of form as an internal factor or principle, possessed by a substance, in virtue of which a thing is the way it actually is. Having an accidental form is what makes a substance exist in a certain way on a non-fundamental level, and having a substantial form is what makes a substance exist in a certain way on the fundamental level.

Form, then, is a principle or explanatory factor in virtue of which a substance is the way it is, and matter is a principle or explanatory factor in virtue of which a substance could be other than it is. But how is this supposed to ward off reification? Isn't all this talk about "principles" and "internal factors" at least as bad? There's no denying that such language is dangerous and misleading. It is very tempting to think that you take some form, and you take some matter, and you put them together to build a cat. In an attempt to avoid this trap, I will carry the analysis further, making use of points laid out previously, especially in §3.3.3.

Recall what we said about properties or features: they aren't mini-things that make a substance be in such-and-such a way, but instead the very being-in-such-and-such-a-way of that substance. This applies to forms, because forms are features. Mickey's lying-down form is not a strange "metaphysical" item that causes his body to be arranged in a certain way. It is, rather, that very arrangement itself. The form is noth-

---

33. But remember a point from §2.6: All this applies only to the sorts of changes that involve trading one form for another. Changes like learning and forgetting are not material changes.

ing other than the particular way of being that Mickey has (in this case, the bodily arrangement that he has). Similarly, Mickey's feline form is not a special mysterious metaphysical item that causes him to be a meowing mammal. Mickey's meowing mammality is what his felinity form is. The form *is* the property or feature.

We can say analogous things about matter. We can say that matter is not some weird special component that gives a cat the potentiality to stand up (an accidental potentiality) or die (a substantial potentiality). It is not some special something that, on its deepest level as "prime" matter, is somehow magically there despite not actually being anything at all. Instead, we can say, the matter of a thing is whatever it is about that thing that allows it to have potentialities to be other than it is.

Remember that form is always in the driver's seat. It's not the case that things have certain forms and then also, as if by coincidence, matter of a certain sort. Instead, what kind of matter something has is dependent on what kind of form it has. And likewise, which kind of potentiality something has is dependent on which kind of actuality it has. Whether something has the potentiality to be changed into a tent peg depends on what kind of actuality it already has. A piece of aluminum has this potentiality, while a bowl of milk does not. Whether something has the potentiality to be changed into a cat depends on what kind of actuality it already has. Cat gametes have this potentiality, while squirrel gametes do not.

For this reason, we will not want to say, without further explanation, both that a substance has certain forms and that it has a certain matter. Instead, we will want to say that it has certain forms, and that, in virtue of those forms, it has certain matter; it has certain actualities, and in virtue of those actualities, it has certain potentialities. At risk of exaggeration, we might even want to say that its potentialities are just further aspects of what its actualities are: being aluminum isn't merely being actually a certain way, but also being potentially in some other way. What aluminum *can* be is a deeper, hidden layer of what aluminum *is*.[34]

Talk of "having matter," then, is systematically misleading insofar as it suggests some kind of stuff that needs to be shaped (like dough); and talk of "having a form" is systematically misleading insofar as it suggests

---

34. Recall something we saw in §2.5—namely, that for Aquinas, a thing's powers are among its necessary accidents, flowing from its essence.

some item that gives shape (like a wire inside a stuffed animal). To avoid misleading ourselves and others, we can translate talk of "forms" into talk of *actuality features*, and talk of "matter" into talk of *potentiality features*. To have an actuality feature is actually to be a certain way; to have a potentiality feature is to be able to be in a different way, and even, at the limit, to be able to pass away in favor of something else, as sperm and ovum have the potentiality to pass away in favor of a cat.[35]

I am proposing unusual ways of speaking that will help ward off a reification danger lurking in the traditional Thomistic way of speaking. But if you want to stick to the tried-and-true Thomistic way of talking about things, proceed like this: form and matter, while not being substances themselves, are, in a sense, parts of substances, with form being a part in virtue of which a substance actually is a certain way, and matter being a part in virtue of which a substance could be in another way, or even be succeeded by a substance of another kind.

3.5 Essence and Existence as Parts

This chapter is already long and difficult, but it's not quite time to end it. There is an important issue that has, from time to time, played an important role in Thomism and that should not go unmentioned, even if we can't actually settle it. Consider this section, then, to be a teaser for something you can look into for yourself.

You and I exist; that's a fact. Tyrannosaurs used to exist, but they don't anymore. There's no longer any fact of their existing. Unicorns don't exist and never have (presumably). There's no fact of their existing, and there never has been. In one sense, then, existence is a fact: it's the fact that something is actual and not just potential. Existence is the actuality of a potentiality.

---

35. Pasnau's reading of Aquinas seems at first sight to be the same as this one, but in fact the two are importantly different. On Pasnau's interpretation, as I understand it, form and matter aren't anything at all. Only substances exist, and the language of form and matter is a way to talk about the actualities and potentialities of substances. On my reading of Aquinas, form and matter—actuality properties and potentiality properties—are more real than that: they are not just our ways of talking or thinking about substances but exist as true "parts" of substances. See Pasnau, "On What There Is in Aquinas."

My understanding of matter has been influenced by numerous conversations with David Cory, which is not to say that he would agree with it.

If existence is actuality, it's only fair to ask what it is the actuality *of*. What is the potentiality that gets actualized by existence? The answer was perhaps suggested in §3.3.3: it's essence. The existence of Mickey is the actualization of felinity, the actualization of the potentiality for something to exist in a feline way.

Existence and essence, understood as actuality and potentiality, are an important pair in Thomistic metaphysics. Are they parts? Well, if you talk only about the existence of something, you're only giving a partial account of it. There's more to something than its existence. And likewise for its essence. This suggests that we can think of the essence of something as one of its parts, and of its existence as another one of its parts. Doing so tends to nudge us toward thinking of existence in a different way: not just as the factual existence of something, but as an internal factor or "part" that results in the factual existence of something. On this way of thinking, shared by more than a few Thomists, every substance has two basic contributing factors: not only its nature or essence, but also its existence, with "existence" now referring not to the fact that the substance actually exists, but instead to an internal factor or principle *in virtue of which* that substance actually exists. This principle is sometimes called existence-as-act or, in Latin, the *actus essendi*. Rusty is the product of two core principles, essence and existence-as-act. It's because of his essence that Rusty is the kind of thing he is, and it's because of his existence-as-act that he is something rather than nothing. The result of them both is Rusty himself, who has existence-as-fact. You'll notice that that gives us two ways of using the word "existence" (*esse*): existence-as-act and existence-as-fact.

In all this talk of essence and existence, we face, once again, the danger of reification. We should not think of essence as being like a little machine, with existence as the electricity inside the machine. We should not think of essences as being like those little animal-shaped sponges that children get, and of existence as being like the water that puffs those sponges up. If you are worried about this enough, you might want to back away from thinking of *esse*-as-act as different from *esse*-as-fact: just as the felinity of Mickey is not some special mini-thing that makes him a meowing mammal, but instead just his very mammalian meowingness itself, so too, perhaps, his existence is not some special actualizer-part but just his being actually there. But the issue is far too complicated to settle here. At least you know now that it's an issue.[36]

If existence and essence are (in some sense) distinct principles or parts, then it seems to follow that an essence doesn't automatically come with existence: instead, whenever something with a certain essence actually exists, something was responsible for the actualization of that essence. That is why it is necessary for Rusty to have a cause, something to bring it about that he is actually there.[37]

And now at last we can tie up a loose thread from §1.2 by discussing the problem of why a creature's dependence on God lies outside of its essence. Rusty's nature is, as noted, such that it doesn't just automatically come with existence: it needs to be actualized by some cause. If this ultimately gets traced to God, then Rusty's existence will be caused by God—in other words, Rusty will depend on God. But note that he depends on God *because* he is a certain kind of thing, the kind of thing whose essence does not automatically possess its own actualization. The fact that Rusty depends on God is derived from the fact that he has that sort of essence. And that means, given the foundational account of essence put forward in §1.2, that Rusty's dependence on God is not part of his essence, but rather derived from his essence. It's not essential but instead a necessary accident.[38]

3.6 Some Summary Thoughts on Parts of Substances

A substance is something that exists as an independent, unified particular of a certain kind. But apart from the possible case of God (see §8.5), these unified particulars are not so unified that one cannot distinguish various aspects, or "parts," of what they are.

Substances can be divided up into spatially distinct parts, such as legs or arms. Here the sense of "division" is a literal one: you actually can cut parts like these off (even if they thereby lose their nature and

---

36. A good place to start, if you want to pursue this further, is White, "Act and Fact."

37. Causation is the subject of chapter four. If you are wondering whether God is an exception, see §8.5.

38. For discussion of medieval claims that dependence on God is extra-essential, see Mark Henninger, *Relations: Medieval Theories, 1250–1325* (Oxford: Clarendon Press, 1989), 78–85.

identity). Or, substances can be divided into various features, and now the sense of "division" is rather more metaphorical: you can't remove the color from Mickey in the way you can remove his tail. Or, they can be divided, perhaps even more metaphorically still, into form and matter, or essence and existence.

These divisions correspond to the fact that substances are complex: they exist in complex ways. Some parts of Mickey are here, while other parts of him are there. Some parts of him are for running or biting, other parts make him gray or agile, and a special and foundational part makes him a cat. Some parts of him make him actually exist in certain ways, other parts make him able to exist in certain ways. One part of him is what he is, while another corresponds to the fact that he is. There's a lot going on.

I have emphasized the danger of taking all these "parts" too literally, as if they were pieces that can be put together. The danger is easiest to fall into when the parts are the sorts of parts that can be spatially distinguished—this part here, that part there. But it's not too difficult to start thinking of other kinds of parts in this way; talk of bundles and substrates, for example, seems always right on the brink of falling into it.

Well, philosophy is hard, and when one thing is in the center of your field of vision, other things are at the edge and therefore not quite in focus. It's probably impossible to find a way forward that runs no risk of error at all (except silence, which isn't a way forward).

At any rate, I think we can help ourselves a lot by remembering, again and again, the distinction between basic beings and non-basic beings. If we remind ourselves that everything that isn't a substance is nonetheless somehow related to a substance, then we will have some protection against reifying those non-substances. Each "part" of a substance is, in one way or another, an aspect of the substance's reality, an aspect that can be understood only in terms of that substance itself: all the parts of Mickey are whole-dependent parts, and he is the whole on which they depend. If we forget this, then we will slide into thinking of them as things on their own, and even as substances on their own, substances out of which he is somehow to be assembled.

Mickey is not assembled out of little substances; he is one substance that exists in various ways. He is complex, and he is complex in a complexity of ways: it's not just that he has various parts, but that he has various kinds of parts. How are these kinds of parts related to each other?

First, it's important to keep in mind that different kinds of parts really are different in kind, with the result that it makes no sense to list them alongside one another without further ado. For example, there's something wrong with merely saying that Mickey's parts include his tail, his left eye, his agility, and his essence. The first two of those are physical parts, while the latter two are features, and acknowledging that difference is part of the process of listing his parts.

Second, it would also be wrong to go to the opposite extreme and say that we can make different lists of parts, but there's no way to relate them to one another at all. For example, having a tail is, in some sense, part and parcel of having a cat essence, and so there's a connection between the tail listed on one of Mickey's parts lists and the essence listed on another of his parts lists.

Third, I don't think there's any general rule about how the items on different parts lists are related to one another. The details have to be worked out in each particular case. So, for example, the physical part *tail* is related to Mickey's essence as follows: it's essential to Mickey that he ought to have a tail. But it gets complicated: which particular bits of cat-tail Mickey has are not related to his essence in that way, inasmuch as it doesn't matter precisely which ones he has. Or, for another example, Mickey's color is not related to his essence in the way that a tail is. Again, one simply has to work out how it goes in each case.

This chapter is finally done. Looking ahead now, we will address directly and in detail some topics that have already come up a number of times: universals and particulars, to be discussed in chapter five, and actuality and potentiality, to be discussed in chapter six. But first we need to discuss causation.

▷ To get started on reading Aquinas himself on the ideas developed in this chapter, begin with *On Being and Essence*, *On the Principles of Nature*, and *On the Mixture of the Elements*.

CHAPTER 4

Causes

4.1 Causes in Cinematic and Snapshot Perspective

CHAPTER TWO WAS ABOUT CHANGE, and chapter three talked more than once about potentiality getting actualized. What makes all this happen?

The word we typically use for what makes something happen is *cause*. This is a familiar word, and most of the time, we know how to use it. The baseball caused the window to break, and so, perhaps, did the bat and the batter; but the passing cloud did not. To talk about causes in this way is to talk about causes in conjunction with the topic of change, or, as I will now put it, to talk about causation from a cinematic or movie perspective—causes as bringing it about that things go from being in one way to being in another way.

But there is, in the Aristotelian-Thomistic perspective, another way of talking about causes, a way that provides a larger context for the first way. We can ask why things *are* the way they are, independently of asking how they changed so as to *come to be* that way. Suppose, for example, we ask why a turtle's shell is so hard to break, and we receive the answer, "because it's made of keratin"; this answer, an answer that uses the word *because*, provides a "cause" of, or explanation for, the shell's being hard to break, and yet it does not focus on any process. This other way of talking about causes we can call the snapshot version—causes as explaining why things are the way they are, largely abstracting from the process by which they came to be the way they are.

In this chapter, we will start with the movie approach, and later we will move on to the snapshot approach. By the end, we will have re-encountered some points made in previous chapters, but from a different perspective.

4.2 Which Items Make Things Happen?

Suppose someone says, "The dog's barking caused the baby to cry." For a statement in everyday speech, this seems fairly unexceptionable. Some philosophers would go further and take it as an illustration of a general truth—namely, that *events* (like a dog's barking) are what make things happen. But this can be questioned. Is it really events that make things happen? Mightn't it be something else, like facts, or substances?

In keeping with the overall Aristotelian-Thomistic approach in this book, I am going to adopt the idea that what makes things happen are substances. Substances, basic beings, are what cause the changes in our world. It's not absurd, of course, to say that the dog's barking woke the baby, but really it was the dog that woke the baby—by barking, of course! The instigators of change, then, are substances. They instigate it by acting, where actions are, in a sense, events of a certain sort, but ultimately, it's the substances that are responsible. I will, then, be allying myself with the "agent causation" approach over and against competitors such as "event causation." Of course, there are reasons for and against taking such an approach, but in a book like this, obviously not everything can be explored, and this is one of the ones that won't be.

4.3 Some Inadequate Understandings of the Movie Version

Despite being a part of our everyday thinking, causation has long been a puzzling topic for philosophy. What is really going on when, as we say, a substance exerts causal influence, or exercises causal powers, or however you want to put it?

Could it be that there is less here than meets the eye? Some have thought so, David Hume most famously.[1] Hume acknowledges that we say that one thing causes another: one billiard ball, let us say, causes another to move. He also insists on the point that if an idea that we have is a real idea, and not an illusion, then it must be a sort of copy of what he calls an "impression"—that is, either an external perception or else an inner feeling, like an emotion. We do indeed have an idea of the first ball moving up to the second one, and we do indeed have an idea of the second ball moving away from the first one, and it is easy

---

1. See his *Enquiry Concerning Human Understanding*, secs. 4–7, and his *A Treatise of Human Nature* I, part 3.

enough to understand where those ideas came from: they came from our perceptions of the first ball moving up to the second one, and the second one moving away from the first one. But we also have, or think we have, an idea of the first one *causing* the second one to move. Do we have any perception of this? Hume insists that we do not, and for that reason, he argues that we do not have a real idea of causation or necessary connection between the first ball's motion and the second ball's motion.

Of course, in some sense we clearly do have such an idea, and Hume acknowledges this. His point is that we misunderstand it. Like all ideas, it arises from an impression; but the impression is inner, not outer. The original impression we actually have, Hume says, is a feeling of expectation: We have so often seen one ball move up to another, with the second one moving away, that now, when we see the first ball approach, we anticipate the second ball's motion in our minds. That inner feeling of expectation is the real source of our idea that the two motions are necessarily connected, such that the one causes the other. But it is wrong to think that this idea is based on something out there, in the billiard balls themselves. It is really only something in our own minds. Our idea of causation is a copy of our inner feeling of expectation, not of some outer perception of causal activity.

Hume holds, then, that whenever we think we have encountered causal relations out there in the world, all we really have encountered is "constant conjunction": it regularly and dependably happens that when one ball moves up to another and touches it, the second one moves away. The two always happen together, in conjunction with one another. Hume does not object to our using the language of "causation" in such cases—he does so himself. But he wants us to realize that we have no reason to think that the first ball is acting on the second in a way that necessitates the second ball's moving. The first ball's motion happens, and so does the second ball's motion happen, but neither the first ball's motion, nor the first ball itself, *makes* the second ball's motion happen. What we call causation is really just constant conjunction (accompanied by a certain inner feeling of expectation).

At this point I feel compelled to mention something that Elizabeth Anscombe said about Hume. In her view, Hume was a sophist, but his sophistries are interesting and important; unlike in the case of ordinary sophistries, figuring out what is wrong with them leads to interesting and important insights.[2] Hume's analysis of causation, while fascinating, seems very off-base. But it is hard to pin down what has gone wrong. Here, at any rate, is a proposal. The real issue, I suggest, is not a metaphysical one, but one having to do with the theory of knowledge. Hume is mistaken to think of ideas or concepts as fainter copies of things we have literally perceived or felt. We do, of course, have faint copies of perceptions or feelings—these imaginings are called "phantasms" in the Aristotelian-Thomistic tradition. But concepts are not phantasms. (Descartes points out that while your concept of a chiliagon, a thousand-sided polygon, is different from your concept of a myriagon, a ten-thousand-sided polygon, your mental images or phantasms of these are indistinguishable. This proves that concepts are not just mental images.)[3] Instead, mysterious as it may be, we have a capacity to form rational concepts that do not correspond in any strict way to perceptions or feelings (even if they do ultimately grow out of them). In fact, metaphysics is impossible if we have no such capacity.

Going into all this would lead us too far astray. This is a book on metaphysics, not on the philosophy of knowledge. For that reason, I will turn to making a different sort of point about Hume's approach to causation—namely, that whatever Hume is discussing, it's *not* causation; causation means, at a bare minimum, making something happen, or at least contributing to its happening. Our idea of causation is more than mere constant conjunction, even constant conjunction accompanied by a certain inner feeling on the part of the observer. To adopt Hume's approach is to abandon the everyday notion of causation. And that, it seems to me, is just going too far. As mentioned in the introduction to this book, if philosophy gets too far from ordinary experience, it loses its way. Causation, real causation, is a concept we cannot do without.

Another approach to causation worth thinking about is the "counterfactual" approach associated most strongly with David Lewis (d. 2001). Counterfactual theories of causation quickly become very complicated—*very* complicated—but the core intuition is this. Suppose that C and E are two events that happen. If it's the case that if C *hadn't* happened, E wouldn't have happened either, then C is the cause of E.

---

2. G. E. M. Anscombe, "Modern Moral Philosophy," *Philosophy* 33, no. 124 (1958): 1–19.

3. Descartes, *Meditations* VI.

Earlier I said that causes are better thought of as substances, rather than events, but for now, let's just ignore that. This basic idea here does seem to capture something important about causation: to say that the dog's barking woke the baby seems to go together with the thought that if the dog hadn't barked, the baby would have slept on. On the other hand, it seems altogether too easy to find ways to object to this approach. Suppose the dog's barking not only wakes the baby but also wakes Mickey. If Mickey hadn't been woken, the baby wouldn't have woken, either, but it seems wrong to say that Mickey's being woken is the cause of the baby's waking.

Philosophers have been talking about Lewis's counterfactual approach for about half a century. Lewis has managed to respond to many objections, either by showing that his account already handles them or by modifying it. Going into all the complications would not be helpful in this book. Instead, what I want to say is, in the end, the same thing that I said about Hume's account. Even if we can find a counterfactual way of talking about causation that doesn't mistakenly call non-causes causes, or causes non-causes, still there is a problem. The problem is that we won't be addressing the core concept of what causation actually is—namely, making something happen. Even if we find all the necessary technical adjustments, causation is still not a matter of what would happen if something else happened, or what wouldn't happen if something else didn't happen. Causation is a matter of something's being responsible for something's happening.[4] Unless we talk about that, we aren't really talking about causation; instead, we are, at best, talking about something that—if you'll forgive this way of putting it—is constantly conjoined with causation.

4.4 A Better Way of Talking about Movie Causation

Consider the following example: You take a length of heavy wire and bend it into a triangular shape. What has happened here, and what had to be in place for it to happen? First, you had to have the power to bend a wire: you had to have the ability to grip it, enough strength to change its shape, and so forth. But that's not all. The wire had to be bendable.

---

4. Cf. John Searle, *Mind, Language, and Society: Philosophy in the Real World* (New York: Basic Books, 1998), 59.

So, you had to have the ability to impart triangularity, and the wire had to have the ability to receive triangularity. Not everything has the ability to bend a heavy wire—a raindrop doesn't. And not everything has the ability to get bent into a triangular shape—an icicle doesn't.

It's not merely that two things happen to be required. The two are related in a very intimate way. One of them is the ability to bring about a certain change, and the other is the ability to undergo that change. The first of these is active, and the second is passive or receptive, but both are real contributions. You can grab an icicle and try to bend it, but it's not going to work, no matter how skillful you think you are: the icicle just doesn't have what it takes. Causation, then, requires both an "agent," an active cause, and a "patient," a receiving cause—that is, something with the ability to receive or undergo the influence of the agent (from the Latin *pati*, to suffer or undergo).

Using traditional language, we can call these an "active potency" or "active power" and a "passive potency" or "passive power." And in accordance with what was said in §4.2, we will take the possessors of these powers to be substances, or anyway as substance-like. You, the wire-bender, are definitely a substance. Given what we said about artifacts in §3.2, perhaps the wire is not really a substance, but an aggregate of little metal molecules. But it would be very inconvenient to keep talking about rearranging a collection of mutually bonded metal molecules into the shape we call "triangular," so we'll just treat the wire as a substance, even if it's only an honorary substance.

In the most straightforward sense—we'll get into complications soon enough—the substance with the active power is the one that we typically call "the cause." But it's not enough for it simply to have that active power; it has to exercise it. Causation, in the movie sense now under discussion, is the actual exercise of an ability to bring about a change in something capable of undergoing the change.

The two potencies—the active and the passive—are distinct but related. One of them exists in the agent, and the other exists in the patient. But when the causation actually happens, there are not two related actualizations, but one. Your actually acting on the wire, and the wire's actually being acted on by you, are the very same reality, described from different perspectives. It can't happen, even by a miracle, that you bend the wire, but it doesn't get bent. (Teachers should remember this: It can't really happen that you have taught the material, but the students haven't learned anything. You may have *tried* to teach the material, but you haven't taught unless they have learned. To use the Aristotelian slogan, "the actuality of the agent is in the patient": the agent's actually being an agent happens *in* the patient—that is, in the very reality of the patient's receiving the causal influence. Teaching, when it happens, happens not in the mouth of the teacher, but in the mind of the student.)

We have seen that you can't bend something into a triangular shape unless it has the ability to be bent into such a shape. Icicles do not have that ability, and for that reason, you cannot bend them into triangles. But here is another thing that does not have the ability to become triangular: a triangular wire. It can't become triangular for a different reason—namely, that it already is triangular. Part of having the capacity to receive something from a cause is not already possessing that something.

This way of thinking about causation makes use of ideas we have seen earlier.[5] Your and the wire's abilities are potentialities, and the exercise of these abilities is an actualization. The wire's passive potentiality is a result of the wire's being material, which is, in turn, a result of its having a certain metallic form, and likewise, your active potentiality relies on your form and matter. Indeed, both your ability to bend the wire, and the wire's ability to get bent, are necessary accidents that flow from your and the wire's essences. And when the act of bending takes place, it boils down to this: the wire, which initially lacks a triangularity form, comes to have one, by the action of something that is capable of imparting such a form—namely, you, the wire-bender. You, the wire-bender, must in some sense have the form in order to impart it: in this case, you have it "in your mind," as we say.[6] So, to sum up, what is required to begin with is form (triangularity), matter (the wire), and privation (the wire's lack of triangularity); you, the agent, bring it about that the form is in the wire, you *form* the wire, thereby removing the privation and actualizing the wire's potential to be actually triangular.

Here I will insert a comment on the type of account that is being given, and I will do so by comparing it to the competing accounts we looked at earlier—namely, the constant conjunction account and the

---

5. See, above all, §2.5.
6. Sometimes the agent has the form not in this way: fire has heat, which it imparts to water, but it doesn't have it in mind.

counterfactual account. Those other accounts, I claimed, do not really tell us what causation is. Instead, they merely offer for our consideration something that, at best, is always there when causation is there: constant conjunction, or a certain counterfactual relation. But someone could object to my alternative Aristotelian-Thomistic account by saying that it has, so to speak, the opposite problem: Although it doesn't describe something other than causality, what it says about causality is uninformative. It simply restates the pre-philosophical intuitive idea ("making something happen") in fancy philosophical terminology, like "form" and "actuality." Either the Aristotelian-Thomistic account doesn't tell us anything new, or else it assumes that we already know what causation is. Either way, it contributes nothing to our understanding.

In response, I think it must be admitted that, in one way, the objection is right. The Aristotelian-Thomistic account doesn't explain what causation is in such a way that someone who didn't understand causation would, as a result of thinking the account through, come to understand it. On the other hand, why believe that this is what a theory of causation needs to be able to do? Philosophy is not the source of our idea of causation. We already have such an idea, before we start doing philosophy. Philosophy helps us make sense of it, purge it of confusion or inconsistency, and relate it to other things, and it helps us do this at as basic and fundamental a level as possible. In one sense, this is clearly more than "just telling us what we already knew," but if, in some other sense, it is telling us what we already know, why is that a bad thing? Again, philosophy grows out of pre-philosophical common sense.

Anyway, enough of this methodological talk about our theory of causation. Let's get back to talking about causation itself. We began by discussing what makes changes happen, but in doing so, we ended up bringing in extra elements, other things that need to be in place for changes to happen, such as recipients of causal influence, forms, potentialities, and so on. What all that points to is that talk of substances causing change needs to be set in a larger context. As we will now see, the Aristotelian-Thomistic way of characterizing that context involves additional uses of the language of causality. Instead of saying that the causes that make things happen need additional factors that allow them to do their causal work, factors that are not themselves causes, the Aristotelian-Thomistic tradition says that the causes that make things happen need other kinds of causes.

On this way of thinking, there are four types of cause: the formal cause, the material cause, the efficient or moving cause, and the final cause. The third of these, the "efficient cause," is the one that has been central to our discussion so far. It's the cause that makes things happen—for example, the person who makes the wire become triangular in shape. But what are the others?

The "formal cause" is the form that the agent imparts to the patient, and the "material cause" is the patient, the entity that receives the form. In the example we have been discussing, the formal cause is the triangularity, the material cause is the wire, and the efficient cause—called this from the Latin word *facere*, to do or to make—is the bender.

The "final cause" can be a little harder to talk about. It's a key part of the Thomist tradition to hold that natural processes don't "just happen"; they are, so to speak, aimed at a certain end point (*finis* in Latin, *telos* in Greek). This end point is "that for the sake of which" the process happens. When the agent or efficient cause has a mind, this is easy to understand: you bend the wire because you want to have an instrument to play in the band (it's a very thick wire). But what about when the agent does not, in any obvious sense, have a mind? Think of Mickey digesting his food. Certain causal processes go on in his digestive system, but Mickey doesn't have any plans about this. (Indeed, plans aren't really making a difference even when humans digest things: If you swallow some food, it's going to get digested whether you think about that or not.) The causal process of digestion has an end point that it tends toward and that makes it, digestion, be what it is; if the process didn't result in nutrition being made available, it wouldn't be digestion.

The final cause, to the extent that we can identify it, helps us see how the others fit together. You choose this matter (the wire) and that form (triangularity) for the sake of achieving a certain goal (having a musical instrument that can be played in a certain way). In Mickey's digestive tract, certain physiological events happen for the sake of getting food digested, and if you want to know *why* certain chemicals are there in his digestive tract, the answer will involve pointing to the role they play in achieving the goal of digestion.

Talking about final causality, then, means thinking of a causal process as being oriented toward coming out in a certain way, as being oriented toward "that for the sake of which" the process happens.

There's such a thing as the natural or correct way for a process to end up, and there's such a thing as a process going astray.[7] The process, when it goes correctly, goes the way it goes so that it can have the correct outcome; the other elements of the process, the efficient, final, and formal causes, are there for the sake of the final cause.

In the wire-bending example, mind is clearly involved. In the digestion example, mind does not seem to be involved at all. Is that a problem? Aristotle seems to hold that final causation does not require mind: nature simply does act for an end, without any thought being required. But Aquinas does not follow him here. Aquinas seems to hold that consistent, goal-oriented activities are evidence of mind: if not of digestive mind, then of divine mind.[8]

Up until now, I have been using, as my primary example, an accidental change, namely, a wire being bent. But it is worth giving an example of a substantial change as well.[9] Rusty's parents, when they mated, acted in such a way that certain gametes merged and became something with a new substantial form. The parents were able to bring this about because they themselves already had the form of cat; putting it differently, they were cats themselves. And the end-goal of the process was clearly to produce a new cat, namely Rusty. Aquinas would have said that Rusty's father imparted the form through the action of the sperm, while Rusty's mother provided the matter in the form of menstrual blood. This, it turns out, is not correct: both parents provide or convey form (this is why offspring look like their mothers as well as like their fathers), and both provide matter. Also, of course, both are efficient causes, jointly producing the new cat. What makes this case different from the wire-bending case is that in the wire-bending case, the causal process brings it about that one entity (the wire) acquires a new accident (triangularity) while persisting through this change, whereas in the case of reproduction, the causal process brings it about that one or, in fact, two entities (sperm and egg) do not persist through change but are instead replaced by a new substance with a new form—namely, Rusty. The details are hard to state exactly right, and this is not a book

---

7. This hearkens back to points about normativity made in §1.5.
8. See the last of the five arguments for God that Aquinas gives in *Summa Theologiae* I, q. 2, art. 3.
9. The distinction between these two kinds of change was explained in §2.3.

on the philosophy of biology. The point is simply that the Aristotelian-Thomistic approach to causation works for substantial change as well as for accidental change—albeit, naturally enough, in a modified version.

Once again, it is worth pausing to purify our concepts in a way that will help us avoid false reification. When you act to make a wire triangular, it is not as if you approach the wire with "a triangularity" in your hand, and then the wire helpfully turns its potentiality side to you, whereupon you slap the triangularity onto the wire. Obviously not. What exactly you do depends on the case in question: Shaping wire is one thing. Baking dough is another. Inflating a tire is something else still. "Imparting the form" can take many forms. In metaphysics we lay out this general structure, but it takes chemistry or other sciences to work out the details.

Earlier in this section, we broadened our use of the language of "cause" to include not only efficient causation, but also the others—formal, material, and final. But someone might object that this is just a gratuitous extension of a word whose meaning was fine as things stood. Why not call those other factors—the "formal cause," "material cause," and "final cause"—by some other name, like "contributory factor" or whatever?

Then again, an altogether different linguistic point could be made, like this: Why did those silly modern philosophers narrow down the meaning of "cause" so that it included only efficient causes?

On one level, I think this is a *merely* linguistic dispute. As long as the realities themselves are discussed, who cares whether they are called "causes" or not? On another level, however, I think that each side actually has a point.

The traditional usage reflects something quite important—namely, that all four of these factors, whatever you call them, interact so that things can happen. Efficient causation, all on its own, is not enough, and those other concepts will in fact always be there in our thinking about causation, whether labeled as causes or not. Everyone knows, for example, that striking with a hammer has a different effect on gold than it does on glass. Whether or not we explain this using the language of "material causation," we need to take it into account.

On the other hand, there *is* something special about the efficient cause, and that is probably what explains why it has tended to become the primary sense of the word "cause." In everyday situations, at any rate, to ask for the cause of something is to ask for the efficient cause. If I ask for an explanation of the window's being broken, I do not want to hear about what it means for glass to break (the formal cause), or about the brittleness of glass (the material cause), or even perhaps whether any purpose was served by its breaking. I simply want to know whether a branch was blown against the pane, or a kid hit a ball into it.

Given the predominance of this use of causal language in ordinary speech, it is unsurprising that it tends to take over philosophical usage as well. On the other hand, even in ordinary speech, causal language isn't restricted to efficient causation. When talking about goals and purposes, we sometimes use the word "cause," as when we say, "the money is being donated for a good cause." And even if we don't use the exact word "cause" for matter or form, we do say that the instrument plays the way it does "because" it is metal or "because" of its shape.

For the most part, I will use the more traditional terminology, calling all four causes "causes," but the important thing is not so much which words we use, but how we understand what makes things happen. And that understanding, however we formulate it, must take significantly more into account than just the efficient cause.

4.5 Onward to Snapshot Causation

We have seen how the theory of four causes applies to what I have been calling movie causation, causation as applied to changes, to things happening. But as mentioned earlier, the concept of causation, in the Thomistic tradition, get used in a "snapshot" version as well, a version that explains why things are the way they are, without examination of the process by which they came to be that way.

Let us start with the example of the triangular-shaped piece of metal. Why is it the way it is? One way to answer would be to say: because it's made of metal. Another would be: because it's triangular in shape. Another would be: because someone made it that way. And still another: because that way it can so readily be used for making a fast series of bright dinging sounds during a band concert.

These answers are different from each other. They are, in fact, different types of answers, and implicitly therefore answers to different types of questions. The first concerns what a thing is made out of. The second concerns the shape taken on by what the thing is made out of.

The third concerns what did the shaping. The fourth concerns the goal for which the shaper did the shaping.

I have been speaking rather vaguely of explanations of why something is the way it is, but in truth, almost no one would ever ask, of a triangle or of anything else, "Why is it the way it is?" To be sure, if one of your friends keeps making dumb jokes, you might ask, in jest, "Why are you the way you are?" But in a case like that, it's clear that you actually mean to ask a rather specific question, like "Why do you keep making dumb jokes?" So it might be helpful to work through all this again, with respect to something rather more specific. Consider a turtle, and consider the question, "Why is its shell so hard to break?" Here are four ways to answer that question. First way, through the material cause: because it's made of keratin. Second way, through the formal cause: because it's rounded. Third way, through the efficient cause: because its parents passed on genes that led to a hard-to-break shell. Fourth way, through the final cause: because having a hard-to-break shell gives you a better shot at living long and prospering.

To be sure, it is possible to ask a very general question about "why something is the way it is," meaning thereby something like "What is the overall explanation of this thing's existing in the way that it does?" Perhaps that's the way you took the question about the triangle from a few paragraphs ago. In any case, we can answer such a general question with general appeals to matter, form, efficient cause, and final cause. A cat is the way it is—overall—because it has a body of a certain sort; because it has a substantial form of a certain sort, along with accidental forms of various sorts; because its parents made it to be in a certain way, and because various additional agents imparted various accidental forms to it; and so that it might live a certain kind of feline life. And to repeat a point made earlier, these causes are not just separate items on a list. It has the matter it does as a result of having the form it does. The matter is formed that way because of the work of the agent. And it is all under the guidance, so to speak, of the final cause, goal, or *telos*. As Aquinas says, the final cause is the cause of causes. It is for the sake of living a feline life that Mickey has a feline body and a feline form. Likewise, the explanation of his parents' having mated is found there too, both in the sense that doing so was part of living out their own feline lives, but also for the sake of Mickey coming into being as a cat. (Remember, regardless of whether you think that Mickey's parents, or

God, had Mickey's coming-to-be in mind, his coming into being was, in fact, the fruition of his parents' act.)

So, then, we can use all four causes to explain why the thing is the way it is: its matter explains it in certain ways, its form explains it in others, and so on. What's more, these causes are related to one another in certain characteristic ways. The matter is what is formed, and the form is the form of the matter. The efficient or agent cause is what imparted the form to the matter, and the final cause explains why the others are as they are.

I have distinguished snapshot causation from movie causation, but it's important not to exaggerate the difference between these two ways of thinking. Including efficient causation in our snapshot account brings in a cinematic element inasmuch as the efficient cause is what makes things happen. And the movie account implicitly points to the snapshot account inasmuch as the account of change is there to explain the final resting-point of change. Skill in thinking about causation involves not choosing one account over the other but understanding how to move back and forth between them.

At this point, we can see a tight connection between our discussion of snapshot causality and our discussion, in §3.4, of parts. Two of the snapshot causes, the formal and material causes, are parts of what they cause. They are internal causes. The efficient cause and the final cause, by contrast, are in some sense external to, or beyond, what they cause.

What's more, these various causes not only explain why the thing is the way it is now, they also help to explain how it will change in the future: in virtue of what it is now, it has various causal powers, both active and passive, which explain how it will participate in further causal interactions. This is why the world as we experience it involves orderly unfolding and not just random happening: the agents and patients have powers of specific sorts, and those powers both restrict and guide how they interact.

4.6 Summary

Substances are causes in the sense of efficient or agent causes. They act upon other substances, substances that are able to play the role of matter with regard to those agents, and they either impart accidental forms to them, or else they transform them into entirely new substances with new forms. And the processes by which substances do this are, as it were, "aimed" at producing the effects that they do. Once a causal process has happened, the result is a substance that is actual in certain ways: as a result of the agent's having acted for a certain end, the result is a substance that now has a certain form and matter that make it exist in this or that way, substantial or accidental as the case may be.

Up until now, much of our investigation has focused mostly on ordinary things: basic beings, their changes, their parts, and their causal entanglements. Now it is time to move on to somewhat less commonsensical considerations, starting with the difference between particulars and universals.

➤ To get started on reading Aquinas himself on the ideas developed in this chapter, begin with *On the Principles of Nature*.

CHAPTER 5

Universals and Particulars

5.1 Universals and the One over Many Problem

PHILOSOPHERS STANDARDLY DISTINGUISH between universals and particulars. This distinction came up earlier, in §1.1 and §3.3.1, but only in a cursory way. Now it is time to look at it in detail.

The world around us is full of beings like Rusty the cat, or the mouse he is chasing, or the rock the mouse is hiding behind. These beings are "individuals" or "particulars." (I will use these words interchangeably.) And these beings have features: Rusty is a cat, and he's red.

Now in one sense, you might say that each being is unique: perhaps there's no cat *exactly* like Rusty. But in another sense, it is important not to carry this too far. Rusty is not utterly unique: he's not different from everything else in every respect. There are other cats, and other red things, and other agile things. Mickey differs from Rusty by being gray, rather than red, but he's similar to Rusty in being a cat. Rusty and Mickey are alike, at least to some extent.

There are a number of ways to express such facts in language. When things are alike, at least in one respect or another, we can, obviously, say that they "are alike." Another thing we can say is that they "resemble" one another, or are "similar" to one another, but this is sometimes a source of confusion. If we say that two things are "similar" in color or "resemble" one another in color, are we, or are we not, implying that they are also slightly different in color? For example, if I say that my blue jacket and your blue jacket are "similar" in color, does that mean that while they are both blue, they are slightly different shades of blue? (If you thought they were exactly the same color, would you reject my assertion that they are a "similar" color and say, "No, they aren't just *similar* in color, they are the *same* in color"?) Some philosophers try to clarify by saying, in a case when two jackets have exactly the same color, that they are *exactly similar* or that they *resemble each other exactly*. Other philosophers think that such language is self-contradictory; for them, resemblance or similarity means *partial* resemblance or similarity.

I do not want to get caught up in an argument about terminology here. I am happy not to use the language of "similarity" or "resemblance" if others find it misleading.[1] Henceforth, I will say either that things are "alike" or that they "match." If two things have exactly the same color, for example, I will say that they match in color or are alike in color.

While we're talking about terminology, let me note further that another way to say that Rusty and Mickey are alike is to say that they "share a nature" or "share a feature." For example, you might say that Rusty and Mickey both share in felinity or share in agility. This way of speaking raises even more questions than words like resemblance or similarity do. If Rusty and Mickey "share a nature," does that mean that the world contains, in addition to Rusty and Mickey, some additional thing—namely, the nature that they share? Consider, as an admittedly rather distant comparison, the idea of sharing an office. One thing we know for sure about office-sharing is that you can't share an office if the office doesn't exist. Does the fact that Rusty and Mickey both share agility mean that agility is in some sense a "thing" that exists? After all, how could they share it if it doesn't exist?

Later, we will consider at some length the possibility that this line of thought is mistaken in a very important way, but for now, let's keep going with it. For now, let's endorse the idea that when we say that Rusty and Mickey share some feature or nature—for example, felinity—it follows that the nature or feature they share is some existing entity. Felinity is the one item that they and all other cats share. It's what some metaphysicians call "the one over the many."

If that's right, then the next questions are going to be: What is this shared nature like, and how do Rusty and Mickey share in it?

What is it like? It seems clear that it doesn't exist in the same way that Rusty and Mickey do. They—Rusty and Mickey—are individuals or particulars, but it, felinity, is a "universal."

That raises a new question—namely, the question of what the difference is between individuals and universals. Let us begin by unpack-

---

1. Some words are worth fighting over—"person" seems like a good example—but not these.

ing something we saw in §1.1 and §3.3.1: A universal is an instantiable, while an individual is a non-instantiable instance.[2]

To say that a universal is an instantiable is to say that it is something that can be instantiated. It is something that there can be an instance or example of. Felinity is a universal because there can be instances of it—Rusty and Mickey, for example.

Typically, instantiables are shareable, capable of being instantiated by more than one thing. Felinity is a good example. But we should at least be open to the possibility that there are universals that can have only one instance. I will come back to this briefly below.

To say that an individual or particular is a non-instantiable instance is to say (a) that it is an instance of something, and (b) that there can be no instances of it. Rusty is an individual because (a) he is an instance of felinity, and (b) there can be no instances of him. (There can, perhaps, be other cats that match Rusty in every respect, but none of them will be an instance of him. None of them will be an example of him, in the way that he is an example of felinity.)

Since universals and particulars are understood in contrast to one another, you might ask why we don't simply say that universals are instantiables, while particulars are non-instantiables.

Why do we also say that particulars are instances of universals? One reason is the simple fact that it really does seem to be the case that particulars are always instances of universals. Nothing is just a being and that's all; every individual is of one kind or another. Another reason is as follows. Think of the property of being both square and circular. Nothing can be a square circle, so therefore square circleness cannot have instances, so therefore it is non-instantiable. If non-instantiability is, all on its own, *sufficient* for being an individual, then square circleness is an individual. And that is clearly wrong.

Why do we say merely that a universal is instantiable, and not add that it is a non-instance? We say it this way because universals can be instances of other universals (or anyway, some philosophers think they can). For example, perhaps felinity is an instance of the universal "universal"![3]

---

2. For a detailed discussion of this approach, and why it is to be preferred to others, see Jorge J. E. Gracia, *Individuality: An Essay on the Foundations of Metaphysics* (Albany: State University of New York Press, 1988), chapter one.

3. Is felinity an instance of the universal mammality? No. Felinity, whatever it is, is not a mammal. It's a universal.

With these clarifications in hand, let's get back to the main line of thought—namely, that since Rusty and Mickey share felinity, felinity must exist as some kind of reality. It's a universal, the one universal shared by the many (Mickey, Rusty, and all other cats). From now on, we'll use capital letters for the names of universals: the cats we've been talking about share Felinity, and Felinity is a universal.

We know what Rusty and Mickey are like. They are cats, they have four legs, they have colors, and so on. What would Felinity be like? It's not a cat, because every cat is an individual. It doesn't have legs, surely, or a color. It has been around a long time; the ancient Egyptians had cats, so it must have existed at least that long. It isn't restricted to any particular country. At this point, it might seem best to go all the way and say that Felinity is not spatiotemporally limited at all, that it's altogether outside of space and time. (After all, it does seem that all spatiotemporal items that we encounter are particulars.) Going further still, it might seem best to say that, unlike Rusty and Mickey, Felinity is the sort of thing that cannot fail to exist. It has to exist. It necessarily exists. (After all, it does seem that all the contingent beings in our experience—that is, the beings that might not have existed—are particulars.) Even if it never had any instances, it would still have been there, able to be instantiated.

If you accept the existence of Felinity, understood in this way, then you accept "Platonic realism" about universals. On this view, the world contains, in addition to individual cats, the universal Felinity. Felinity exists as a timeless, non-spatial reality that individual cats share in. A view like this is called "realism" because it holds that universals are really there, objectively, regardless of what anyone thinks or says.[4] It's called "Platonic" because it seems to line up with the views of Plato, who held that universals are not only objectively real, but also outside of time and space in the way described just above. To be sure, some scholars don't think that Plato actually believed in universals (or at least not in this way). But even if he didn't, this kind of view gets discussed in his works, and it has come to be attached to his name. So even if Plato was not himself a Platonic realist, Platonic realism is still a thing that some philosophers believe in.

---

4. The word "realist" can mean various things in various parts of philosophy. For example, someone who believes that there are objective norms of right and wrong can be called a "moral realist." In this chapter, realism only means believing that universals exist.

Let's think a bit more about what it means to believe in Felinity along these lines. It means believing that Mickey exists, and that Rusty exists, but also that Felinity exists. All three of them, it seems, are existing beings. Not, however, in the same way: Mickey and Rusty are individuals, non-instantiable instances, and Felinity is a universal, an instantiable. And it is not just that Mickey and Rusty are both instances: They are instances of the same thing, Felinity. They share in Felinity. So although we can say that Rusty and Mickey "are not the same," in that each is an individual distinct from the other (Rusty is not Mickey, and Mickey is not Rusty), still in another sense we can say that they "are the same," inasmuch as each of them is an instance of the one universal Felinity. Although Rusty and Mickey are not "one in number," they are "one in kind," and Felinity is that kind.[5] Likewise for all other cats, of course! Felinity is the one nature that brings together or unifies the many cats in the world.[6]

Remember that we had two questions: What is Felinity like, and how do Rusty and Mickey share in it? Felinity, we have been saying, is a universal, a being that exists outside of space and time, a being that many entities can instantiate. And the way Rusty and Mickey share in Felinity is that each of them is an instance of it. So far, so good, or so it seems. We had a problem—namely, how can Rusty and Mickey both be the same, given that they are obviously different individuals? And the following looks like a solution: there is some special kind of being, Felinity, that each of them is an instance of.

And yet, some philosophers do not accept this. It's easy enough, they say, to believe in the existence of Rusty and Mickey: those cats are just straightforwardly there, in the everyday world, as physical individuals. But Felinity is not like that. Felinity is not part of the physical world. Felinity is not even a non-physical individual, like a ghost or an angel, because Felinity is not an individual at all. And Felinity exists in a way that stands outside of time. In short, Felinity is quite unlike the beings we encounter in our normal, everyday world of particulars. Felinity, and all other universals, are very weird. According to some philosophers, they are just too weird to believe in.

---

5. See §2.4 for different senses of identity.
6. Is Felinity "one" in the same sense in which Rusty is "one"—namely, one in number? This is a difficult question, which I will return to, briefly, in this section.

This argument feels somewhat persuasive to me, but I'm not sure that it should. Maybe reality contains weird things, and we simply have to get used to it. And anyway, what counts as weird? As it happens, universals seem weirder to me than angels do, but some intelligent people feel exactly the opposite way. Perhaps it's unwise to put too much emphasis on considerations of this sort.

Instead, let's move on to a firmer kind of worry. If we believe in universals, it's not because we've seen them or touched them or encountered them in any ordinary way. It's because we accept, on the basis of philosophical reasoning, that they serve a theoretical purpose. They explain something. They do some philosophical work, so to speak, by helping us understand how two or more individuals can be of the same kind. The universal is the one over the many, and it is meant somehow to explain the unity of the many. But how does Felinity explain their unity? What does it do? How does it accomplish this work of unification? We have said that they are instances of it, but what does this really mean?

The difficulties are related. If Felinity is so very different from Rusty and Mickey, doesn't that make it hard to understand how they can be related to it? They are in a particular location, but it is not; they are at a specific point in time, but it is not; they are physical, but it is not. It's as if Felinity belongs to an entirely different zone of reality. How can it possibly have any bearing on Mickey and Rusty?

I've been asking a lot of rhetorical questions, but I don't mean to bully you. A rhetorical question is, after all, not an argument. You may think that these questions make no sense or that they can be answered. I'm not trying to convince you that universals don't exist, merely by asking a lot of questions. I'm simply trying to bring out the sort of difficulties that people who believe in universals must face up to.

Suppose I'm hiking in the dark, and something heavy rolls down the hill, bangs into my leg, and then rolls farther on. I literally "don't know what hit me," but that's no reason to doubt that something did. Even without any understanding of what hit me, I have reason to believe that something did: I felt it. But universals are not like that. We don't encounter universals, in the grocery store or on the hiking trail, and then later wonder what they are. We believe in them *only* as a way to solve a philosophical problem. If they don't explain anything—if they don't solve our problem—then the whole point of believing in them is lost. Above I said that they are accepted because they do some explanatory work for us. The worry we are trying to face now is that maybe they actually don't do any work. Just because some philosopher says they do doesn't mean it's true. And the cold, harsh truth here is that the world of metaphysics is a dog-eat-dog, ultra-libertarian kind of world. There's no unemployment insurance or welfare payments or universal basic income. If universals don't do the explanatory work that we need them to do, they starve. We don't keep them around out of pity, we exclude them from our theory.

If we do exclude them from our theory, then we will be not "realists" but "nominalists."[7] Nominalism has the advantage of not believing in those strange entities called universals. (That said, it still must address the questions that led realists to believe in universals.)

So far, then, we have the following situation. On the one hand, it seems that a multiplicity of beings, like Rusty and Mickey and all other cats, are alike or, as we say, share a nature. And it might seem that natures can't be shared unless they exist. On this basis, it might seem we should become realists by believing in natures or universals, like Felinity, as an explanation of the fact that all cats share a nature. On the other hand, Felinity is rather weird, and on top of that, it's not clear how it is related to Mickey and Rusty, and therefore it's not clear how it explains what it is meant to explain. This might lead us to reject universals and become nominalists. In short, we started with a question or a problem, and we have been considering a possible answer or solution, but we're not sure whether the proposal actually works as an answer or solution.

One way of responding to this situation is as follows. Instead of accepting the Platonic realist solution to the one over many problem, and instead of proposing a different solution, one can deny that any solution is needed at all, on the grounds that things were never alike or matching in the first place. One can say, for instance, that it's not true

---

7. This term comes from the Middle Ages, when it was used as a label for philosophers who say that universals aren't real entities, but only names (*nomina* in Latin). As we will see, however, there is a difference between the medieval and the contemporary uses of this term. What's more, the word "nominalist," in a medieval context, is sometimes used to describe positions that are at best distantly connected to the question of universals, such as certain positions on how moral law relates to human nature. In this chapter, we are discussing nominalism *only* as a position on the existence of universals.

that Rusty and Mickey are both cats. They aren't alike, they don't match, and therefore, there's no point in discussing whether the nature that they allegedly share exists or not. There's nothing to discuss.

This is the most extreme kind of nominalism, well expressed in the sentence "Not one of them is like another" and which I will therefore call "Dr. Seuss nominalism."[8] Dr. Seuss nominalism says that no matter which two things you choose, they are going to be different, and not just different in some way, but different in *every* way. To be sure, we may say that Rusty and Mickey are "both cats," and we may put them in the same compartment in our minds, but there is nothing out there that makes it correct to do so. It's entirely an arbitrary choice on our part.

In my judgment, Dr. Seuss nominalism takes things way too far. Even if no two things can be exactly alike, matching in every respect, still, they can match in at least some respects. Mickey and Rusty may differ in size or color, but both are cats; Mickey and my car differ in essence, but they are both gray. Alikeness is an unavoidable fact about our experience of the world, a fact that metaphysics needs to explain, not deny. Dr. Seuss nominalism is wrong, then, and the One Over Many Problem still needs discussing.

I now turn to two "intermediate" solutions. They are intermediate in the sense that they don't go as far as Platonism, and they don't go as far (in the opposite direction) as Dr. Seuss nominalism. I will explain how all four relate to one another in more detail below; for now, let me simply describe the two intermediate solutions.

One intermediate solution agrees with the Platonist by accepting the existence of universals but disagrees with the Platonist by re-thinking the nature of universals and how they relate to individuals. This view says that while universals do exist, they don't exist above and beyond individuals, or apart from them; instead, they exist in them. Felinity isn't something that exists in a timeless and placeless zone of reality that is distinct from the zone of reality that Rusty and Mickey exist in; instead, Felinity exists in Rusty and Mickey themselves.

This view is often called "Aristotelian" realism. The contrast between it and the "Platonist" view is famously depicted in the painting

---

8. Theodor Seuss Geisel, *One Fish, Two Fish, Red Fish, Blue Fish* (New York, NY: Random House, 2013), 15.

that adorns three-quarters of the philosophy department websites in the universe—namely, the painting titled *The School of Athens*. It depicts a large number of Greek philosophers, with Plato and Aristotle in the middle. You can tell who is who because one of them is gesturing upwards, as if to the heavenly universals, while the other is gesturing downwards, as if to indicate that the natures of things exist here, within the world of individuals.

This first intermediate solution, the less Platonic and more moderate version of realism, can also be called "immanent realism"; it takes universals to be within things, immanent in them, rather than "transcendent," above and beyond them. It accepts the force of the One Over Many Problem by agreeing that if Mickey and Rusty share the nature of being cats, then Felinity must exist, but it does so while hoping to avoid some of the apparent problems of Platonic realism. If it seems like a problem to say that Felinity is timeless and spaceless, yet still somehow related to Mickey and Rusty, then perhaps it's not so much of a problem if you say that Felinity exists here in time and space.

On the other hand, this approach gives rise to a different difficulty. If Felinity is really a universal, and not a particular, you might wonder how it can exist within particulars. If it exists in Mickey, then presumably it exists wholly and entirely in him. Otherwise, he'd be only a half-cat, a semi-feline. And the same, of course, would hold for Rusty. But in that case, one reality, Felinity, would exist entirely in one place at one time while also existing entirely in another place at the very same time. And that sounds strange.

So much, for now, on the first intermediate solution. The second intermediate solution accepts that Rusty and Mickey are both truly cats, regardless of how anyone chooses to speak or think about them. In this way, it rejects Dr. Seuss nominalism. However, it does not accept the One Over Many Idea, and in that way it is nominalistic. It says that Mickey and Rusty can be alike as cats without the existence of the universal Felinity. But how?

Let us come at this question indirectly, by setting the question of alikeness aside for a while and talking about just one cat. What makes Rusty a cat? Rusty is a cat, one might say, because of certain facts about him. Suppose, just for fun, that the right definition of cat is "meowing mammal." Rusty is a cat because he is a meowing mammal. He is a mammal inasmuch as he has the power to regulate his own body temperature, to bear live young, and so forth.[9] These are individual facts about him: For example, he is warm-blooded because he has his own personal hypothalamus that can secrete his own personal hormones to regulate his own personal body temperature. He is meowing because he has his own personal throat and so forth. Having all these individual features—the features that make him a mammal, and the features that make him a meower—is what makes him a cat.

Now let's talk about Mickey and ask what makes *him* be a cat. The answer will be, of course, that he has *his* own personal hypothalamus, *his* own personal throat, and so on. Mickey is a cat because of individual facts about him.

Now, in explaining why Rusty is a cat, I made no mention of universals. And likewise, in explaining why Mickey is a cat, I made no mention of universals. Rusty is a cat in virtue of individual facts about Rusty, and Mickey is a cat in virtue of individual facts about Mickey. But if we don't need universals to explain why Rusty is a cat, and if we don't need universals to explain why Mickey is a cat, then why would we need universals to explain why Mickey and Rusty are both cats?

The second moderate or intermediate position says that we don't. All we need for Mickey and Rusty to both be cats is (a) for Rusty to be a cat and (b) for Mickey to be a cat. If we don't need universals for one to be a cat, and if we don't need universals for the other to be a cat, then we won't need universals for both to be cats. That comes along for free, so speak.[10]

On this way of thinking, widely-used expressions such as "sharing a nature" are systematically misleading. When we say that Mickey and Rusty "share felinity," all we really mean is that Mickey is a cat and Rusty is a cat. It may sometimes be more convenient or elegant to use the language of feature-sharing, and even to speak of "Felinity" as if it were some special kind of entity, but we should not let this trick us into thinking that there really exists some nature to be shared. The parallelism between "share a nature" and "share an office" is, you might say,

---

9. OK, you're right, Rusty doesn't bear live young; he gets his mate to do this.
10. See the entertaining and instructive exchange in Michael Devitt, "'Ostrich Nominalism' or 'Mirage Realism'?" *Pacific Philosophical Quarterly* 61, no. 4 (1980): 433–39; D. M. Armstrong, "Against Ostrich Nominalism: A Reply to Michael Devitt," *Pacific Philosophical Quarterly* 61, no. 4 (1980): 440–49.

deceptive and something that we need to be wary of. Regardless of whether or not we like to say things like "Rusty and Mickey both have Felinity," we should not fall into thinking that there really is a universal Felinity. Each cat is what he is, and each cat matches the other, and that's all. Mickey and Rusty are alike, and we therefore say that they share something, but we should avoid the error of thinking that there's literally some thing that they share.[11]

Is saying this another instance of taking a stand against reification? In a way, yes; the moderate nominalist faults the realist for holding that universals are, in some sense or other, things that belong to the landscape of reality. However, this form of anti-reification is stronger than what we have seen previously. In talking about accidents, for example, in §3.3.3, I urged that we not think of them as things, as substances or quasi-substances, but I did not deny any reality to them at all. The moderate nominalist, by contrast, while not denying real conspecificity, is denying reality to universals.[12]

At this point I would like to introduce a bit of terminology that will make it easier to state the four views compactly. We have been saying that things can "be alike" or "match" or (perhaps misleadingly) that they can "share a nature." Let us now say that anyone who believes that this is possible—anyone, in short, who isn't a Dr. Seuss nominalist—is someone who believes in "real conspecificity." It's "conspecificity" because there's likeness according to kind or species, and the conspecificity is "real" because it holds objectively, independently of what anyone thinks or says.

Using that terminology, we can say that there are two types of realists and two types of nominalists. Let's start with the realists. (a) Platonic or transcendental realists believe in real conspecificity and believe in universals as existing in a transcendent (non-spatial, non-temporal,

---

11. And now for a technical point. If there are no universals, and if individuals are instances, then why doesn't that mean that there are no individuals? In the face of this question, the nominalist will perhaps say that explaining individuals and universals by contrasting them was a useful explanatory device, but something we ultimately need to abandon. If pressed nonetheless to give an account of individuals, the nominalist could perhaps say that an individual is something that has features or characteristics, but that isn't itself the sort of thing that can be a feature or characteristic of anything else: Socrates is human, but nothing "is a Socrates."

12. But see §8.8 and §8.12.

etc.) fashion. (b) Aristotelian or immanent realists believe in real conspecificity and believe in universals as existing in a more immanent, this-worldly fashion.

By the way, you can call Platonic realists "extreme" realists, as long as "extreme" isn't automatically taken as having a negative connotation; sometimes extremism is good! And likewise, you can call Aristotelian realists "moderate" realists, as long as "moderate" isn't automatically taken as having a positive connotation; sometimes being moderate is just a way of being timid.

Let us turn now to the nominalists, who deny the existence of universals.[13] Again there are two types. At the opposite extreme from Platonic realists there are (d) Dr. Seuss nominalists, who are extreme nominalists. They not only deny the existence of universals but also deny real conspecificity. In between them and moderate realists are (c) moderate nominalists. They deny the existence of universals but affirm real conspecificity.

You can see it all in Table 5-1.

TABLE 5-1 THEORIES OF UNIVERSALS

Deny universals	Deny universals	Affirm (immanent) universals	Affirm (transcendent) universals
Extreme nominalism	**Moderate nominalism**	**Moderate realism**	**Extreme realism**
Deny real conspecificity	Affirm real conspecificity	Affirm real conspecificity	Affirm real conspecificity

---

13. This way of using the word "nominalism" (as a position on the existence of universals) is fairly standard in contemporary metaphysics, although there are exceptions. It's particularly important to note that this usage deviates from the usage of many scholars of medieval philosophy, including many Thomists. For some, the only kind of "nominalism" is Dr. Seuss nominalism. For others, being a nominalist requires denying that substances have features as parts, that is, being a "blob theorist" (see §3.3); for a recent article that falls into this category, see Jeffrey E. Brower, "Aquinas on the Problem of Universals," *Philosophy and Phenomenological Research* 92, no. 3 (2016): 715–35. These terminological differences can lead to enormous misunderstandings. On the way I'm using the word in this book, it might make sense to call Thomas Aquinas a "nominalist," but on either of the other two senses mentioned in this footnote, it would be completely ridiculous to call him one. Be careful!

The view in the rightmost column, Platonic or transcendent or extreme realism, affirms real conspecificity. To support real conspecificity, this view is willing to make a very strong metaphysical claim—namely, that there is a special transcendent realm of being containing special transcendent universals.

The view in the leftmost column, Dr. Seuss nominalism or extreme nominalism, rejects special universals, and indeed any kind of universals, and this rejection goes hand-in-hand with its denial of real conspecificity.

The middle two views agree in affirming real conspecificity, and they agree that transcendent universals are not the right way to explain real conspecificity, but they disagree over whether you need universals at all: the moderate nominalist thinks that universals are not needed, while the moderate realist thinks they are. You will learn a lot by studying the chart and thinking through which views agree with which, and on which issues.

The difference between Dr. Seuss nominalism and the others is very large and very clear. But what about the other views? They all agree on real conspecificity, but they disagree on how to explain it.

The difference between extreme realism and the others seems clear enough. Extreme realism says that there is a separate realm of non-individual entities, entities whose existence does not depend on how the ordinary world is. The other views, in contrast with extreme realism, either deny the existence of universals altogether, or else assert that universals exist only in particulars. The two forms of nominalism do the former. Moderate realism does the latter. It says that Felinity exists, but only in actual cats: if the world had unfolded differently, in such a way that there never had been cats, and never would be, then there would also be no such thing as Felinity.

Another way in which extreme realism differs from the other views is this: It seems to see universals as basic beings. It either sees them as basic beings in addition to individuals like Mickey and Rusty, or else it sees them as the only basic beings, with Mickey and Rusty somehow secondary to them.

What about the middle two views? How different are they? At first glance, they seem as different as different could be: one of them says that universals exist in things, and that's what explains real conspecificity, while the other says that universals aren't needed for real conspecificity. However, at least in my experience, when you press the advocates of each view for further explanation, it starts to become at least a little harder to be sure that the views are different. The moderate realist admits that Felinity in Rusty is tied up with Rusty's individuality: it's Felinity, but *Felinity as existing in him*. It exists only as individualized in individual cats. Meanwhile, the moderate nominalist admits that Rusty's personal felinity and Mickey's personal felinity are truly just alike. Close inspection, then, reveals the views to be closer than they seem at first.

One way to press the issue is this: Is there *one thing* that belongs to both Rusty and Mickey, namely, their Felinity? Rusty and Mickey are numerically distinct and the same in kind, but are they the same in kind because of something—Felinity—that is, in itself, numerically one?[14] If the moderate realist says yes, then I think his view is, in the end, clearly different from the view of the moderate nominalist, because the moderate nominalist would say that there is nothing that is numerically the same between the two of them. But if the moderate realist says that when we say that Rusty and Mickey share "one nature," we *don't* actually mean that the nature is anything *numerically* one, despite the terminology of "one" nature, then it remains unclear whether the views are actually different. On this version of moderate realism, when we say they have "the same nature," it's somehow a sameness that's not as strong as numerical sameness, and yet stronger than the mere sameness in kind that the moderate nominalist would allow for.[15]

Philosophy is hard, and the point is subtle. It could be that each view is emphasizing a different aspect of the problem, resulting in the views sounding different: the moderate nominalist, perhaps, is reluctant to sound like a Platonic realist, so he pushes hard against universals, while the moderate realist, perhaps, is reluctant to sound like a Dr. Seuss nominalist, so he pushes hard in favor of there being something shared.

---

14. Armstrong adopts this version of moderate realism toward the end of *Universals: An Opinionated Introduction*. In his view, it is a theoretical advantage to say that there aren't two types of unity, specific and numerical, but only one. Specific unity is reducible to numerical unity. (By contrast, you might say that the bundle of universals theorist thinks that numerical unity is reducible to specific unity—see §3.3.2.)

15. Rightly or wrongly, many understand the medieval philosopher John Duns Scotus (d. 1308) to take this line. For an attribution of something close to it to Aquinas, see Brower, "Aquinas on the Problem of Universals."

I firmly reject Dr. Seuss nominalism. Real conspecificity is real. And if the only way to accept real conspecificity is to accept universals, then bring on the universals. However, it seems to me that moderate nominalism is a good position. What makes something a cat, or red, are certain particular realities about that cat. It's hard to see how a universal is needed to make Rusty red or feline.[16]

It also seems to me that if Rusty has what it takes to be a cat, and if Mickey does too, then they "are both cats." We don't need any universal to come along and somehow join them into one species. Each has what it takes to be a cat, so they just automatically are both cats. Admittedly, we do say "they share in Felinity," but that can be reinterpreted as a systematically misleading expression.

Bringing this discussion to a tentative conclusion, then, let me say that I find the moderate nominalist position the best of these four. It accepts real conspecificity without asking us to take on the special burden of believing in universals. I call this a "tentative" conclusion, however, because I will add a wrinkle in §8.8 and §8.12.

5.2 Universals and a Linguistic Argument

So far, in talking about the problem of universals, we have been focusing exclusively on the main reason why philosophers have discussed them: the One Over Many Problem. Now I want to shift our focus to considering another reason philosophers have had for believing in universals. Because we already know what universals are, we can move much more quickly.

Let's start with an obvious fact: we say things like "Red is a color." And then let's add another obvious fact: when we say that, we say something that's true. But, you might ask, how can it be true to say "Red is a color" if there is no such thing as Red? This seems to lead to the conclusion that Red exists. And obviously the sentence "Red is a color" isn't about this or that instance of red, but instead about Red-in-general, the universal Redness. We have, then, the following argument: The sentence "Red is a color" is true; that sentence can be true only if

---

16. Just to be clear, although I am saying that Rusty is feline because of particular realities about him, I do not mean to imply that he therefore has a felinity-trope. As I argued in §3.3.3, it is better to understand essential and accidental features differently from each other. Accidents are tropes, but essences are not.

Red exists; and by "Red exists" we mean that Redness the universal exists; therefore, the universal Redness exists.

Behind this argument is the following sort of thought: Sentences are true only if key parts of those sentences represent, or refer to, items in the world. If the sentences are going to be true, those aspects of the world must really be there to be referred to.

Someone who is on the nominalist side (whether extreme or moderate doesn't matter for this purpose) needs to have a response to this sort of argument. And the most interesting kind of response says that the argument makes a mistake about the relationship between language and reality.

As we have seen in previous chapters, the relationship between language and reality is complicated. In particular, in §1.3 we saw that not every predicate stands for a property: "Taylor Swift is popular" may appear to indicate a property belonging to Taylor Swift, but it does not. Here we can consider a different way in which language can be misleading.

Consider the following two sentences:

The tallest person in the class is 5′7″.
The average person in the class is 5′7″.

The first of these sentences cannot be true unless there actually is someone in the class who is 5′7″. But the second sentence is different. For the average person in the class to be 5′7″, it is not necessary for there to be someone in the class who is 5′7″. If half the people are 5′9″, and the other half are 5′5″, then the average is 5′7″, even though no one is 5′7″.

The two sentences look similar. The only difference in wording is that one of them has "average" where the other has "tallest." Since the sentences contain different words, it's not surprising that they mean different things, but perhaps it's surprising that their meanings are so very different. But they are. The two sentences work in very different ways. To say that the tallest student is 5′7″ is to say that some person in the class is tallest, and that that person is 5′7″. But to say that the average student is 5′7″ is not to say that some person in the class is average, and that that person—the average one—is 5′7″. Even if someone in the class is 5′7″, and indeed average in every other way, still no one in the class is The Average Student. There simply is no such thing as The Average Student. There are just students, whose heights can be averaged. To say that the average student is 5′7″ is not to talk about any student at all, but instead to say that if you take the heights of all the students, and add them together, and divide the result by the number of students, you will get 5′7″. (Of course, it's precisely because that's such a complicated thing to say that normal people just say, "the average student . . . ")

What does this show? It shows that the relationship between language and reality is complicated, and that sentences that look very similar on the surface can function very differently from one another. More particularly, it shows that a piece of language that seems to refer to some particular object in the world ("the average student") might not actually work that way at all. When we say, "the tallest student," there is some particular student we mean to talk about, but not when we say, "the average student."

With that in mind, let's return to "Red is a color." At first glance, it might seem obvious that this sentence works like "Rusty is a cat." The sentence "Rusty is a cat" can't be true unless Rusty exists, so then why not say the same thing about "Red is a color"? Well, we know that "Rusty" is a name, but is "Red" a name?[17] Sometimes it is, of course—there used to be an entertainer named Red Skelton—but that's not the question I'm asking. The question I'm asking is whether the word "Red" is a name in the particular sentence we are dealing with—namely, "Red is a color." If it is, then it would seem right to say that "Red is a color" can't be true unless Red exists. But maybe "Red" isn't a name. Maybe the sentence doesn't work that way at all. Maybe "Red is a color" is just a less-complicated way of saying something like "Red things are colored." If that's what it really means, then there's no pressure to believe in the universal Redness, only pressure to believe in red things, which any nominalist would be happy to do.

How do we know which is right? How do we know whether "Red is a color" is talking about the universal Redness, and saying that it's a color, or instead talking about red things, and saying that they are colored? I think that linguistic analysis cannot answer this question. In cases in which we already know that two sentences are in fact functioning differently—like the sentence about the average student and the sentence about the tallest student—linguistic analysis can shed a lot of light

---

17. For my medieval friends: I'm asking whether it's a name in the ordinary, 21st-century sense of that term, not whether it's a *nomen* in the medieval sense of that term.

on what is happening, and why the sentences might appear to be similar even though they are not. But that works only because we already know that there's a difference between "tallest" and "average." In the case of "Red is a color," if we don't already know whether Redness is a universal or not, analyzing the sentence isn't going to tell us. Philosophers who believe in universals will say that the word "Red" is the name of the universal Redness; philosophers who do not believe in universals will say that "Red is a color" is a shorthand way of saying something like "red things are colored." Linguistic analysis, in my view, is very helpful for helping us understand what's going on once we have taken a metaphysical position, but it can't tell us which metaphysical position to take. Everyday language wasn't invented for metaphysics, it was invented for everyday purposes like describing the weather, or ordering beer, or asking someone to marry you. It's not reasonable to think that metaphysical truths can be easily read off of everyday sentences.[18]

However, it's only fair to note that not all philosophers see it my way. Some think that linguistic arguments can establish the existence of universals. And so it is important for me to make the following remark. Someone could think that the one over many argument was a good argument while thinking the linguistic argument was a bad argument. Or someone could think that the One over Many argument was a bad argument while thinking the linguistic argument was a good argument.[19] If you want to be a nominalist, you have to think that *all* the arguments for universals fail. But if you want to be a realist, you need *only one* such argument to succeed. Realists and nominalists can agree that a certain argument for universals is a failure while ultimately disagreeing about the existence of universals. That is what would happen if there was some other argument for universals that they didn't agree about.

5.3 A Hybrid Position Worth Considering

A nominalist, in either sense, holds that there are no universals, and so a nominalist holds that everything that exists is a particular, an individ-

---

18. For more on the relation between linguistic analysis and metaphysical analysis, see Willard Van Orman Quine, "On What There Is," *Review of Metaphysics* 2, no. 5 (1948): 21–38; William P. Alston, "Ontological Commitments," *Philosophical Studies* 9, no. 1 (1958): 8–17; van Inwagen, *Material Beings*, 98–114.

19. For example, Devitt, "'Ostrich Nominalism' or 'Mirage Realism'?"

ual. A realist, in either sense, holds that universals exist. Could a realist hold that there are no individuals, but that only universals exist? A moderate, immanent, Aristotelian realist could not: the whole point of being this sort of realist is believing that universals exist in particulars. But at least in theory, it seems that an extreme, transcendent, Platonist realist could hold that only universals exist. This would, however, be a very strange theory; the existence of individuals seems to be one of the most basic facts of experience. So, leaving aside that extreme version of extreme realism, it seems best to say that nominalists believe only in individuals while realists believe in both universals and individuals.

In a sense, then, realists typically hold a hybrid position: they believe in both individuals and universals with substances being the individuals and features being the universals. It turns out, however, that there is a different kind of hybrid position that one can take. One can say that while substances are indeed individuals, features can be either universals or individuals: there are not only universal features, like Felinity, but also individual features, like Rusty's felinity. This position, which came up very briefly in §3.3.2, believes there are universal features and also tropes corresponding to them.

Why would anyone adopt such a view? Well, suppose first that you already believe in universals. Next, suppose the following scenario occurs to you: there are two yellow sheets of paper, and one of them gets burnt up in the fire. When that happens, you say to yourself, yellowness is lost in the case of the one sheet, but not in the case of the other; therefore, there must be two different individual yellownesses, one of which went out of existence, and the other of which did not. But since, as noted, you already believe in universals, you infer that reality contains not only the universal Yellowness, which is obviously immune to being destroyed by fire, but also individual instances of yellow, yellowness tropes, which can indeed be destroyed by fire. These yellowness tropes are instances of the universal Yellowness.

5.4 The Problem(s) of Individuation

For a nominalist, there seems to be no point in asking what makes individuals be individuals: Being individual is the only option on the table. But realists, even moderate realists, can ask what makes individual things individual. They can ask, in other words, what "individuates" them.

Let me note right away that sometimes, a different question receives the label "individuation." If there are two different individuals that both share in the same universal, what makes this one *this* one, and the other one *that* one? "Differentiation" might be a better label for this question, but "individuation" has become pretty standard. Philosophers have proposed many answers. Some say that two instances of a universal are different from one another because they differ in some of their other universals; for instance, two instances of Felinity are different because one of them is also an instance of Grayness, while the other is also an instance of Redness. But others do not think this will work, because they think that it should be possible, at least in theory, for two different individuals to instantiate *all* the same universals.[20] So other theories have been proposed. For instance, some philosophers think that which individual you are is determined not by which universals you instantiate, but by which portion of matter takes on those universals; others think it is determined by a special metaphysical principle called a *haecceity*, a "thisness." I am not going to discuss this sense of "individuation" further here.[21]

But what about the meaning of "individuation" that I first mentioned? Using "individuation" in that sense, the question is not why this instance of a given universal is different from that instance of it, but instead why this thing is an individual and not a universal. We already know that individuals are non-instantiable instances, while universals are instantiables, so in a way, you could just give that as your answer: what makes an individual an individual is its being a non-instantiable instance, and what makes a universal a universal is its instantiability. But it would be understandable if someone asked *why* some things are instantiable while others are non-instantiable instances.

One possible answer would be that anything that exists in three-dimensional space is a non-instantiable instance, while anything that exists outside of three-dimensional space is instantiable. But that does not strike me as a promising answer. I don't see any reason for thinking

---

20. We discussed this in §3.3.2.
21. In case you are wondering, it seems to be Aquinas's view that what differentiates two individuals of the same kind is matter. For this reason, Aquinas holds that angelic natures have only one instance: there cannot be another angel of the same species as Michael, because angels are immaterial and thus do not have the matter that would allow there to be more than one per species. Other angels, like Gabriel, differ from Michael in kind, not just numerically.

it is true. If there are angels—meaning not blond guys with harps, sitting on clouds, but instead immaterial intellects—then they exist outside of three-dimensional space, and yet, surely, they are individuals instead of universals.

I am not going to say more about this question. But I will note in passing that one advantage of being a nominalist is that you don't have to answer it.[22]

5.5 Could Aquinas be a Nominalist?

Since this book is an introduction to Thomistic metaphysics, I feel I need to mention that scholars have disagreed a lot about Aquinas's views on realism and nominalism. Everyone would agree that Aquinas is neither a Dr. Seuss nominalist nor a Platonic realist. But is he a moderate nominalist or a moderate realist?

Some philosophers think that rejecting universals automatically means rejecting real conspecificity. For them, moderate nominalism is a fantasy position: it's wanting to have the benefits of universals (real conspecificity) without paying for them (by accepting universals). Anyone who thinks like this, and who also thinks that Aquinas is a really good philosopher, is not likely to classify Aquinas as a moderate nominalist, because that would be to classify him as someone who indulges in metaphysical fantasies! But anyone who thinks that moderate nominalism is at least reasonable will be open to the thought that Aquinas is a "nominalist" in this sense of the word.

I think that's probably the best interpretation of Aquinas. He discusses the issue in chapter two of his little book *On Being and Essence*. However, it's important to note that he doesn't discuss it using the language of universals. Instead, he uses the language of *natures*. As I interpret him, his view is that every existing thing is an individual. Rusty is an individual cat, and cat-nature in him exists as individual. Parallel points hold about his accidents: his color or agility are individual accidents, and the natures of agility and redness in them exist as individual.

Aquinas says, furthermore, that natures like cat-nature or redness also exist in minds: when you and I think of cat-nature, cat-nature has

---

22. For a good discussion of various questions concerning individuation, see the prolegomena to Gracia, *Individuality*.

a special mental or conceptual mode of existence. This mode of existence is also individual. You have your concept of cat, and I have mine, in the sense that these concepts are numerically distinct from each other. (Of course, they are also specifically the same, in the sense that they agree or match in content.)

However, cat-concepts are different from cats in an important way, and explaining this leads Aquinas to deploy the language of universality. For Aquinas, to say that something is "universal" is to say that it is one thing that is common to many. Mickey is one thing, and so is his cat-nature, but neither of them is common to many. Your cat-concept, however, is one thing that is common to many. It is one thing—your concept, existing in your mind—that applies equally to Rusty and to Mickey and to all cats. This concept, then, is "universal" in Aquinas's sense.

Is Aquinas saying that universals exist in the mind? Not in a way that would make him a Dr. Seuss nominalist! Do not be misled. If Aquinas wanted to affirm Dr. Seuss nominalism—which he certainly doesn't—he would say that *natures* exist only in the mind. When he says that universals exist in the mind, he is merely saying that it is not items like Rusty, or Rusty's felinity or redness, that exist individually while also belonging indifferently to many, but concepts instead.

Let me acknowledge that Aquinas also talks about the nature "absolutely considered," that's to say, the nature considered neither as it exists in individuals like Rusty nor in individual concepts like your idea of cat-nature. It is tempting to think that here Aquinas is, after all, affirming the existence of natures ("universals," in contemporary lingo) in a realist way. However, I think it would be mistaken to understand Aquinas in this manner. Aquinas is talking about natures absolutely *considered*. He means that we can *think* of natures apart from their existence in things or in minds. But in his view, they do not have existence like that; they have existence only in individual things or individual minds.[23]

If I am right, then, Aquinas is (using contemporary lingo) a kind of moderate nominalist. However, I hasten to add that many Thomists would strongly reject this interpretation of Aquinas. Some of them might reject it because they thought I was accusing Aquinas of being a Dr. Seuss nominalist. That would be an inaccurate interpretation of my interpretation. But some of them would understand my interpretation

23. Again, all this is based mostly on Aquinas, *On Being and Essence*, c. 2.

correctly and still reject it. They would say that Aquinas is some sort of moderate realist.[24]

One thing for sure: it's just not entirely clear what, in detail, Aquinas's view was on the status of natures. I think the explanation for this is that it wasn't enough of a burning issue in his day for him to spend pages and pages talking about it. He spent his time on other things, and addressed this question, which *we* find so very interesting, only from time to time. In the end, I think, we must live with the idea that we can't be entirely sure what his view was. But ultimately, that's not what matters. What matters is what the right view is, and the only way we can find that out is to think for ourselves.

5.6 A Tentative Conclusion

In this chapter, I have described various views on individuals and universals, and I have come down in favor of so-called moderate nominalism. Some readers may feel that while there's a lot to be said in favor of this position, universals are still, after all, somehow *there*.[25] However that may be, it is time to move on to a new topic, namely, how things might have been.

▷ To get started on reading Aquinas himself on the ideas developed in this chapter, begin with *On Being and Essence*, especially chapter two.

---

24. For a review of some of the various interpretations of Aquinas to be found in the literature, see Brower, "Aquinas on the Problem of Universals."

25. I will come back to this in §8.8 and §8.12.

CHAPTER 6

The Way Things Might Have Been

6.1 Introduction to the Idea of Possible Worlds

IN EARLIER CHAPTERS OF THIS BOOK, we have talked about what's possible, about ways things might possibly be. People do this all the time. It's a beautiful spring day, and we're inside mopping floors. Suddenly one of us says sadly, "You know, we could be out fishing!" We aren't fishing, but we might be: that we're mopping floors is part of the way things are, but so too is it part of the way things are that we could be fishing. Or suppose you say to an annoying co-worker, "You know, there's a way to have meetings where you don't do ninety percent of the talking." Possibilities are part of the landscape of being. "Do you really mean that if I climb to the top of Everest, I might die?" "Yes, extreme mountaineering brings with it the chance of death; that's just the way it is."

With this much in hand, it's time to introduce a bit of technical terminology. When philosophers talk about ways things might be, or might have been, they often call them "possible states of affairs." The expression "state of affairs" is not really an everyday expression for most of us, but it's not entirely foreign, either. If a dog does something unpleasant to your new shoes, there are a lot of things to say, but if you want to keep it classy, you can say, "Oh my, this is a most unpleasant state of affairs." Often, we formulate possible states of affairs using the possessive case and an "-ing" word, like this: *your reading this book, our mopping the floor, Mickey's napping*. These are ways things might be. They are possible states of affairs. Perhaps you could also call them "possible situations."

It's important to note that while some possible states of affairs are incompatible with others, that's not always the case. The possible state of affairs *Mickey's napping* is incompatible with the state of affairs *Mickey's chasing a mouse*, but it's not incompatible with the state of affairs *our mopping the floor*. Sometimes—most of the time, in fact—two possible states of affairs are compatible with one another: they could both be actual at the same time. It really is possible for us to mop the floor while Mickey is napping; it really is possible for *our mopping the floor* to be actualized while *Mickey's napping* is actualized. What that means is that there's a more complex way for things to be: *our mopping the floor AND Mickey's napping* is a possible state of affairs.

We can go on thinking of larger and larger possible states of affairs, simply by adding more possible states of affairs (as long as they aren't incompatible with the ones we've thought of so far). For example, here is a possible state of affairs: *our mopping the floor* AND *Mickey's napping* AND *the weather's being fine* AND *three's being greater than two*.

Is there any limit to this additive process? There is. It stops when you have added everything that might possibly be added. Here's a way to think of it. First, you list every possible state of affairs (of course no one could actually do this; but pretend). Then, to each one, you say "yes" or "no": we *are* mopping the floor, Mickey is *not* napping, and so on. When you have said "yes" or "no" to all of them, you have gone as far as you can go. Now, if you said "yes" and "no" in a consistent way, meaning that you didn't say "yes" to any pairs of incompatible possible states of affairs, then adding up all the ones you said "yes" to gives you what's called a "maximal" possible state of affairs. It's maximal in the sense that it's literally impossible to add to it.

Philosophers have a name for maximal possible states of affairs. They call them "possible worlds." A possible world is a way things might be, but it's special because it's a way *everything* might be. It's a fully specified way for reality to be, in every possible detail.

It's worth thinking about possible worlds for a little while. The first thing to note is that any difference is enough to give us a different possible world. There's a possible world in which Mickey is napping, you are reading this book, I am fishing, etc., etc., and, finally, the temperature in Washington, DC is 95°F. The possible world in which Mickey is napping, you are reading this book, I am fishing, etc., etc., and, finally, the temperature in Washington, DC is 96°F is a different possible world. Even if that's the only difference, it's enough of a difference to make those two possible worlds distinct.

A second point is this. When you realize that even little differences are enough to differentiate possible worlds, you realize just how many possible worlds there are. Without yet getting into the question of whether there can be infinitely many of them, it's clear that there is a truly amazing number of them. Think of all the different temperatures it can be in Washington, DC. Think of all the different things Mickey can be doing. And think of the extraordinarily large number of possible states of affairs hidden in the "etc., etc." part of those sentences you just read. If it's not mind-blowing yet, you need to keep pondering.

Third, I want to bring out something that's implicit in what's been said so far. Possible worlds "include" smaller possible states of affairs: many possible worlds include, for instance, the possible state of affairs *Mickey's napping*. Putting it the other way, *Mickey's napping* "belongs to" many possible worlds, or "is part of" many possible worlds, or (you might say) "happens in" many possible worlds. We can even say: "there are possible worlds in which Mickey is napping."

Fourth, it's worth keeping in mind that when we talk about possible worlds, we never talk about them in every detail. If one says to one's annoying co-worker, "There's a possible world in which you don't monopolize the meeting," one doesn't add "and in which the sun is shining, the grass is green, etc." One reason why not is that it's simply impossible to complete the description. But another reason, a reason that's more important, is that saying more would bring in too many irrelevancies. For your purposes, it actually doesn't matter whether the sun is shining or not—the point is simply that it's possible for the annoying coworker not to be so annoying. So, strictly speaking, if you say to your coworker, "There's a possible world in which you don't monopolize the meeting," you don't mean that there is only one such possible world. There are many of them, and right now you'd be quite happy to see any of them actualized, rather than going through one more torture session with this person; for that reason, you mention only the important part—namely, *this person's talking less*.

We have seen the notion of possible worlds, and we have seen some interesting facts about them. At a certain point, however, you might be inclined to say that we need to break out of this dreamland and talk about the way things actually are. Let us begin that process now. As you will see, it gets complicated fast. There will be five key concepts to keep track of, concepts that philosophers call "modal" because they concern different modes of truth or even modes of being.

Let's begin with something obvious. There's a way things are, and there's a way things aren't. You are reading right now, and (probably) you aren't skydiving right now. That's the way it is.

Now sometimes, when things are a certain way, it's not merely that they are a certain way, but also that they *must* be that way, in the sense that there's no alternative to their being that way. The universe could not have unfolded so that they weren't that way. Here are some examples:

2 + 2 = 4.
If something is a dog, then it's a mammal.
If you have a fence, then either it's green or it's not green.

There's just no way for things not to be like this. It's literally impossible for the world to be so arranged that it's not like this—even God couldn't do it![1] These are examples of (1) how things are "necessarily." That's the first key modal concept, necessity.

By contrast, sometimes things are a certain way, but they don't have to be that way. They are that way, but (2) they are that way "contingently." They are that way, but they could have been otherwise, if the universe had unfolded differently. Here are some examples:

You are reading right now.
The United States is not a monarchy.
The Earth contains mammals.

These are the way things are, but things might have gone differently: you might have gone skydiving; a coup might have led the United States to be a monarchy (or would it have destroyed the United States and replaced it with a different country?—see §2.3); and so on.[2]

---

1. But wait, can't God do everything? Yes, he can do everything in the sense that he can do everything that's possible to do. But he can't do things that involve contradictions, because those are not possible to do. There's no such thing as 2 + 2 equaling five, so there's no such thing as making 2 + 2 be five. Here's an analogy: no football player, no matter how good he is, can hit a home run in a football game; in football, there's no such thing as a home run. (For a number of reasons, this is only an analogy. Divine omnipotence is a complicated topic.)

2. Think back to the distinction between possibilities for change and alternative possibilities discussed in §3.3.2. It's alternative possibilities we're discussing now. The question isn't "can you get there from here?" but rather "could we have ended up there instead of here?"

To avoid confusion, let me insert here a brief terminological remark. Sometimes we say that something is "contingent on" something else. For example, suppose someone says, "Your admission to college in the fall is contingent on the successful completion of your high school studies." Here, "is contingent on" means pretty much the same thing as "depends on." But to say that things "are a certain way contingently" is not, all by itself, to say anything about what depends on what. To say that it's only contingently the case that you are reading means nothing more than that you are reading but needn't have been.[3]

Back to the main line of discussion. As noted already, of the ways things are, some can't be otherwise, and hence are necessarily the way they are, while others could be otherwise, and hence are only contingently the way they are. There's a distinction, in short, between necessity and contingency. But what about the ways that things are not?

Some of the ways that things are *not* are ways they simply *cannot* be: no matter what, things cannot be like that. The universe could never unfold *that* way. These are (3) "impossible." Here are some examples:

2 + 2 = 5
Some dogs are reptiles.
I have a fence that is entirely green and entirely white.

Even God can't make things turn out like this.

Not every way things aren't is like this, however. There are ways that things aren't but that are, nonetheless, ways that things could be. If the universe had unfolded differently, things would be that way. These are (4) the "merely possible" ways for things to be. Here are some examples:

My hair is blue.
You are skydiving.
The United States is a monarchy.

These are "possible" ways for things to be, but they are "merely" possible because, in actual fact, things aren't that way.

---

3. To be sure, there might well be a connection here. It's reasonable to suspect, for example, that if something holds contingently, then its doing so is contingent on something else. In fact, as we'll see in §8.2, that way of thinking might lead us toward an argument for God's existence.

Now note the following. If you take (4) the merely possible ways for things to be, and (2) the ways things contingently are, and (1) the way things necessarily are, and put them all in one box, then you get (5) the "possible" ways for things to be, or, to put it differently, the ways things could be. (Or, to say it all again, using the language of "situations": if you take the merely possible situations, and the contingently actual situations, and the necessarily actual situations, and put them together, you get the full range of possible situations.) This is, of course, what we started the chapter with—ways things could be. Some of them are merely possible ways for things to be, while others are ways things actually are, and some are ways things have to be.

One way to set out the distinctions just made is shown in Figure 6-1.

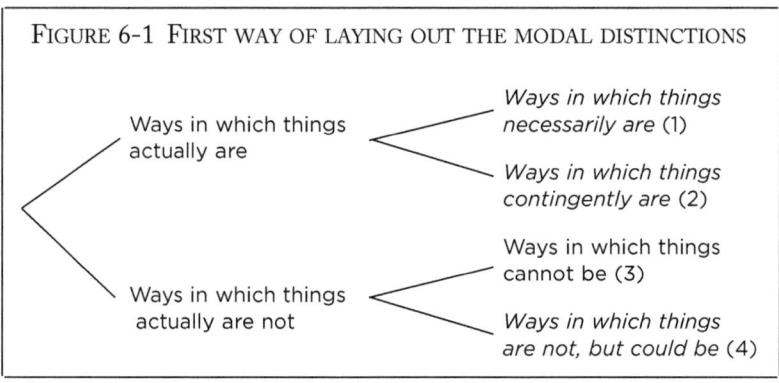

Of the four items along the right-hand side of Figure 6-1, the ones in italics together make up (5), possibility.

The same points can be presented differently, as in Table 6-1.

TABLE 6-1 SECOND WAY OF LAYING OUT THE MODAL DISTINCTIONS

	...are	...are not.
Ways in which things necessarily...	1	3
Ways in which things contingently...	2	4

The shaded areas in Table 6-1, which correspond to the italicized items in Figure 6-1, together give us (5). What the table view reveals is that there are actually two crisscrossing distinctions at work.

The key concepts can be arranged in another way. Consider Figure 6-2, where we start not with the distinction between ways things are and ways they aren't, but with the distinction between ways things could be (5) and ways they couldn't be (3)—the distinction between possible situations and impossible situations.

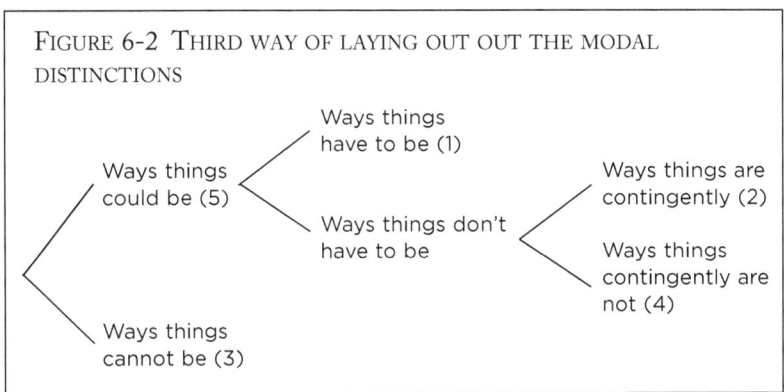

FIGURE 6-2 THIRD WAY OF LAYING OUT OUT THE MODAL DISTINCTIONS

There are ways things could be, and there are ways they can't be. Of the ways things could be, some are ways that things must be, and some are not; of the ones that are not, some are ways that things are, while others are ways they aren't.

For still another way to think of it, consider Table 6-2.

TABLE 6-2 FOURTH WAY OF LAYING OUT THE MODAL DISTINCTIONS

	What's actual	What's not actual
What's possible (ways things could be)	1, 2	4
What's not possible	x	3

Again, the shaded areas together give us (5).

Now you have a few ways of relating the five key concepts. Perhaps you can think of still other ways. If you spend time going back and forth between them, seeing how they work together, you will learn a lot.

It's good to have a five-way distinction, and it's good to have a few different ways of organizing that five-way distinction, but you might be forgiven for wishing there was a more unified way of presenting this material. As it happens, there is. It involves using the notion of possible worlds, with a special eye on how possible states of affairs belong to possible worlds.

Let's just plunge right in.

(a) a state of affairs is necessary **iff** that state of affairs belongs to every possible world.[4]
(b) a state of affairs is impossible **iff** that state of affairs belongs to no possible world.
(c) a state of affairs is possible **iff** that state of affairs belongs to at least one possible world.
(d) a state of affairs is actual **iff** that state of affairs belongs to *this* possible world—the actual one.
(e) a state of affairs is contingent **iff** that state of affairs belongs to *this* world but not to all.

If a state of affairs belongs to every possible world, then that state of affairs will be actual *no matter how reality turns out*, in every possible situation, which is to say that it is necessary; and vice versa. If a state of affairs belongs to no possible world, then that state of affairs will not be actual, no matter how reality turns out, which is to say that it is impossible; and vice versa. And so on. It will most definitely repay the effort to work through each of these, working both in the left-to-right direction and in the right-to-left direction.

Now let's come at it from a different perspective. Many philosophers hold that every state of affairs corresponds to a proposition. For example, to the state of affairs *Mickey's napping* there corresponds the proposition *Mickey is napping*. If the state of affairs is actual, then the proposition will be true, and vice versa. If the state of affairs is not actual, the proposition will be false, and vice versa. Based upon this correspondence, we can go through the list again, using p to stand for a proposition:

(a*) p is necessarily true **iff** p is true in all possible worlds.
(b*) p is impossible **iff** p is true in no possible world.
(c*) p is possibly true **iff** p is true in at least one possible world.

---

4. Iff = "if and only if." "A iff B" means the same as "if A then B <u>and</u> if B then A." If a state of affairs is necessary, then it belongs to every possible world, and vice versa.

(d*) p is true iff p is true in *this* possible world—the actual one.
(e*) p is contingently true iff p is true in *this* world but not in all.

Again, it will most definitely repay the effort to think through these carefully. You should both memorize them and make sure you understand what they mean.

Understanding what they mean includes understanding their interrelationships. Notice, for example, the relationship between (d) and (c), or (d*) and (c*). (c) and (c*) talk about what belongs to at least one possible world, but they don't say anything, one way or the other, about what belongs to *this* possible world, which is what (d) and (d*) require for a state of affairs to be actual, or a proposition to be true. That's why something can be possible without being actual: actuality requires that the state of affairs belong to this world, the actual world, not just some world; truth requires that the proposition be true in this world, the actual world, not just some world. Or note the connection between (e) and (e*), on the one hand, and (a) and (a*), on the other. If a state of affairs belongs to this world, but not to all, then it will be actual but not necessary; likewise, if a proposition is true in this world but not in all, then it will be true but not necessarily true. Necessity, or necessary truth, requires every world, not just this one. Or note the connection between (c) and (b), and (c*) and (b*). (c) says that a state of affairs is possible if it belongs to at least one world, while (b) says a state of affairs is impossible if it belongs to *no* world; (c*) says that p is possible if it's true in at least one world, while (b*) says that p is impossible if it's true in *no* world.[5]

Now let me add a wrinkle. Suppose you feel tempted to say that *Socrates's being rational* is necessary, or that "Socrates is rational" is a necessary truth. Be careful. Do you really mean that it's true, in every possible world, that Socrates exists and is rational? Probably you don't, because probably you don't think that Socrates exists in every possible world. He's important, but he's not *that* important; he might never have existed at all. It's better to say that Socrates is rational not "in every world" but instead "in every world in which he exists."

---

5. By the way: We don't say that p is possible if it *can* be true in some world, nor do we say that p is necessary if it *must* be true in all worlds. On the right-hand side of these formulas, it's always just plain old "is."

We have spoken at some length of possible worlds and of how they can be used to think through important distinctions. But what actually *are* possible worlds? In the third paragraph of this chapter, I said, "Possibilities are part of the landscape of being." But what does that really come to? If I say, "There's a book on that table," you feel confident that I mean that there is some thing on the table—namely, a book. But if I say, "There's a difference between Rusty and Mickey," you might wonder whether I really mean that, in addition to Rusty and Mickey, there is some third item, a difference. You might suspect that I don't, and that "there's a difference . . ." is a misleading expression. Well, how should we think about our talk of there being possible worlds? If we say that there are maximal states of affairs, possible worlds, are we really attributing existence to certain entities? If so, what are they like? If not, what do we mean instead? The rest of this chapter is devoted to such questions.

6.2 What Are Possible Worlds?

As we have just seen, talking about possible worlds gives us a way to organize our thoughts about what's possible, what's necessary, and so on. But are possible worlds "really there"?

One way to proceed is to say that no, they aren't really there, but talking about them gives us a powerful metaphor that makes it easier for some people to understand modal concepts like necessity and possibility. If someone was unsure what was meant by saying that a certain proposition was necessarily true, perhaps things would click for that person if I said, "Well, it's true *in every possible world*." Responding like that might provide the insight that this proposition is true *no matter what*. Or if someone was unclear on the idea that a proposition was only contingently true, perhaps things would click if I responded, "Well, it's true *in this world*, but there are *some other possible worlds* in which it's not true." Responding in that way might provide the insight that while this proposition is true, it doesn't have to be true: it's *true*, but it's not *true no matter what*. So, on one level, talk of possible worlds can simply be used as an insight-triggering metaphor that might work for some people. And there's nothing wrong with that!

Going further, however, many philosophers treat talk of possible worlds not just as a useful metaphor, but as a literal way of describing reality. For them, possible worlds really are really there. For philosophers who take this route, there really are possible worlds, literally; and things are true in them, literally. Since the 1960s or so, a number of ways of working this out have been developed. I will now give brief explanations of the two most important ones.

The first is associated most of all with the philosopher Alvin Plantinga (b. 1932).[6] Plantinga believes that possible worlds are real entities. But they are not physical individuals like rocks or dogs. They are somewhat like Platonic universals; they are not universals, not really, but they are akin to them inasmuch as they exist necessarily and transcendently, outside of time and space.[7] There are as many of them as there are possible ways for everything to be. And that means that there are infinitely many of them.[8]

And now a tricky point. In the previous section, I spoke rather casually, a few times, about ways that things can't be. If there are possible states of affairs, are there also impossible states of affairs? If there are possible worlds, are there also impossible worlds? It's hard to avoid *talking* like this—"I'm sorry, but the scenario you are discussing right now is simply impossible"—but most modal metaphysicians do not endorse the existence of impossible worlds.[9] On the most common way of thinking, if we say that *Mickey's being a lizard* is an impossible situation, that's just a potentially misleading way of saying that there isn't any possible

---

6. See especially Alvin Plantinga, *The Nature of Necessity* (Oxford: Clarendon Press, 1974).

7. If they exist necessarily, does this mean that each world exists in every world? Yes. For Plantinga, each possible world contains the other possible worlds, at least in the sense that no matter which world is actualized, all the others are still possible. For Plantinga, what's possible doesn't depend on what has been actualized. As we will see in section three of this chapter, there's a very important issue lurking here.

8. That might be a problem. Aristotle says that however many things there are, the number must be finite. If Aristotle is right about this, then there can't be infinitely many possible worlds.

Modern mathematicians have worked out interesting theories of infinities; does this prove that Aristotle was wrong? It depends on the relationship between metaphysics and mathematics, and that's a question that cannot be answered without going deep into the philosophy of mathematics.

I'm not going to discuss these issues further, but now you know about them.

9. I said "most modal metaphysicians," but most is not all. See Francesco Berto and Mark Jago, "Impossible Worlds," *The Stanford Encyclopedia of Philosophy* (Summer 2023 Edition), Edward N. Zalta & Uri Nodelman (eds.), https://plato.stanford.edu/archives/sum2023/entries/impossible-worlds/.

situation that includes Mickey's being a lizard. It's not, in other words, to say that there *is* a situation that includes his being a lizard—a situation that is impossible. (This is a bit like the idea that to say "Santa Claus is non-existent" is to say not that Santa is there, although unfortunately non-existent, but instead that he is not there at all.)

All these possible worlds actually exist, for Plantinga, but only one is actualized or realized.[10] We live in the actualization of that possible world. The other worlds, although they do actually exist, as possible worlds, are not actual*ized*; they are analogous to universals that have not been instantiated. That is why they are ways reality might have been, but not ways reality is.

Importantly, if Socrates belongs to this world (the world that's actualized, the world that obtains) and to some other world, then it is Socrates himself that belongs to both of them. He is a "transworld individual." The world that got actualized contains Socrates, but if a different world had been actualized, and if it had been one of the other worlds that also contain Socrates, then in that case too, Socrates himself, the same man, would have actually existed.

There are many, many more details of Plantinga's view that have been left out here, but what's been said is enough for our purposes. For Plantinga, possible worlds are maximal possible states of affairs, truly existing in an abstract, non-spatiotemporal way. You and I exist in many of these possible worlds, and luckily for us, one of those worlds actually obtains.

Now let's look at a contrasting view, the one put forth by David Lewis (d. 2001).[11] Lewis doesn't ask us to believe in any beings that are different in nature from the ordinary beings we already believe in. For this reason, you might suspect that his view is going to be less daring, less extravagant (perhaps not daring and extravagant enough). But in actual fact, many people consider Lewis's views to be much wilder than Plantinga's.

For Lewis, the way to know what a world is is to look around you: there's a rock, there's a person, there's a cat, and all that stuff, together, makes up a world. Worlds are not understood to be any special kind of

---

10. Plantinga sometimes says that the world that gets actualized is the world that "obtains." This is an adaptation of an expression like "Hey, you, stand up! The custom of rising when the president of the United States enters the room still obtains!"

11. See especially Lewis, *On the Plurality of Worlds*.

transcendent entities. A world is just what plain ordinary people think of. But there is one special point that needs to be added: there are infinitely many of them—that is, infinitely many concrete, physical universes. There's this world, and then there's a world that's slightly different, and then there's a world that's slightly different in a slightly different way, and so on, for every possible difference. But they are all just as down-to-earth and non-Platonic and individual and concrete as this one is. You can't get to them, so don't bother trying. They are completely inaccessible. But they all exist, in just the way this one does.

Now a theory involving possible worlds doesn't accomplish anything unless there is a difference between this world, the actual one, and the others, which are merely possible. Lewis understands the difference as follows: The reason that only this one is actual is that "actual world" means "the world inhabited by the person using the world 'actual.'" On his account, the word "actual" is like the word "home": I'm at home when I'm here, and you're at home when you are there, and there's no contradiction, because the meaning of the word "home" depends on who is using it.[12] In a parallel fashion, when we say that the chair we are sitting in actually exists, we are right, and when the people in other worlds say that the chairs they are sitting in actually exist, they are right, too. (You might think that this sort of defeats the whole point of the language of actuality. Actuality, you might think, is supposed to indicate a difference of status, not merely a difference in who is talking. I'm with you one hundred percent on that. But for now, I'm presenting Lewis's view.)

I just mentioned something about the other people sitting on other chairs in other worlds. You might wonder whether those "other" people could be you and me, the same people as us but in different worlds. For Lewis, unlike for Plantinga, that can't happen. Individuals as Lewis understands them are sometimes called "world-bound": they exist in only one world. And if you think about what Lewis means by possible worlds, you can see that that's the right thing for him to say. If a possible world is a physical, concrete thing, or a collection of physical, concrete things, then it would indeed be strange if I existed in more than one of them, especially because each is inaccessible from the others.

---

12. So "actual" for Lewis is an "indexical" expression, like "home" or "here" or "now" or "I" or "you"—an expression whose referent (the thing it refers to) depends on the occasion of its use. The philosophy of indexicals is very fun and interesting.

But this raises an interesting question. How, using possible worlds language, can we say that Socrates, while not currently being sunburned, could be sunburned? The Plantinga answer would be this: "In the actual world, he is not sunburned, but in some other possible world, he is." On Lewis's understanding, however, Socrates does not exist in any other possible world, and that means that it can't be literally true that Socrates is sunburned in any other possible world. Similar problems arise for other uses of modal concepts. For example, if we say that Socrates is necessarily human, that means that he is human in every world in which he exists. If, as Lewis would have it, Socrates exists in only one world, then obviously he is human in "every" world in which he exists—namely, in this one; but that's not really what we are trying to say.

Lewis has an answer.[13] His approach is called "counterpart theory." In this world, we have Socrates, and he's not sunburned. In some other world, there's some other guy who is sunburned, and although he is not Socrates, he is Socrates's "counterpart."[14] So "Socrates is not sunburned, but he's possibly sunburned" means that although Socrates is not sunburned, one of his counterparts is sunburned.

Lewis is somewhat flexible about the details of the counterpart notion, but the basic idea is something like this: Socrates's counterpart in world W is the entity in W that is the most similar to Socrates. That's only an approximation of the idea. For one thing, suppose world W contains no humans, and in fact no living things, but only sand. Perhaps one of the grains of sand is more similar to Socrates than any of the others is (maybe it looks most like him, if you look through a magnifying glass). But presumably we don't want to say that it's one of his counterparts, because then we would have to say that Socrates is possibly made of quartz. Instead, in that world, even though something is most similar to him, nothing is similar enough to be his counterpart. He just doesn't have a counterpart in a world that contains only sand. For another thing, perhaps in world W there are two things that are similar enough to him to be his counterpart, and they are equally close.

---

13. For better or for worse, Lewis has an answer to pretty much everything. He was an extremely skillful philosopher. That doesn't mean his answers are right, but they are often extremely creative and nicely developed.

14. Actually, at a certain point in his career, Lewis decided that a counterpart needn't exist in a different world; for our purposes, however, it's fine to ignore that option; see Lewis, *On the Plurality of Worlds*, 232n22.

In that case, which is his counterpart? Are both of them his counterparts, or should we pick one? Lewis thinks of this as a matter of context, at least to a certain extent.[15]

Suppose all these difficulties about the exact meaning of "counterpart" can be resolved. Still, there's a really big problem, a problem often called "the Humphrey objection." Back in 1968, Hubert Humphrey lost the US presidential election to Richard Nixon. Imagine that he tried to make himself feel better by saying, "Well, I *could* have won." On Lewis's account, that means: "In some other world, some other guy actually did win." But how, to Humphrey, is it any consolation to think that although he lost, some other guy won (some other election)? Of course, the point isn't really about the emotional states of American politicians. Instead, the point is that it's hard to see how "Humphrey could have won" could be made true by the victory of someone other than Humphrey.[16]

Many people think that Lewis's view is too weird to adopt. They think it's close to crazy to think that reality contains infinitely many other worlds, similar to this one in many ways, but spatiotemporally inaccessible from it. Quasi-Platonic possible worlds might be wild, but this seems even wilder. On top of that, there's the problem of the Humphrey objection.

Plantinga understands possible worlds to be necessarily existing quasi-Platonic entities. Lewis understands them to be physical, concrete universes like this one. Plantinga's view might seem extravagant in one way, but then again, Lewis's might seem extravagant in another. From Lewis's point of view, it's mistaken to believe in new types of being—eternal and timeless ones—when we can solve all our problems just by believing in more of the same kind of physical and temporal beings we already believe in. From Plantinga's point of view, it's mistaken to believe in a multitude of concrete worlds (almost) just like this one, especially when (as he sees it) doing so doesn't really help.

Modality is a hard problem. Possible worlds are puzzling. Perhaps you, like me, find it hard to believe in possible worlds in either the Plantingian or the Lewisian sense. Is there a way to understand modality without invoking possible worlds at all?

---

15. See Lewis, *On the Plurality of Worlds*, 251–55.
16. The locus classicus for this objection is Saul A. Kripke, *Naming and Necessity* (Cambridge: Harvard University Press, 1980), 45n13.

6.3 Modality without Possible Worlds

The Aristotelian-Scholastic tradition gives us ways to talk about modality without possible worlds. Let us start by noting an important principle in that tradition: actuality is prior to potentiality. True, whenever there is an actual chicken, there first had to be a potential chicken in the form of an egg, but then again, there had to be an actual chicken to get that egg. On the Aristotelian way of looking at things, where the buck stops has to be with chickens, not eggs: with actuality, not potentiality. Actuality can give rise to potentiality, but mere potentiality can't give rise to anything. Indeed, potentiality only leads to actuality if there's some *other* actuality that actualizes the potentiality. "Those dishes aren't going to wash themselves, you know!" What this suggests is that whatever we point to as being the *ultimate* explanation of modal facts, it's going to be something actual.

It might seem that the actuality-before-possibility principle simply excludes possible worlds theories, but that's not the case. One can always say that the huge vast array of possible worlds is itself the basic actuality from which all possibility follows. Worlds as Lewis understand them are certainly actual in the sense that they all exist (even if Lewis will use the word "actual" only for the one he is in). As for worlds in Plantinga's sense, well, obviously only one of them is actual*ized*, in the sense of being enacted or implemented, but each Plantingian world has its own actual reality apart from, and prior to, any actualization or realization of it, somewhat as a play has a reality prior to its being performed.

Nonetheless, there are reasons for doubting that arrays of possible worlds are the right actualities to base all the potentialities on. Here are three, drawn from the philosopher James Ross (d. 2010).

First, believing in all these worlds appears to violate the already-mentioned Aristotelian principle that there can never be infinitely many of anything.

Second, when thinking about the full infinity of possible worlds, we are invited to think about the full number of *all* the possible humans, *all* the possible dogs, etc. But, says Ross, there is no such thing as "all the possible humans." There can always be more.

Third, possible worlds as normally understood seem like obstacles to correct thinking about God. If reality includes a necessarily-existing array of possible worlds, it seems that God's role is only to decide which world will be implemented. It's as if the worlds are plays written down in books, with his job being merely to pull a book off the shelf and arrange for the play to be performed; or as if each world has a switch, with his job being to decide which switch to flip. This doesn't seem to respect the full idea of God as creator.[17]

Let's step back and think about all this differently, and let's start small, by asking a very simple question. Why is it possible for a certain window to break? It's because (a) the window has certain capacities or potentialities or dispositions (its fragility), and (b) there's something else (a baseball, a hammer, whatever) that has the capacity to actualize the window's capacities. The first of these is a "passive potency"—a potentiality for being acted on—and the second is an "active potency," a potentiality for acting.[18] To approach things in this way is to explain the possibility of the window's breaking in terms of actually-existing agents and their powers (together with the things they act on and their passive powers, although I will not always add that).

If that makes sense, then let's scale it up, all the way. The entirety of what *could be*, given where we are now, is based on what *already actually is*. For each thing that is possible, there is some actual thing (or collection of things) whose causal powers make it possible: either it's possible immediately, because something already actual can bring it into existence, or it's possible mediately, in the sense that something already actual can bring into existence something that could bring it into existence (of course there can be many steps inserted here). What's possible isn't a matter of which possible situations or possible worlds there are. What's possible is a matter of (all the) actual agents and (all their) powers.[19] And notice, by the way, that this respects the actuality-before-potentiality rule.

---

17. For these and other arguments, see James F. Ross, "God, Creator of Kinds and Possibilities," in *Rationality, Religious Belief, and Moral Commitment: New Essays in the Philosophy of Religion*, ed. William Wainwright and Robert Audi (Cornell University Press, 1986), 315–34.

18. These notions were introduced in §4.4.

19. That's the second time I've said "powers." Isn't that like saying "potentialities"? How does it respect the actuality-prior-to-potency rule to have everything based on powers? The answer, in a nutshell, is that strictly speaking I should just have referred to agents, agents as they actually exist. The powers that they have are necessary accidents of those agents, flowing from those agents' essences (see §1.2, §4.4). So, while talking about powers is an important part of explaining how things are *possible*, the rule is still being respected inasmuch as the powers are ultimately rooted in the actual essences of the agents.

So far, we have been discussing what could be brought about, causally, in the future. But we need to discuss not only this, but also alternative possibilities, that is, how things *might have been*: not only how things could be in the future, given where we are now, but also how things might have been now, other than how they are now. Can thinking in terms of agents shed light on this as well?

It can. Things are the way they are now because, previously, certain causal powers were actualized. But, back then, when those causal powers were actualized, different powers might have been actualized instead. If those other causal powers had been actualized, then things would have been different—in other words, the present would be different. For example, if you want to say that my hair, although brown, might have been blue, it goes like this: yesterday, or at some other time in the past, I had the power to dye my hair blue, and I might have actualized that power.

The basic idea is that possibility is based not on possible worlds, in whatever sense, but on the immediate or mediate powers of actually existing agents. This is a very Aristotelian way of thinking. It respects the actuality-before-potentiality rule in a very clear way, and the actualities it appeals to are understood straightforwardly as existing substances with causal powers.[20]

So far, so good, but now let's notice something. The kind of possibility you get by focusing on agents and their powers appears to be a limited kind of possibility. Something is possible (in the relevant sense) only if it's *causally* possible—there's an agent that could bring it into existence, or else there's an agent capable of bringing such an agent into existence (repeat as needed). But if there isn't (and never was, and never will be) an agent capable of bringing it into existence, then it's not possible (in the sense now under discussion).

I say "in the relevant sense" and things like that because there's a different sense of "possible," namely, non-contradictoriness: If *x* is non-

---

20. For a few discussions of this way of thinking, see Alexander Pruss, "The Actual and the Possible," in *Blackwell Guide to Metaphysics*, ed. R. M. Gale (Oxford: Blackwell Publishing, 2002), 313–33; Timothy Pawl, "A Thomistic Account of Truthmakers for Modal Truths" (PhD diss., St. Louis University, 2008); Jonathan D. Jacobs, "A Powers Theory of Modality: or, How I Learned to Stop Worrying and Reject Possible Worlds," *Philosophical Studies* 151, no. 2 (2010): 227–48; Alexander R. Pruss, *Actuality, Possibility and Worlds* (New York: Continuum, 2011).

contradictory, then *x* is possible. To use one of Lewis's pet examples, if there's no internal contradiction to the idea of a talking donkey,[21] then talking donkeys are "possible"—even if there aren't now, and never were, and never will be agents capable of bringing talking donkeys into existence.

I don't want to say that one of these uses of the word "possible" is right while the other is wrong. Both are legitimate uses. However, paying attention to the difference is important. There's an important difference between saying merely that something is non-contradictory and saying that it really could come into existence. For something to come into existence, for it to pass from possibility to actuality, it's not enough for it to be non-contradictory; an actual agent is required. And in this stronger causal sense, many things that seem to be possible might not really be possible after all. They are non-contradictory, but there is no agent to bring them about, so therefore they are not really possible.[22]

Where does this leave us? The good news, perhaps, is this: we have a theory of possibility that doesn't involve possible worlds. (It's good news if you'd rather avoid possible worlds.) The bad news, perhaps, is this: we have a theory where possibility is rather tightly constrained. (It's bad news if you think that possibility extends farther than the powers of finite agents, especially if you think it extends as far as non-contradictoriness.)

6.4 From Possibility to God

The following conversation was overheard at a café near the university recently.

> Ari: I can't accept this possible worlds stuff. I think that my account in terms of agents and their powers is better.
> Al: But your agency account can't be right; it saddles us with too limited a sense of possibility. I can't shake the feeling that whatever is non-contradictory really is possible.
> Ari: So you are willing to accept all those crazy possible worlds?

---

21. It's a big "if."

22. Some people speak of this as the difference between what is "essentially possible" and what is "existentially possible."

Al: If it's the only way to avoid having possibility restricted to mere causal possibility, yes.

Ari: You pay a high price, my friend.

Al: So do you, my friend.

Ari & Al [in loud, plaintive tones]: If only someone could show us how we might both be right!!!

Tom [approaching table]: Hey, guys, what's up?

Ari: He is willing to believe in possible worlds in order to make room for saying that everything that's non-contradictory is really possible.

Al: And *he* is willing to deny that everything non-contradictory is really possible, just to avoid possible worlds. *He* thinks the only real possibilities are the ones that hold in virtue of agents' powers.

Tom: Can I make a suggestion?

Al: Sure. I've read some of your stuff, and it's good.

Ari: I also want to hear. By the way, I like some of the ways you've used my ideas.

Tom: Well, you guys are good at philosophy too! I probably would have used some of your ideas, Al, but, you know, time travel is not really a thing.

Al: No offense taken!

Tom: As for you, Ari, well, there's a reason why I call you The Philosopher.

Ari: Aw, shucks, Tom.

Al: Shouldn't you call him St. Tom, Ari?

Ari: Well, I'm not Catholic.

Al: Neither am I! I'm Protestant.

Ari: But I'm, like, a pagan.

Al [aside to Tom]: We'll work on this later.

Tom [winks to Al]: OK, so let's get back to the issue we were discussing. I like Ari's agency idea . . .

Ari: [beams]

Tom: . . . but I also like Al's wide and expansive sense of what is possible.

Al: [beams]

Tom: What if—are you guys ready for this?—what if there was an agent that could do anything that was non-contradictory? A kind of, you know, super-agent? Oh, I might as well just say it: God! Then you could explain possibility without those bizarre possible worlds . . .

Al: [looks unhappy]

Tom: . . . while taking seriously the idea that anything that isn't contradictory is really possible.

Ari: [looks unhappy]

Tom: Now, Al, as a Christian, shouldn't you have thought of this already? And shouldn't the thought of possible worlds that are independent of God bother you a bit? You sometimes make it sound like they are out there, as something God has to just deal with. That undercuts God's sovereignty. And we all thought you were a Calvinist!

Al: Well, it has bothered me, and I have written about it a bit,[23] but, well, . . .

Ari: You didn't really settle things!

Tom: And Ari, do you actually insist, for the record, that talking donkeys or whatever are just not really possible at all?

Ari: Well, I follow what you're saying here, but for me, God isn't really a creator.[24]

Tom: We've all got problems. Anyway, let me restate the thought. If you have an agent who is capable of doing anything that isn't self-contradictory, then you can understand possibility in terms of agency while keeping a wide sense of real possibility.

Al: So, no more possible worlds?

Tom: Well, that depends on what you mean.

Al: [looks hopeful]

Tom: What if you put them in God's mind? I mean, what if you think of them as very complex divine ideas?

Ari: Did you get that from Jim Ross?

Tom: No, not really. He would say it doesn't go far enough. But I don't entirely understand his view.[25]

Al: We can talk about Ross some other time. I have a different concern. If we think of possible worlds as ideas that God has, isn't he under an obligation to have correct ideas? Don't his ideas of what is possible have to measure up to what is really possible? If so, then doesn't that mean that he, God, is subordinate to realities outside himself? How is this better than possible worlds?

Tom: I think there's a way out of it. In a nutshell, God's ideas are beholden not to things independent of him, but to himself—to his very own being and nature. What things measure up to is God's own infinite being.

Ari and Al: You are blowing our minds. Can you say more?

---

23. See Alvin Plantinga, *Does God Have a Nature?* (Milwaukee, WI: Marquette University Press, 1980).

24. See Aristotle, *Metaphysics*, Book XII.

25. See Ross, "God, Creator of Kinds and Possibilities."

Tom: Actually, I've got to run. But if you turn to §8.8 and §8.12 of *A Contemporary Introduction to Thomistic Metaphysics*, you'll find an account of how God is, so to speak, the infinite standard that everything imitates.
Ari and Al: Is it a Thomistic account?
Tom: You guys are embarrassing me, but, well, yeah, pretty much.

In this chapter, we have distinguished among key modal concepts like possibility, necessity, and contingency, and we have considered some of the mainstream contemporary understandings of modal metaphysics.

I find possible worlds approaches to be fascinating but, in the end, unacceptably extravagant. It's far better, in my view, to adopt a more Aristotelian approach, grounding possibility in the powers of actual agents. At the same time, however, there is a problem with understanding possibility in too restricted a way. By rooting what's possible in the powers of a finite number of finite agents, we get the problematic result that only some non-contradictory "possibilities" are really possible. If, however, there were some actual agent with *infinite* power, rooted in an *infinite* essence, then everything that's non-contradictory will be really possible. This possibility will be based not on something external to that infinite agent, but on that agent itself. Or maybe we should say: that Agent Himself. At this point, we have traveled to the edge of metaphysics, and possibly beyond it. But there's one last set of issues to explore before we go there.

▸ To get started on reading Aquinas himself on the ideas developed in this chapter, begin with *Summa Theologiae* I, q. 25, on divine power, and especially article 3; then turn back to *Summa Theologiae* I, q. 15, on divine ideas.

CHAPTER 7

Thoughts about Everything

7.1 Introduction

SO FAR IN THIS BOOK, much of our thinking has depended on distinctions between different regions or types of reality: basic beings as distinct from their features, essential as distinct from accidental features, parts as distinct from wholes, parts as distinct from other parts, universals as distinct from particulars, the actual as distinct from the possible, and so on. Now I would like to step back and consider what there is to say about everything at once: not just about substances, or accidents, or causes, or parts, but about *everything*. It turns out that in one way, it's not possible to talk about everything: there is no all-encompassing category or kind that everything belongs to. In another way, however, it is possible: everything in reality has actual existence, and it is possible to talk about what is common to all actual existents. To bring out the first point, we will inquire into categories. To bring out the second, we will inquire into the transcendental properties of being.

7.2 Categories

If you are trying to get your desk organized, one thing you might do is put things into piles: books, papers, pens, paper clips, and so on. A way to describe this activity is "categorizing." You are putting things into categories.

There is nothing wrong with this use of the word "categories," but there is another use that is found in Aristotelian metaphysics. On this much more technical use of the word, paper clips do not make up a "category," and neither do books or pens. Categories in the technical sense, which I will sometimes call "metaphysical categories," are *highest* categories. Many questions arise here.

7.2.1 What Metaphysical Categories Are

The first order of business is to understand what is meant by "highest category," and the way to do this is to think hierarchically. You can group all cats into one class, or "category" in the everyday sense, and likewise you can group all dogs into one class (a different class). But there's another class, a higher class, that both the dogs and the cats belong to—namely, the class of mammals. So, there are two lower classes, dogs and cats, and then a higher and more inclusive one that encompasses them both. It doesn't end there. The class of mammals includes both dogs and cats, but it doesn't include snakes, which belong to the class of reptiles; but reptiles and mammals both belong to a still-higher class—namely, the class of vertebrates. There are higher classes still, like the class of animals.

This cannot go on forever. It must come to a stop somewhere. It comes to a stop when you reach a class that has lower and narrower subclasses within it, but that is not itself a subclass of any higher class. Such a class is a "category" in the technical, metaphysical sense. There are classes below this one, but not above it. It has subclasses, but no super-classes. It is a highest category. And perhaps you will not be terribly surprised if I say that the highest category to which cats, mammals, vertebrates, and so on belong is *substance*.

The point can be made more clearly with the help of Table 7-1.

TABLE 7-1 A TABLE OF CLASSES

Types of classes	Examples (with their differentiae)
Metaphysical category	substance
Even higher genus...	animal ("having sensation")
Higher genus	vertebrate ("with a backbone")
Genus	mammal ("lactating")
Lowest species	cat ("meowing")
[Individual]	[Mickey]

In the right column, you have hierarchically related classes, and in the left column, you have words that indicate the type of class in question, which essentially means indicating how high up in the hierarchy the class is.

The table is a table of classes, or categories in the everyday sense, rising to a category in the technical and metaphysical sense. But its bottom row contains not a class, like cats, but an individual, Mickey. In a sense, that row is really not a part of the table at all, and that is why I have put it in square brackets.

The table really begins with "lowest species," *infima species* in Latin, which are classes that have no subclasses.[1] "Cat," in this example, has no subclass. (Mickey is not a subclass of the class "cat," he is a member of it.)

At the top of the table is a proper metaphysical category, a class that is not a subclass of any higher class. So the two extremes are lowest class, a class without subclasses, and highest class, or "category," a class without super-classes.

In between are some items that I have vaguely labeled "genus," "higher genus," and "even higher genus. . . ." The " . . . " at the end there is meant to indicate that there may be no fixed number of genera in between the lowest species and the highest category: maybe there are two, maybe there are twenty, but for our purposes it doesn't matter. What matters is that there are classes with no super-classes, classes with no subclasses, and classes in between—that is, classes with both super-classes and subclasses.

Also worth mentioning are the items in parentheses in the right-hand column. These are *differentiae*, "differences" in a certain technical sense of that word—namely, the features that divide subclasses from other subclasses. For example, cat is a subclass of mammal, and what separates cats out from other subclasses of mammal (like dogs) is that cats meow.[2] So mammal is the genus, meowing is the difference, and the resultant species is cat. The same pattern appears higher up. For example, vertebrate is a subclass of animal, and what separates vertebrates out from other subclasses of animal is that they have backbones: animal is the higher genus, having-a-backbone is the difference, and the resultant sub-genus is vertebrate.

---

1. I need to mention that my presentation of some of this material will be rather frustrating for specialists in medieval logic and category theory. Among other shortcuts, I will be using words like "genus" and "species" in ways that correspond much more to contemporary everyday usage than they do to medieval logical usage. In particular, I am glossing over the distinction between terms of first intention and terms of second intention, with the result that I will not be carefully observing the intricate ways in which metaphysics and logic are intertwined in the thought of authors like Aquinas. I think this strategy is best for my purposes here, but I want to acknowledge its limitations as well.

2. This is not meant as a serious biological proposal, of course.

Now I would like to expand our view of things by adding another column. See Table 7-2.

TABLE 7-2 A BROADER TABLE OF CLASSES

Types of classes	Examples (with their differentiae)	
Metaphysical category	substance	accident
Even higher genus...	animal ("living")	quality ("what the substance is like")
Higher genus	vertebrate ("with a backbone")	color ("reflecting light in a certain frequency range")
Genus	mammal ("lactating")	gray ("reflecting light in the frequency range XYZ")
Lowest species	cat ("meowing")	Mickey's special shade of gray ("reflecting light in the frequency range Z")
[Individual]	[Mickey]	[Mickey's grayness trope]

The right-most column bottoms out not with a substance, but with an accident: Mickey's particular grayness trope, which is not a class but a particular instance or member of one. Above it, as lowest species, is the maximally specific shade of gray that Mickey's color-trope is an instance of. Above it, as a genus, is gray in general; above that, color; above that, quality; and then finally, as a metaphysical category, accident (but see next paragraph). Mickey's special shade is differentiated from gray-in-general by involving light in a very specific frequency range; gray-in-general is differentiated from color by involving light in a broader frequency range; color is differentiated from other qualities by being the sort of quality that involves the reflection of light, rather than involving sound waves, or the ability to do math, or whatever other kinds of qualities there might be; and qualities are differentiated from other accidents by being what substances are *like* as opposed to, say, *how big* substances are.

Some readers may have noticed that there is something rather un-Aristotelian and un-Thomistic about this table—namely, the way it embodies the idea that "accident" is a metaphysical category. As will be discussed later, thinkers in the Aristotelian tradition distinguish different kinds of accident and treat each of them as its own highest category.

For now, however, I think it better not to get into such details. The main point, for now, is not how many categories there are, but simply the bare idea that there is more than one. The idea that there is more than one metaphysical category, more than one class-without-a-super-class, is momentous. It means that in some sense, although you can group beings into broader and broader classes, more-and-more inclusive classes, you can never arrive at a class that includes them all.

7.2.2 Why Being Is Not a Category or Genus

It is a traditional part of Aristotelian-Thomistic metaphysics to say that "being is not a genus." The highest categories—substance and accident, or whatever they turn out to be—are as high as it goes. The point is not easy to grasp, but trying is very much worthwhile, because doing so will give us deeper insight into some important metaphysical topics.

Let me start with an initial, rather logic-oriented reason for thinking that being is not a genus. Here is something we know: Being is divided, in the sense that there is more than one being, and even more than one type of being. Now beings that are different from one another are different in virtue of something or other—if they were exactly the same as each other in every respect, then they wouldn't be different. Let's use the expression "being-dividers" for those realities in virtue of which being is divided. Now, how are being-dividers related to being overall? Are they related in the way that *difference* is related to *genus*? Aristotle, and Aquinas and others after him, have given the following as a reason for saying "no." On the one hand, one never predicates the genus of the difference. On the other hand, one must be able to predicate "being" of the being-dividers; otherwise the being-dividers would not be beings, in which case they wouldn't exist at all, with the result that being wouldn't be divided (as we know it is). The upshot is that being doesn't fit one of the requirements for being a genus—namely, the inability to be predicated of its differences. Therefore, being is not a genus.[3]

Structurally, this argument is fairly straightforward. However, it's not entirely clear what it is really saying. For example, what does it mean to say that a genus cannot be predicated of its differences? Exactly what

---

3. See Aristotle, *Metaphysics* III, 998b20–27, and Aquinas's commentary on *Metaphysics* III, lect. 8, §§432–33. See also, for example, Aquinas, *Summa theologiae* I, q. 3, art. 5.

is being denied here? Is "rational is an animal" an example of a genus being predicated of a difference? It does seem right to deny that "rational is an animal"—indeed, it's not clear that "rational is an animal" means anything at all. But maybe that's not the right way to think about the idea of a genus being predicated of a difference. Perhaps the following is an example of a genus being predicated of a difference: "a rational being is an animal." Especially if that means that *at least some* rational beings are animals, it seems not false but true! And there are still other possible ways to interpret "one cannot predicate a genus of a difference." Does it mean that the concept of the genus does not include the concept of the difference?—for example, that the concept of rationality does not include the concept of animality? There are arguments for and against saying that, but whichever way you go, you might be forgiven for wondering why facts about *concepts* have such large implications for *being*. To sort all this out would lead us deep into theories of logic and language, much deeper than would be appropriate for this book.[4] For that reason, I would like to set this logical approach aside.

Let us approach matters in a more strictly metaphysical way. I will propose two lines of thought. The first has to do with what it really means to have metaphysical categories or highest categories. Note how talking about beings in terms of genera and species means talking about them in terms of their kinds—that is, talking about them in terms of their natures and essences.[5] That could mean the specific natures of substances, like felinity, along with higher, more abstract and less determinate genera, like mammality and animality; or it could mean the specific natures of accidents, like the precise shade of red found on a Scarlet tanager, or higher, abstract, less determinate genera, like redness or even just color. Belonging to this species rather than that one, or this genus rather than that one, is a matter of the kind of thing you are. It's a matter of your nature.

The fact of hierarchy means that things can be different in nature on one level, while being alike in nature on another. Consider the cat

4. For such questions and more, as part of a wide-ranging exploration of the argument and its fate across many centuries, see Lukáš Novák, "Conceptual Atomism, '*Aporia Generis*' and a Way Out for Leibniz and the Aristotelians," *Studia Neoaristotelica* 6, no. 1 (2009): 15–49.

5. Here again I will mention, blushingly, that I am glossing over the medieval logical uses of terms like *genus* and *species*.

Mickey and the dog Fido. Consider also the highest level at which they differ—in this case, it's the very first level, the species-level, where the difference between cat and dog shows up. And finally, consider the lowest level at which they are the same, which on our table is the genus-level of mammal. Mickey and Fido belong to different species—cat and dog—but to the same genus, mammal. They differ according to their specific kinds or natures (cat vs. dog), but they are the same according to their generic kind or nature (mammal). And of course, their similarities go higher up the hierarchy, because they are the same in terms of higher genera as well: they are both vertebrates, they are both animals, and they are both substances.

But now let us change examples by thinking of Mickey and a certain snake, Twisty. The highest level at which they differ is not the species level, but the genus level, where mammal is different from reptile. And the lowest level at which they are the same is not the genus level, but the higher genus level, vertebrate. Now in one way, the situation is just like the previous one: difference of kind from a certain level on downwards, and sameness of kind from a certain level on upwards. However, it's important that the sameness starts higher up. Rusty the mammal and Twisty the reptile are less similar to each other than Rusty and Fido were. There is less commonality of kind, and there is more difference of kind. They do indeed share higher genera, but they share fewer of them. They differ in terms not only of lowest species (snake vs. cat) but also in terms of genus (mammal vs. reptile).

Now let's go straight to the top. Let's consider not two mammals, or two vertebrates, or even two animals, but a substance and an accident, like Rusty and his redness. When you get to this point, there's not just *less* commonality of kind, there's *no* commonality of kind. They are different on every level. Why? The only thing they have in common is that they are both beings, but that's not a commonality of *kind*. To have a commonality of kind is to share a way of being, but when two things share nothing but the fact that they are existing beings, then they do not share a way of being. That's because simply existing, simply *being* a being, is not a *way* of being at all. If someone asks, "What kind of being is that?" it is completely off-target to say, "Well, it's a being," or even "It's an existing being."

If being were a kind, then there would have to be some other kind that it was contrasted with. Would that kind be *non-being*? This seems to make no sense; nothing could ever belong to *non-being*, even in principle. "Non-beings" don't have a special type of being; they don't exist in a non-being sort of way; rather, they don't exist at all. True enough, we can *say* things like "centaurs are instances of the kind *non-being*," but this is merely a misleading way to say that there are not actually any centaurs. Felinity and substantiality are ways something could be, and maybe even centaurhood is a way something could be, but non-being is not. It's possible for there to be instances of cat or substance, and in fact, there are such instances. It's possible, perhaps, for there to be instances of centaur, but there aren't any such instances. But it's not possible for there to be any instances of *non-being*: it's not possible for anything *to be a non-being*. The difference between being and non-being, then, is not a difference between different kinds or natures or essences. It's not a difference between things that exist in different ways. It's a difference between what is there in actual reality and what isn't there at all. Once you get to the level of metaphysical categories, all differences in kind are maximally radical. You can talk about "all beings," but you won't be talking about things that all belong to one kind. You will be lumping together things of radically diverse kinds. You won't be talking generically anymore. Being is not a genus.[6]

Here is a second way to see that being is not a genus. Take substance and accident as two categories and ask whether there might be some category higher than they. Well, what are substance and accident? Oversimplifying some of the material we saw in §1.1, we can say that a substance exists in itself, while an accident exists in another. But this doesn't mean that there's such a thing as generic being, which then gets specified in two ways, "in itself" and "in another." To say that an accident exists in another is really to say that it exists *in something that exists in itself*—that is, in substance. Substance and accident aren't related by being different ways to implement or determine some one generic kind that they both share in. Instead, one of them shares in the other. As Aquinas puts it, substance and accident are related to one another as prior and posterior—accident is what it is only in dependence on substance. But that sort of relation is not how things that share a genus are related, and so again, being is not a genus.

I have given some Thomistic reasons why we should be willing to accept the idea that categorization comes to an end with multiple cat-

---

6. For discussion of this line of reasoning, see Wippel, *Metaphysical Thought*, 74ff.

egories, not with one top category of "being." This brings us back to a topic considered in §1.7—namely, analogy. Being is spoken about in different ways, and that's because there are different ways to be. But now we can put the point more strongly: being is spoken about in radically different ways, and that's because there are radically different ways to be. There is, in the end, no generic sense of the word "being," and that's because there is, in the end, no single kind or way of being that we are indicating when we speak of something's being "a being." To be sure, the various kinds of being are related—substance is the primary way to be, and other ways are related to it—but this relation doesn't amount to there being some single higher way that they all belong to or boil down to or share in. Reality is diverse from bottom to top.

7.2.3 So Which Are the Categories?

In how many ways is reality diverse, and which are those ways? What, in short, are the categories? Given how things have been unfolding since the beginning of this book, and given the tables in §7.2.1, it would be reasonable to guess that this book's answer to that question will be "substance and accident." But that turns out to be too fast and too simple. It's too fast because there are possible examples of metaphysical categories that are neither substance nor accident. It's too simple because there are good reasons to think that "accident" is not really a category, but just a label for what is, in a reality, a whole set of categories.

Let us start with the "too fast" problem. Philosophers have proposed a surprisingly large number of metaphysical categories other than substance and accident. For two examples, consider Events and Places.[7] Suppose you think, for example, that to make sense of the idea that physical objects move around, we need to be able say things like this: "First the object was at place #1, and then it was at place #2." And suppose you followed up with the thought that this couldn't be true unless those *places* existed: place #1 is a being, place #2 is a being, and so on. But then, what are places? Are they substances? Are they accidents? Perhaps, you will conclude, they are neither of those, nor are they any-

---

7. For a longer list, see Joshua Hoffman and Gary S. Rosenkrantz, *Substance among Other Categories* (Cambridge: Cambridge University Press, 1994), for discussion of, *inter alia*, properties, tropes, places, times, limits, events, privations, and collections.

thing else except simply themselves. In short, you might conclude, they belong to a metaphysical category all their own.

Switching now to the other example, suppose you think that events, like Rusty's running, are neither substances nor accidents, or anything else, again in such a way that they, events, are just themselves. If that is right, then they too belong to a metaphysical category of their own.

There are many such lines of thought, and it's not possible to deal with all of them here. In fact, it would be hard to deal definitively with even just one of them; the issues they raise are deep and complex. First, I will simply state the Thomistic approach to putative categories other than substance and accident.[8] Then I will indicate, in an admittedly sketchy fashion, how that Thomistic approach might be worked out, at least in a preliminary and hand-waving way.

Putting things in broad terms, the Thomistic approach holds that the only real categories are categories of substances and accidents, and that whenever we think we have discovered some other category, what we really have discovered is some combination of substance and accidents. That's stated rather abstractly. Let me try spelling it out concretely in terms of the two examples mentioned already, events and places.

First, let's think of events. Oversimplifying a bit, an event is a combination of (i) a substance and (ii) some action that it is performing. The event of Rusty's jumping is the combination of (i) Rusty and (ii) his jumping, which is one of his accidents. It's perfectly fine to speak of this as "an event," but there's nothing to this "event" beyond Rusty and his jumping. We don't need a distinct metaphysical category to explain it.

Some philosophers use the word "event" more broadly, to encompass things like "Rusty's being red." This use of the word "event" leaves out the notion of something happening, and in that way, I think it involves stretching the meaning of the standard English word "event" rather far. For our purposes, however, it doesn't really matter, because the Aristotelian explanation is essentially the same. An "event" in this broader sense is still nothing above and beyond (i) a substance and (ii) one of its accidents. Whether we take event in the narrow sense or the

---

8. "Putative" is like "alleged," but without the snarkiness. If I speak of "your alleged solution," it sounds like I think your solution is bogus. If I speak of "your putative solution," I just mean that you have a proposed solution, and it may or may not be a good one.

broad sense, it is going to turn out to be just a substance and one of its accidents—either an action type of accident, or any kind of accident at all. The event is real, but it doesn't constitute a distinct category: it's just what you get when there are entities in two different categories (substance and some category of accident), related in the correct way.

Now let's talk about another putative category, places. Earlier we talked briefly about the idea that physical substances have locations only relative to other physical objects. If there was only one physical object in the entire universe, it would make no sense to ask *where* it was; where-questions always presuppose a landscape of objects with numerous interrelations.[9] That idea is related to this one: there are no objective or absolute "places," as if empty space were already there, divided into places, waiting to be filled by objects showing up at this place or that place. Instead, when multiple physical objects exist, we can talk about how they are related to one another, and places exist only in a way that is parasitic upon those interrelations. An imaginary example can make clear what this means. Suppose we live on a plain on which bushes grow, more or less randomly, a dozen or so yards from one another. We pick two bushes several hundred yards away from one another, and we mark one of them with a blue flag and the other with a red flag. The line between them is now one axis (we can drag a stick along the ground to mark it if it helps). Then we pick two other bushes that make an axis perpendicular to the first one, and we mark them as well, this time with green and yellow flags (and maybe make a line in the dirt there too). Where these axes cross, we place a large rock and call it "the origin." I hope you remember enough math to realize that if we do all of this, we will have essentially created a real-life Cartesian coordinate system, one which we can use to identify the locations of any objects around. If I want to tell you where a treasure is buried, I can hand you a certain stick and say, "Start at the origin, and go four hundred and fifty-five stick lengths toward the blue flag; then go seven hundred and forty-two stick lengths in the yellow direction, parallel to the green-yellow line." In so doing, I will have sent you to "a place," but all this is done only relative to the original bushes. If some joker had come along in the night and moved the rock, you would not find the treasure.

9. See §3.3.2.

The point is not the details of the example, of course, but just to give a sense of how we can speak of where things are located without presupposing that there are pre-existing "places" for the things to be located in. The original axis is created at random, the second one is created perpendicular to it, and everything else is explained relative to them. In short, then, we don't need to believe in places as a distinct metaphysical category. We just need (say) bushes and rocks and sticks, and the ability to tell whether two lines are perpendicular or not.[10]

In the preceding few paragraphs, I have sketched out, in a rather quick-and-dirty fashion, ways to think about events and places that do not require thinking of events and places as belonging to distinct metaphysical categories. If all we have are substances and accidents, then that is enough to explain events or places. There is no space here to work out how to do this for all putative categories, still less to do so in a really detailed and rigorous way. But something like that has to be possible if we are to have a category system that is, at its heart, Aristotelian and Thomistic. There are basic beings, and there are accidents, and everything else is constructed out of those.

Once again, I may be giving the impression that on the Thomistic way of thinking, there are two categories: substance and accident. But, as indicated, that's too simple. Aristotle, in the work we call the *Categories*, distinguishes nine different accidental categories. Now this is a tricky point. Because they are all accidental categories, it's tempting to believe that they are *sub*-categories of the truly metaphysical category Accident, leaving us with a two-category system after all (substance, accident). But on the traditional way of thinking, different types of accidents are too different from one another to fall under one category.

Here is Aristotle's full list of nine accidental categories, with examples:

Quantity: being six feet tall, or weighing 200 lbs.
Quality: being red, or being asleep
Relation: being someone's father
Habitus: being clothed, or shod
Time when: being today, or tomorrow
Place where: being in Paris, or in Washington, DC

---

10. It's possible to invent a version that doesn't even require perpendicularity, but it's harder to explain.

Position or posture: being sitting, or lying down
Action: punching someone
Passion: getting punched by someone

You can see them all in Table 7-3, with classes lower than the categories removed. It is important to remember that items in the non-substantial categories are accidents belonging to some substance. In some cases, the point is obvious enough: quantity and quality, for example, are easy to think of as accidents that belong to substances. Rusty's weighing fifteen pounds, and his redness, are both accidents of him. But in other cases, it is easy to get confused. For example, the category of "place where" includes not places, like Montreal, but accidents of being in some place. The item in this category is not Montreal but being-in-Montreal.

As mentioned, you can find this list in Aristotle, and Aquinas adopts it as his own as well. Acquiring a full understanding of the list is not easy, however. One important question is whether it really makes sense to see distinctions among types of accident as being true categorical differences, rather than sub-categorical differences within one generic category "accident." It seems to me that this does make good sense. Being a certain height is very different from being red or being asleep. These are deeply different ways for a substance to be; they do, it is true, share the fact that they are both *in* a substance, but this is not really a kind or genus, if only because "in" here covers such a deeply diverse multitude of relationships.

Another question is whether this list of nine is really the right list; in particular, one can ask whether the list is too long. Think of the category *habitus*, like "being clothed," "having one's hat on," or "being armed."[11] Why doesn't "Socrates is clothed" simply mean "Socrates is

---

11. Perhaps you are wondering about the strange word *habitus*. The Latin verb *habere* means to have, and a *habitus* is something that one has. Think of how the garb worn by those in religious life is called a "habit."

Or perhaps whether you are wondering whether I was joking when (in Table 7-3) I gave Rusty's wearing a collar as an example of *habitus*. After all, doesn't Aquinas restrict this category to humans? He does. I was trying to be funny. But then again, it's complicated: while he says that instances of this category are found only among humans, he adds (*In Phys.* III, lect. 5, §322) that the category can be extended to animals that serve humans, so that a horse's being saddled would count as a *habitus* in some sense.

TABLE 7-3 TEN ARISTOTELIAN CATEGORIES

Types of classes		Examples								
Categories	Substance	Quantity	Quality	Relation	Habitus	Time when	Place where	Posture	Action	Passion
[Individuals]	Rusty	His weighing fifteen pounds	His redness	His being a father (of Fluffy)	His wearing a collar	His being alive on Tuesday	His living in Montreal	His lying down	His waving his tail	His being warmed by the sun

related in such-and-such a way to his clothing," which requires no more categories than the categories we need for Socrates, his clothing, and the relation between them?[12]

For our purposes, it is not necessary to sort it all out in detail. The crucial thing is not exactly how many categories there are, but the idea that there really are multiple metaphysical categories, that there really are a number of highest-level genera of beings, rather than one unitary top-category "being." This is of great significance: it means that reality is marked by radical internal diversity. What holds everything together is not similarity of kind, but the relation between substance and accident, on the one hand, and, on the other, the fact that it all has a common source.[13]

7.2.4 A Brief Digression on Relations

Here I want to insert a brief digression on one category of accident—namely, relations. It's worth a bit of discussion because there's a rather large difference between the way in which philosophers like Aquinas think about relations and the way in which philosophers nowadays tend to think about relations. What's more, it's a difference that makes a difference.

Suppose you have two substances, Vader and Luke, and suppose as well that they are related to one another—let's say that Vader is Luke's father.[14] According to a way of thinking about relations that is quite common in contemporary analytic philosophy, "being the father of" is a relation, and Vader and Luke both share in it. Vader shares in it from

---

Does a cat's wearing a collar count here? For a recent discussion of the category *habitus*, see Mark K. Spencer, "The Category of *Habitus*: Accidents, Artifacts, and Human Nature," *The Thomist* 79, no. 1 (2015): 113–54.

12. For discussion of Aquinas's presentation of the categories, see Wippel, *Metaphysical Thought*, 208–28. For a complication I have so far avoided, namely how action and passion are different categories when they are—as we saw in §4.4—the same reality, see Gloria Frost, *Aquinas on Efficient Causation and Causal Powers* (Cambridge: Cambridge University Press, 2022), 171–81. For a look at how some early post-Thomistic thinkers raised doubts about the need for all nine accidental categories, see William E. McMahon, "Reflections on Some Thirteenth- and Fourteenth Century Views of the Categories," in *Categories: Historical and Systematic Essays*, ed. Michael Gorman and Jonathan J. Sanford (Washington, DC: The Catholic University of America Press, 2004), 45–57.

13. This last point will come to the fore in §8.8.

14. Just an example, of course.

one side, so to speak, and Luke from the other, but it's one thing that they share in. The accident belongs to both *relata*—that is, to both "related things."

The Aristotelian-scholastic way of thinking about relations is different. It refuses to say that relations—which are accidents, after all—are shared by the two relata, but says instead that an accident, even a relation, is always had by only one substance. So instead of saying that "being the father of" is some single item that both Vader and Luke share in, the scholastic approach would say that "being the father of" is something that only Vader has, and that Luke has something else—namely, "being the son of." These are two distinct accidents, belonging to two distinct substances. Vader has a "being the father of" accident, and Luke has a "being the son of" accident. Of course, we need to add that Vader's fatherhood accident is, so to speak, directed at Luke, and Luke's sonhood accident is directed at Vader. Vader is the "subject" of his father-of accident, with Luke as its "term," while Luke is the subject of his son-of accident, with Vader as *its* term.

When two substances are related in the usual way, each has a relation pointing to the other as its term: A has a relation with B as term, and B has a relation with A as term. Because the relations come in pairs like that, it might seem that there is no important difference between this approach and the approach that thinks of A and B as both sharing in one relation. However, there are unusual cases, and in those cases, the difference between the two approaches comes out.

Suppose Luke is thinking of Rusty. When this is happening, Luke has a thinking-about relation with Rusty as its term. But does Rusty have a corresponding accident? It seems, on reflection, that he does not. To be sure, we can say of Rusty that he is "thought about by" Luke, but this is another one of those cases where language can be misleading. Being thought about by Luke is not an accidental feature of Rusty's. It is not a modification or enhancement of his being. When Luke is thinking about Rusty, all the metaphysical machinery, so to speak, is on Luke's side, not Rusty's side. Of course, both Luke and Rusty are involved in the relation "thought about": Luke is the subject, and Rusty is the term. But that doesn't require us to say that Rusty has a corresponding relation with Luke as term.

If we think about relations in the usual contemporary way, as one item shared by both relata, then the difference between the Luke-Rusty case and the Vader-Luke case is difficult to see. It is difficult to see how, in the Vader-Luke case, being related is a real metaphysical component of both relata, whereas in the Luke-Rusty case, it's not. It is difficult, that is to say, to see how Rusty is left untouched, metaphysically unaffected, by being thought about by Luke. But if we think about relations in the scholastic way, then it is easier to distinguish the two cases: in the Vader-Luke case, both relata are affected, and each has an accident, while in the Luke-Rusty case, only one relatum is affected, and only one has an accident.[15]

Relations is a difficult topic, and it would take us too far afield to explore it in depth, but that is enough to at least give you a sense of how it is approached in Thomistic metaphysics. Now it is time to return to categories in general.

7.2.5 A Brief Remark on Categories and Universals

In an earlier section, we considered whether there are metaphysical categories that are neither the category of substance nor any of the categories of accident—for example, whether we should consider "event" or "place" as categories. Some philosophers have proposed that we take universals as forming a separate category, contrasting with individuals. On their way of thinking, the category of individuals would include, say, Rusty and his particular redness, while the category of universals would include, say, Felinity and Redness.

One could do this in the way just laid out—lumping all individuals into one big category, and all universals into another—or one could do it in a way that respects the division between substance and accident, and even in a way that respects the divisions among kinds of accidents. One could, that is, think of there being a category for individual substances, and another category for individual quantities, and another category for individual qualities, and so on; and then add, on a separate level, a category for kinds of substances, a category for kinds of quantities, and so on. If you believed in the full set of Aristotelian categorical distinctions, this would give you twenty categories.[16]

---

15. The ability to think about relations in this way will have a further payoff when we get to §8.10.

16. A recent philosopher who took such an approach, on a smaller scale, is E. J. Lowe (d. 2014), for whom there were four categories. He called them object, mode,

If you are a realist about universals—and some Thomists are—then perhaps it would make sense for you to include categories for your universals. This book, however, advocates moderate nominalism (see §5.1), and so I do not recommend this approach. Categories contain beings, and universals are not beings.

7.2.6 De-Reifying Categories

A final word about categories, namely, a warning against reifying them. We talk about things "belonging to the same category," and that's fine, but we have to be wary, lest language bewitch our intelligence. Talk about things "being in categories," and even more so, talk about "putting things into categories," can make it sound as if categories are buckets. When we say that Rusty and Mickey belong to the same category, we shouldn't fall into thinking that there is some strange metaphysical thing, a metaphysical bucket, that both Rusty and Mickey can be put into. It's just a way of saying that the way in which Rusty is, and the way in which Mickey is, are similar in a certain very abstract respect. As noted in the introduction, in metaphysics we mostly do not talk about abstract, highly generic, extraordinary things, but rather we talk abstractly and highly generically about ordinary things. "Putting things into categories," as we call it, is one of the most abstract and generalizing ways in which we do this.

7.3 Transcendentals

We have discussed metaphysical categories, and a lot of emphasis has been placed on the idea that categorical differences are maximally radical. There is no type or genus that all beings belong to. But that raises a certain difficulty. If talking about things means saying what kinds they belong to, whether that means essential kinds (like felinity) or accidental kinds (like agility), and if being is not a kind, then it looks like there is nothing to say that applies to all beings. Does that mean that at the highest level, the most authentic form of metaphysical discourse is silence?

---

kind and attribute, but they correspond quite closely to individual substance, individual accident, substance-kind, and accident-kind. See, above all, E. J. Lowe, *The Four-Category Ontology: A Metaphysical Foundation for Natural Science* (Oxford: Clarendon Press, 2006).

It's true enough that what is common to all beings is only being itself, existence, but that doesn't mean that there is nothing to say about all beings. We can unpack what it means to be. We can uncover various aspects of what it means to exist. We won't do this by putting beings into a kind, but we'll still be saying something.

Discourse of this sort—discussion of what is common to all beings—involves talking about the "transcendental properties" of being. To do this is not to talk about unusual entities that exist in a far-away realm—about transcendent beings—but to talk about everyday entities with an eye on what they share with all other entities. Such properties or features are "transcendental" in the sense that they go beyond the categories, and they go beyond them by showing up in all of them and thereby not being restricted to any of them.[17] The tradition of thinking along these lines goes back at least to Aristotle, with contributions made along the way by many philosophers both before and after Aquinas. To use a list found in one of Aquinas's works, everything that exists is a being (*ens*), it's a thing (*res*), it's one (*unum*), it's something (*aliquid*), it's good (*bonum*), and it's true (*verum*).

Compared to the richness of detail that you get by describing a thing's essence, proper accidents, and other accidents, a discussion of the transcendentals can seem pretty thin. But it's not nothing, and furthermore, it's very important, because it's what everything else is based upon and presupposes. In what follows, I will discuss the transcendentals listed above, and then I will go into extra detail on one of them—namely, goodness. Focusing on goodness will provide us with an opportunity to explore the metaphysics of good and evil, an interesting and important topic. But first we need to untangle the following puzzle: How can there be more than one transcendental?

---

17. One of my undergraduate philosophy teachers, Thomas Langan, said that whenever someone uses the word "transcends," you should stop him and ask, "*What* goes beyond *what*, *how*?"

I derive this helpful contrast between transcendental properties and transcendent entities from Jan Aertsen, *Medieval Philosophy and the Transcendentals: The Case of Thomas Aquinas* (Leiden: E.J. Brill, 1996), 168.

7.3.1 The Multiplicity of the Transcendentals

If you were asked to list a few properties or features, you might say something like this: agility, redness, furriness. And it's clear that each of these gives rise to a distinct class: the class of agile things is different from the class of red things, and likewise for the class of furry things. To be sure, the classes do overlap: some things are both agile and red, some things are both agile and furry, and so on. But not everything that is agile is red, not everything that is furry is agile, and so on.

If all lists of properties are like that—if every list of different properties gives rise to a corresponding list of different classes—then it will follow that there can't be more than one transcendental property. Transcendental properties apply to all beings, and obviously there's only one class of *all* beings, so if properties line up one-to-one with classes, then for the one class of all beings, there will be only one property.[18]

It turns out, however, that it's not always the case that multiple properties correspond to multiple classes. Imagine someone trying to define "human being." His first attempt is "warm-blooded biped," but that's wrong, because it casts the net too widely: there are warm-blooded bipeds that are not human, like birds. His second attempt is "bearded mammal," but that's wrong too, because it casts the net too narrowly: there are humans that are not bearded. Finally, he hits upon the following: featherless biped.[19] Now in one way, this isn't so bad. It appears to be neither too broad nor too narrow.[20] In another way, however, there's clearly something not quite right about this definition. It doesn't seem to really get to the heart of things, in the way that "rational animal" does.

For our purposes here, it's not important to figure out what's wrong with "featherless biped." What's important is simply to realize that there can be two features—the feature of being a featherless biped, and the feature of being a rational animal—that capture the same class of beings. To use some technical terminology, these two features have the same "extension"—they extend to all the same entities—but they differ in

---

18. Of course, given something we saw in §7.2.2—namely, that being is not a genus, this "class" of all beings will not be the sort of class whose members all share a kind or genus.

19. This is given, not too seriously, as a definition of human in Plato's *Statesman*.

20. Or is it too broad after all? Are kangaroos bipeds or quadrupeds?

"intension" or conceptual content (from a Latin word, *intentio*, that can be used for thought or for the mind's stretching out to grasp reality).

Holding that there are multiple transcendental properties requires holding that they are the same in extension but different in intension. They pick out the same items—all beings—but they do so in different ways. Each distinct transcendental represents a unique way of thinking about what it is to be a being. It expresses a unique perspective or point of view on what it is to exist.

7.3.2 A List of Transcendentals

Thomas Aquinas talks about transcendental properties of being in a number of works. He does not give the same list every time, however, nor, even for those transcendentals that show up on more than one of his lists, does he always offer the same explanations. To present any list as "the" list of St. Thomas would, therefore, be a historical error. It would certainly be possible for a philosopher to present the list that he or she considered to be most in line with Aquinas's deepest principles, but doing so would require more argumentation than would be appropriate for a book like this. What I will do in this section, then, is present the longest list that Aquinas gives, the one found early in his *Disputed Questions on Truth*, and comment on it in various ways. I will not attempt to convince you to adopt this or that precise list of transcendentals, but only to bring out what is at stake in the issue of transcendentals overall. That will set you up to think about them on your own.[21]

The list itself is the one I gave earlier: everything that exists is a being (*ens*), it's a thing (*res*), it's one (*unum*), it's something (*aliquid*), it's good (*bonum*), and it's true (*verum*).

The first thing to bring out is what these mean. It's even less obvious than it seems, because to some extent, Aquinas gets his points across by appealing to certain aspects of particular Latin words, aspects that don't always transfer over into English. We'll have to be careful not

---

21. For a very detailed look at Aquinas's views, see Aertsen, *Medieval Philosophy and the Transcendentals: The Case of Thomas Aquinas*. For a more general introduction to the problem of transcendentals, see Wouter Goris and Jan Aertsen, "Medieval Theories of Transcendentals," *The Stanford Encyclopedia of Philosophy* (Fall 2019 Edition), Edward N. Zalta (ed.), https://plato.stanford.edu/archives/fall2019/entries/transcendentals-medieval/.

to get tripped up by these verbal differences, so that we can grasp the core philosophical points.

To say that something is a being, an *ens*, is to say that it exists, that it has actual existence. *Ens*, being, is a Latin present participle, like "running" or "jumping," but it's a present participle used as a noun, so it means, roughly, a thing that is existing or be-ing. If something that runs is a running thing, a runner, then something that exists is an existing thing, an exister or be-er.

When Aquinas says that everything is a *res*, a "thing," he means to get across the idea that everything has an essence. This is considerably more specific than the way we've been using "thing" language in this book up until now. The important point, however, is not the English word "thing" or the Latin word *res*, but instead Aquinas's point that it's universally true that every being has an essence.

To say that something is *unum*, one, is to say that it is undivided, a whole, a unity. Even a being that has multiple parts must somehow hang together as a whole if it is to count as *a* being and not instead a group of beings.

Next comes *aliquid*, "something": every being is something. Taken out of context, it's far from obvious what that might mean in ordinary English, but Aquinas uses the Latin equivalent in the following way. He sees the Latin word *aliquid* as boiling down to *aliud quid*, "another what," and so he uses *aliquid* to get across the idea that every being is distinct from every other. And perhaps this even works in English to some extent: you wouldn't call Rusty "some thing" unless there were some *other* thing for him to be distinguished from.

Still another transcendental is *verum*, or true. This is, in a way, the oddest of all, at least verbally. It seems senseless to say that everything is true: surely the only things that have even a chance of being true are sentences or beliefs! What Aquinas means here is sometimes called "ontic" truth, the truth of being (Greek *on*). "Everything is true" means that everything is knowable or intelligible. Only thoughts, or sentences expressing thoughts, are true in the sense of accurately representing reality, but everything that exists can be understood and accurately represented, and that is what is meant by saying that everything "is true."

The last on our list is *bonum*, or good. The claim is that everything is good. This too is surprising, but in a different way. "Everything is true" sounded like something that didn't make sense at all. "Everything is good" sounds like something that makes perfectly good sense, but that is obviously false: surely tumors are not good! This is a very important issue, important enough that I will devote a separate section to it below.

As indicated, Aquinas sometimes gives shorter lists, and he has more than one way of explaining the lists that he gives. Here is one way to think about his long list, a way inspired by some of Aquinas's thoughts even if not corresponding too closely to any one of his presentations.

Think of the distinction between existence and essence. That distinction is brought out in the transcendentals *ens* and *res*: everything is existing, and everything has an essence. Nothing is non-actual, and nothing is devoid of all features, nor does anything have only accidental features.[22]

Next comes another pairing—namely, *unum* and *aliquid*. This reminds me of the clichéd slogan about identity discussed by David Lewis and others: "Everything is identical to itself; nothing is ever identical to anything else except itself."[23] To say that each thing is one is to say that it exists unto itself as a unified being, and to say that each thing is something rather than something else is to say that it is distinct from all others. You are you, and no one else.

Verum and *bonum* give us a final pairing: Everything that exists is true in the sense that it is knowable, and good in the sense that it is desirable (at least on some level—see next section). Everything is a potential target of both reason and will.

All six of these transcendentals are co-extensional. They all share the same extension, namely, everything. The class of beings is the same as the class of unified entities, the class of good entities, and so on. Nothing can have only some of these transcendentals. You have all of them, or you have none of them; and if you have none of them, then you simply don't exist at all. And yet they are different conceptually: to think of something *as existing* is different from thinking of it *as having an essence*, which is in turn different from thinking of it *as unified*, and so on. Each transcendental represents a distinct perspective on what it is to be.

That last point is worth expanding. Often one hears not just of "the transcendentals" but of "the transcendental properties of being." Putting it that way might seem a bit strange. If "being" is one of the tran-

---

22. Essence and existence were discussed in §3.5. The idea that everything has an essence came out in §3.3.2 and §3.3.3.

23. Lewis, *On the Plurality of Worlds*, 192.

scendentals, then how are the transcendentals transcendental properties *of being*? Is being a transcendental property of itself?! The answer is that each transcendental is a property of everything: we could, in a sense, speak of "the transcendental properties of the unities," or "the transcendental properties of the somethings," and so on. However, "being" is, in an important sense, the root concept. After all, without actual existence, there's nothing to talk about. So "being," which signifies actual existence, is the most basic of the transcendentals.

The transcendentals are the properties that belong to everything—to every being. Every being is actually existing, every being has an essence, every being is a unity, and so on. To say all this is, again, not to identify *kinds* to which every being belongs. "Actual being" is not a kind of being, as if there were also non-actual beings; "essence-having being" is not a kind of being, as if there were also beings without essences; and so on. Being is not a kind, but talking about things does not always require talking about kinds that they belong to, and therefore we can bring out what all beings have in common, over-and-above whatever kinds or categories they may belong to.

7.3.3 Goodness (and Beauty)

Above I mentioned the idea that goodness is a transcendental property of being: every being is good. This claim is startling enough to merit a section of its own. Perhaps instead of "startling," I should have said "flat-out implausible." Is it not obvious that some beings are bad? Think of tumors, or hurricanes, or a bird's broken wing.

The easiest way to see why someone would want to say that every being is good involves bringing in the topic of God. That topic will not properly arise until the next chapter, but I hope you will forgive this bit of disorderliness (remember the baseball problem!). Suppose you believe in God. It's pretty plausible that if you do, you also believe that God is good and that God is the creator of everything other than himself. Those are not, in fact, the only possible views about God, but just consider them for the sake of argument. If God is good, and God is the creator of everything, then there is a lot of pressure to say that everything is good. After all, how could a good God create something bad?

There's reason, therefore, to think that everything is good. But it's obvious that some things are bad. We need some sort of conceptual breakthrough. The solution proposed by St. Augustine (d. 430) is essentially this: Evil or badness—*malum* in Latin—is not a being, but instead a lack of a being. Think of a bird missing a leg. This is bad, but what's bad is not a thing. It's not as if "missing leg" is one of the bird's parts! No, what's bad about this situation is not that something bad is there, but that something good is not there. Something is missing. Evil is a lack, a lack of something that should be there. On this way of thinking, sentences like "evil exists," while certainly true, are systematically misleading. They give the impression that evil is a special kind of reality, when in fact it's a lack of ordinary reality.

Right away I should add some clarifications. The standard way of formulating this view is by saying "evil is a privation," but the word "evil" here is perhaps not ideal. It makes sense to say that cruelty is evil, but it sounds bizarre, and even just false, to say that missing a leg "is evil." The Latin word *malum*, in other words, covers more ground than the English word "evil." We use the word "evil" primarily for moral evil, evil embodied in free choices that are wrong. We would be far more likely to say that missing a leg "is bad."

Second, as mentioned above, evil or badness isn't just any lack, it's a lack of something that should be there. Humans don't have wings, but that's not bad; humans are not supposed to have wings. A bird's not having wings is bad, however, because birds are supposed to have wings.[24]

The third thing to say is that working out the theory that evil or badness is a privation is not always easy. The case of the bird missing a leg is pretty obvious, which is why I started there: the bird's missing leg is clearly not a being, but a lack of a being (that should be there). But what about a tumor? A tumor is definitely *there*. The right analysis depends, of course, on exactly what a tumor is, and the metaphysics of disease is a tricky matter. But when a tumor grows inside of an organism, it should *not* be there, and the way it grows is a way in which it *shouldn't* grow. It lacks the growth patterns and growth limits that the parts of living organisms of this type should have. It's either a part that's gone wrong, through lack of correct development, or it's not a part at all, but something in the wrong place. Either way, what makes it bad, what makes it *malum*, is not the way it is in itself, but the way in which it is *not* as it should be. So even in the case of something that is most

---

24. What's good or bad for something turns on what its essence is, and on the norms connected to that essence. See §1.5.

emphatically there, like a tumor, the badness of its being there is rooted in some lack—a lack of proper relationship or development, perhaps.

How bad can things get? How thoroughly can something fail to live up to what it ought to be? Can anything be entirely bad? If something *completely* failed to be what it should be, in every respect, then it would not exist at all. If it does exist at all, that's because it has, at least to some small extent, managed to be as it ought to be. This might not amount to much—maybe the poor bird has no legs, no wings, and no feathers—but it's still something. It still exists as it should, to some degree. Everything that exists has at least some goodness.

It's worth pausing over the fact that goodness comes in degrees. Doing so will help us grasp better the connection between goodness and being. If something's development has been thwarted or damaged, then this is bad. But to say that something's development has been thwarted or damaged is to say that its *being* has been thwarted or damaged, and that its *becoming* has been thwarted or damaged. When there's badness, that's because something exists other than as it ought to, and less fully than it ought to: its being has been imperfectly actualized. So while nothing can exist if it is completely unactualized—it wouldn't be actual at all!—something can certainly exist while being incompletely actualized. Alas, this happens all the time.

These thoughts about goodness and being even apply to morality. That is part of what it means to speak of "natural law" morality, morality as rooted in human nature. Human actions are beings—accidental beings in the category of "action." They can exist as they ought to, or they can fall short of this. When they fall short, they are bad actions—sometimes slightly bad, sometimes horrible. But they still have *some* goodness in them inasmuch as they exist at all. Of course, what goodness they have can be ruined by incompleteness and misdirection. It's bad, very bad, to shoot an innocent person, but there can be goodness in the marksmanship. It might have been, as we say, "a good shot," even though it should never have happened.

To say that everything is good, then, is not to hold the absurd view that everything is awesome. It's to say that everything is good to the extent that it is fully actualized. It's tempting to say, "to the extent that it is actualized *as it ought to be*," and that would not be wrong, but it might be misleading. It might give the impression that incorrect actualization is a special kind of actualization. Incorrect actualization is not a species of actualization, it is a failure of actualization. If everything were fully developed, everything would be fully good. The fact that many things are bad proves not that some counterforce has entered the world, as if anti-being were at war with being, but only that being has failed to develop as fully as it ought to.

Of course, there are deep questions about *why* being fails to come to fruition. Inquiry quickly runs in a theological direction here. Christians talk about evil coming into the world through the Fall, the first sin of Adam and Eve, but why did they fall? How did their tempter fall before them? And how does God fit in? The theory that evil is a lack saves us from saying that God created evils, that he created bad things, but it doesn't explain why God allows things to be thwarted or damaged. I'm not going to explore these questions here. Suffice it to say that while the origin of evil or badness is mysterious, its nature can be understood in metaphysics as a lack, a lack of being that should be there.[25]

I would like to close out this section with a brief remark about beauty. Aquinas holds that beauty is what pleases in being perceived: Merely *hearing* a Beethoven piano sonata is pleasing. He articulates certain aspects of what makes something beautiful—integrity, or completeness; proportion; and clarity, or brightness. It is not entirely clear what all of these are supposed to mean. Aquinas gives us no extended discussions of beauty. What is important for present purposes is the question of whether beauty is a transcendental property of being.

If it is, then presumably it is similar to goodness at least in the following way: just as we say not that everything is perfectly good, but only that it is at least somewhat good, and would be fully good if its being were fully actualized, so too the point would be not that everything is stunningly beautiful, but rather that it is at least somewhat beautiful, and would be fully beautiful if its being were fully actualized.

Aquinas never includes beauty on a list of transcendentals, but a number of Thomists have tried to argue that Thomistic principles lead to this conclusion. Others have argued that this is not the case.[26] I will not pursue the question here.

---

25. For a detailed recent discussion of this classical account of good and evil, see David Oderberg, *The Metaphysics of Good and Evil* (London: Routledge, 2020).

26. For Aertsen, beauty is important in Aquinas's thought, but it is not sufficiently distinct from the good and the true to count as a transcendental in its own right; see

7.4 Final Remarks on Categories and Transcendentals

We have been talking about what can and can't be said about everything. When talking about something depends on putting it into a category, nothing can be said about everything, because there is not a category that everything belongs to (again: being is not a genus). But there is a different way to talk about things: Instead of putting things into categories, we can unpack various aspects of what it means for something to be at all. We can discuss, from different perspectives, what it is for something to exist as an actual being; in that sense, we can talk about everything, by talking about the transcendentals.

What was just said depended on the Thomistic idea, discussed at some length in §7.2.2, that reality involves diversity on a very radical level. But Aquinas believes that what exists involves even more diversity than we have considered so far. No matter how different any ordinary being is from any other ordinary being, there is something more different than that. That maximally different being is God, the topic of our next chapter.

▹ To get started on reading Aquinas himself on why being is not a genus, begin with *On the Principles of Nature*, chapter six.

▹ To get started on reading Aquinas himself on the tenfold schema of categories, see his commentary on Aristotle's *Metaphysics* V, lecture 9 and his commentary on Aristotle's *Physics* III, lecture 5.

▹ To get started on reading Aquinas himself on the transcendentals, begin with *Disputed Questions on Truth*, q. 1, art. 1.

Aertsen, *Medieval Philosophy and the Transcendentals*, 335–59. For a somewhat different perspective, set in a much larger discussion of Aquinas on beauty overall, see Christopher Scott Sevier, *Aquinas on Beauty* (Lanham, MD: Lexington Books, 2015).

CHAPTER 8

To the Edge of Metaphysics . . . and Beyond!

8.1 God and Metaphysics

PERHAPS IT'S NOT TOO SURPRISING for God to come up in a book about metaphysics. If metaphysics is about wisdom, if it is the science of first principles, then the metaphysician can hardly avoid the question of God. After all, if there is a God, then God will somehow be the most important or basic entity that there is.

On the other hand, as we will see later in this chapter, God is *very* different from anything else. That's enough to make us wonder whether God is really part of what metaphysics studies. Some philosophers, including Thomas Aquinas, hold that being *qua* being is the subject matter of metaphysics, but also that God isn't part of being *qua* being, but instead different from it and outside of it. From that point of view, although God is very important to metaphysics inasmuch as he is the source of being *qua* being, still, he's not part of metaphysics in a direct way. Metaphysics cares about God not because he's *part* of the subject matter, but because he's the *source* of the subject matter.[1] To be sure, not all philosophers agree with this. Some think that God actually is part of being *qua* being. One way or the other, metaphysics will want to talk about God.

Our discussion in this chapter will be limited in two ways. First, we will discuss only topics that are relevant for metaphysical inquiry. Theorizing about God that helps us understand modal metaphysics, or other things in metaphysics, will be included in this chapter; but theorizing about God that considers God for ethical topics, or just for the

---

1. For discussion of this difficult issue, see Wippel, *Metaphysical Thought*, 11–22.

sake of thinking about God in himself, will not be very important here. Our discussion, then, will address only a small part of what belongs to the overall philosophy of God. We will limit ourselves to what's relevant to an introduction to metaphysics.

Second, we will be discussing God only insofar as he can be considered philosophically—that is, by using philosophical reasoning alone without reliance on supernatural revelation (from the Bible and the Church, or whatever). If there is no such thing as supernatural revelation, then obviously philosophical knowledge about God will be the only kind available. If, however, there is such a thing as supernatural revelation, we will not be relying on it in this chapter. And yet, that might seem like a strange thing to do. If you have a car, why walk? If you believe in divine revelation, why pursue knowledge of God without resorting to it?

One reason is that doing so creates a basis for talking about God to people who don't believe in divine revelation. Another is simply that God has given us the natural power of reason, and it is good to exercise our powers within their own domains. Still another reason is this. The Bible needs interpretation, and correct interpretation requires a lot of intelligence, including philosophical intelligence. To get the most out of what's in the Bible, it can help to do some extra-biblical thinking.

So much for methodological preliminaries. Let's talk about God, starting with the question of whether there even is one in the first place.

8.2 Arguments for God's Existence

God's existence is a big, big topic. There are different arguments for God's existence, and different types of argument. Some arguments stand (or fall) on their own, but others rely on background philosophical ideas about, for example, causation. And, in a way that I'll explain in §8.4, the arguments don't all prove the same thing, or if they do, it's not obvious that they do.

One big divide between types of argument for God's existence goes like this. One type of argument starts from the concept or definition of God and then tries to show that a being fitting that definition must exist. Another type of argument starts from familiar facts about the world and then tries to show that these facts can't be true unless something else is true as well—namely, that God exists.

The first type of argument is sometimes called "ontological," even though that's hardly a good name for it. The most famous version is the one found in a short work called *Proslogion* by the medieval monk Anselm (d. 1109). It starts by saying that God is that being than which no greater being can be conceived. A lot of smart people have worked hard to figure out whether this argument works. It has an amazing way of being simultaneously attractive and implausible. It has been proposed and re-proposed, in varying versions, by a number of authors, including Alvin Plantinga. But we're not going to talk about it here.

Instead, we're going to talk about the other type of argument. Speaking very generally, what arguments of this type have in common is the following. They start from some familiar fact about the world—for instance, that things change. Then, they say that careful analysis of this familiar fact reveals that if *all* facts were like that familiar fact, then that familiar fact couldn't actually be true. The familiar fact can be true only if there's some other fact, very different from the familiar one. And that unfamiliar fact is the existence of some being that, in some sense, has a title to being called "God."

Stated so generally and so abstractly, it's not easy to see what this means. To flesh it out, I will give a rough sketch of two arguments that run along these lines. These rough sketches are *very* rough. If they seem unconvincing, that's fine, because as they stand, they don't have anything like enough detail to be convincing. My purpose is simply to provide some insight into how the arguments are structured. Each begins from a familiar and hard-to-deny fact, and then proceeds by non-obvious reasoning to the conclusion that God exists.

The first is based on Aquinas's "First Way" and Aristotle's argument in the *Physics*.[2] The sketch goes like this:

(1a) Things get changed.
(1b) If something gets changed, it has to get changed by something other than itself.
(1c) So let's say that A gets changed, and it gets changed by B. Does B get changed? If yes, then let's say it gets changed by C. Can this go on forever? No.

[2]. In *Summa Theologiae* I, q. 2, art. 3, Aquinas offers five arguments for the existence of God, which have come to be known as "the Five Ways." For Aristotle, see *Physics* VIII.

(1d) Since it can't go on forever, at some point you must reach something—let's call it Z—that causes other things to change without getting changed itself. It's an unchanged changer—an unchanged source of change. Or, to use more traditional philosophical vocabulary, it's an "unmoved mover." ("Motion," in technical Aristotlespeak, is basically change.)

(1e) Something like that—an unchanged changer—can legitimately be called "God."

The first step of the argument is an obvious and familiar fact. But some of the subsequent steps involve non-obvious claims. Step (1b) says that things can't change themselves, but why believe that? Step (1c) says that a series of changed changers cannot go on forever, but why believe that? A fully-developed version of the argument would have to address such questions.

Now let us turn to another argument sketch. This one is a bit like Aquinas's "Third Way."

(2a) Some things are contingent—it's possible for them to exist, and it's possible for them not to exist.

(2b) But not everything can be like that.

(2c) Therefore, there must be something that is not contingent but necessary: something that cannot not exist, that *must* exist and that explains why the contingent things exist rather than not.

(2d) Something like that—a necessarily-existing explainer of contingent existents—can legitimately be called "God."

Again, the starting point is something familiar and obvious, but later claims are not obvious: (2b), the claim that not every being can be contingent, clearly needs support.

To repeat, these are not really the arguments, but just their bare skeletons; indeed, skeletons that lack important bones. I've tried to indicate some of the points that need support. I have left out some details so that the common structure will stand out more visibly. Each argument starts with something fairly non-controversial that has nothing to do with God: things get changed, or things are contingent. Then each argument says that not everything can be like that: it can't be that everything gets changed, or that everything is contingent. Then it says: therefore, there must be something that is very different from these everyday things: something unchanged, something necessary. Or, more precisely: there must be something that is not only very different from these everyday things, but that is also somehow *responsible for* these everyday things. There must be not just something unchanged or unmoved, but an unchanged source of change or an unmoved source of motion; not just something necessary, but a necessary source of contingency. The everyday things lack something, and for this reason, they are not self-sufficient. They need something other than themselves, something that is self-sufficient. Everyday things have sources, and those sources may themselves have sources, but ultimately there must be an unsourced source.

Here's a comparison of sorts. Suppose you are looking at a moon. It's shining because light is shining on it. Suppose further that the light shining on it is coming from some other moon (pretend you are on a planet with more than one moon, like Mars or Jupiter). The moon you are looking at is a shined-on shiner, and so is the second moon. But at some point, there has to be an unshined-on shiner: in other words, a sun.

8.3 Why Sourced Beings Can't Be The Whole Story

The arguments we have been looking at can be thought of as sourcing arguments. Things in the world around us have sources in other things: they receive their motion from other things, or they receive their existence from other things, or whatever. The sources they depend on may themselves have sources. But all sourced things ultimately require an unsourced source.

A series of sourcing relations is something like a chain—a sourcing chain or a supply chain. A receives from B, and B receives from C, and C receives from D, and so on. Coming at it the other way, B gives to A, but C gives to B, and D gives to C, and so on. It's like a chain because one thing is connected to another.

It's worth asking how long a sourcing chain can be. Building on a point made earlier, there are Aristotelian reasons for saying that a chain's length is "potentially infinite, but not actually infinite."[3] "Potentially infinite" doesn't mean that it has the potentiality to become infinitely long. It means, rather, that there is no limit to how long it can

---

3. See §6.2.

be. You can always add another link.[4] But no matter how many you add, the number of links you have will be finite: 1 followed by a trillion zeros is still a finite number.

Interestingly, it turns out not to matter how many links there are. Let's think more about links and chains—and for now I mean literal chains made of literal links of literal metal. Given what a link is, a link can't move itself: it needs to be moved by something else. The something else can be another link, but only if that link is itself moved by something else. If that something else is a third link, then the same issue will arise. It should be easy enough to see that you can't explain the motion of the chain by increasing the number of links, even if you increase it to infinity. Even if Aristotle is wrong, then, and you can literally have an infinite number of links in the chain, that still won't get you any motion. You'll just have an infinitely long chain that's going nowhere. You need something other than a link; more to the point, you need something that does not itself need to be moved by something else.

What holds for literal chains in physics holds, analogously, for sourcing chains in metaphysics. The sourcing might involve change, as in the first argument sketch. It might involve coming-into-existence, as in the second argument sketch. But however we flesh out the notion of sourcing, not every source can be a sourced source. That would be like saying that a chain can move itself. Sourced sources are in debt, and these debts cannot be paid off unless someone has cash money. We need an unsourced source.

An unsourced source of sourced things will not be an ordinary source. It will not belong to the world where things are changing, or receiving, or passing from potentiality to actuality. It will not receive from anything. It will be without ever having been brought into being; it will be actual without ever having been actualized.[5]

It might be objected that while we do need unsourced sources, that doesn't lead to God. Maybe animals, for instance, can serve as

---

4. For physical reasons, it's not always quite that simple: if the sourcing chain is literally a physical chain, then there will be a limit, because that sort of chain, once it becomes long enough, will be so heavy that pulling on it would break the links. But in the cases we are considering when talking about God, that sort of issue won't arise.

5. I want to repeat that I'm just giving sketches of arguments, not complete arguments. For one recent book that goes into a few arguments in a lot of detail, see Edward Feser, *Five Proofs of the Existence of God* (San Francisco: Ignatius Press, 2017).

unsourced sources—in particular, as unmoved movers. Doesn't Mickey just get up and go? Well, neither Aristotle nor Aquinas would accept that. First, humans or other animals don't act unless they are motivated—*moved*—to act. Each time we move, something has moved us to act. Animals, even human animals, are moved movers.[6] What's more, there is the following more general point. Ordinary things act according to their natures, but they did not give themselves those natures. They received their natures from their causes. Mickey, for example, is a cat because his parents made him that way, and his parents were cats because their parents made them that way. Mickey's overall character as a moving thing, then, is traceable outside himself to his causes or sources. For this reason, then, animals cannot be appealed to as unmoved movers or unsourced sources.

In this section I have tried to explain in more detail something that got presented quite briefly in the preceding section: how the fact that beings have sources requires that there be an unsourced source. Whether or not there can really be an infinite chain of sourced beings, there needs to be something utterly different from all of those sourced beings. As will become apparent in the next section, its difference turns out to make all the difference.

8.4 From Small Conclusions to the Start of Something Big

A sourcing argument, if successful, proves that there is an unsourced source of sourced things. Strictly speaking, that is all it proves. For Aquinas, that's enough to count as a proof of the divine; he concludes each of his Five Ways by saying something like "and everyone calls this God." But you might accept a sourcing argument while thinking that the conclusion isn't really that God exists, on the grounds that being an unsourced source isn't enough for something to deserve being called "God." In what follows, I will, for the sake of convenience, use the

---

6. Focusing now just on humans: If we are moved movers, does that mean we have no free will? It doesn't, because what moves us moves us to act *in accordance with reason*, on the basis of our belief about what we should do. And that means acting freely. A rational moved mover is a free moved mover. (You are right if you suspect this makes the issue of free will sound simpler than it is; see my "Intellect and Will: Free Will and Free Choice," in *The New Cambridge Companion to Aquinas*, ed. Eleonore Stump and Thomas Joseph White (Cambridge: Cambridge University Press, 2022), 211–30.)

word "God" to mean the unsourced source of other things, but it's absolutely correct to say that what's been proved so far is quite minimal. For all that's been shown so far, an unsourced source might lack a mind. It might not be omnipotent, but merely very powerful. Even if what the argument has proved is truly the existence of a god, it might not be a very impressive god.[7]

Furthermore, just because we have proved that there is a God, in the sense of an unsourced source, that doesn't mean that we have proved that there's only one. Perhaps there are quite a few such entities; perhaps there are multiple gods.

The question of multiple gods arises in another way as well. Suppose we have figured out a way to show not merely that there is an unsourced source, but also that there is only one. But suppose further that other arguments for God work as well. If those other arguments for God work, are they different ways of proving the existence of the same unsourced source, or do they prove the existence of some other unsourced source? The proofs, as they stand, simply don't address this issue.

These are just a few examples of a much more general point. Proofs of the sort we have been examining (assuming they succeed) are definitely an accomplishment, but they have serious limits: they leave open whether the being whose existence was proved has many of the traditional properties associated with God. They leave open whether this being has knowledge, whether this being loves us, and even whether this being is the only one of its kind.

It turns out, however, that even though these arguments do not, in and of themselves, establish a robust picture of God, they contain the seeds for such a picture. That's because knowing that something is an unsourced source allows us to derive certain further truths about it, among them its perfection and uniqueness. And that will, in turn, enable us to learn some things about its role in metaphysics.

Earlier, I said that our discussion of God will restrict itself to material that is relevant to metaphysics, but even that is too much for just one chapter. Topics about God that are relevant to metaphysics are so numerous and difficult that we can't get into them all. What you will be getting is a selective look at what God is and how he serves as the source of the basic and non-basic beings that metaphysics studies.

---

7. See David Hume, *An Enquiry into Human Understanding*, sect. 11.

8.5 God's Essence and Existence

Let's think back to a topic that we explored in §3.5: essence and existence. There we said that existence and essence are distinct "parts" of substances: essences do not automatically bring actual existence with them, and so existence is something over-and-above, and added to, essence. But does that apply to God? Are essence and existence distinct in God as well?

Here is an argument in favor of the view that, in the first being, God, essence and existence are not different, but entirely the same.[8]

If a being A contains anything other than its essence, that extra something has to be caused either externally (by something that lies outside of A altogether) or else internally (by something that lies inside of A). Let's consider these two options as applied to the case when A is God and the something extra is existence.

God's existence can't be caused by something that lies wholly outside of God, because God is uncaused; if the existence of what we call "God" was caused by something from outside, then what we call "God" wouldn't be God.

The alternative is for God's existence to be caused by something inside of God. The only reasonable candidate here, it seems, would be God's essence. But there are at least two reasons to deny that God's existence is caused by his essence. First, if God's existence were caused by his essence, then the "God" whose existence was thus caused would be a caused being; it would be downstream from, and secondary to, the divine essence. But then this "God" wouldn't be God at all; instead, the divine essence would be the real God, the real uncaused or unsourced being. Second, it doesn't even seem to make sense to talk about God's essence causing God's existence. An essence can't "do" anything unless it is actual, but if God's essence is actual, then God already exists, in which case there could be no question of causing him to exist.[9]

---

8. The argument is based on, but not exactly the same as, the argument given by Aquinas in *Summa Theologiae* I, q. 3, art. 4.

9. If God's existence isn't caused by the divine essence, could it be caused by divine accidents? No. As we saw in §1.1 and §3.3.3, accidents depend on substances. If divine accidents exist, therefore, they depend on God; but then they can't cause him, because nothing can cause what it depends on. In any event, as I will mention later in this section, God doesn't have accidents at all.

If there are only two ways for God's existence to be different from God's essence (by being caused internally or by being caused externally), and if neither of those ways makes any sense, then God's existence is not different from his essence. Instead, God's existence and God's essence are the same thing as each other. We talk and think about them as if they were different—they are conceptually distinct—but really, in reality, they are the same.[10] His essence is his existence. His essence is not to be this sort of thing, or that sort of thing, but simply: to be.[11]

Now there are two ways to think about the claim that God's essence is identical to his existence. One way is to think of existence minimally. On this way of thinking, to exist is to just barely be there at all, and anything that's even a tiny bit interesting must have not just existence, but more: life, rationality, or whatever, with all of those understood as accidents.

The other way to think of existence is to think of it maximally, as unlimited in itself. Essences don't add to existence, they delimit and restrict it. To be a cat, for example, is indeed to be mammalian and meowing, but it's also *not* to be a rock or an angel or a fish. To have an essence is to be of a certain sort *in contrast with* being of any other sort. Essences are how we define things, and anything that is defined, or definite, is defined or definite precisely in virtue of having a limit.[12] On this way of thinking, then, to say that God's essence is existence is not to say that God is just barely there, but on the contrary to say that God has unlimited existence. Obviously, this is the better way to go.

---

10. Aquinas's denial of any distinction between God's essence and existence is part of a larger teaching of Aquinas's—namely, that God is *simple*—meaning that God is non-complex, without parts or constituents. In God there is no multiplicity of physical parts, no distinction between form and matter, no distinction between act and potency, no distinction between essence and accident, and so on. This is a difficult and important idea, but not one that we can explore here. See *Summa Theologiae* I, q. 3.

11. Thomists have sometimes pointed with delight to *Exodus* 3:14: "God said to Moses, 'I AM WHO I AM.' And he said, "Say this to the people of Israel: 'I AM has sent me to you'." All Scripture quotations taken from the English Standard Version (ESV).

12. The word "definition" comes from *finis*, a Latin word for limit. By the way, can you see how this is related to material in §7.2.2?

8.6 God's Perfection

Once we have the idea of God's unlimited existence in hand, we are in a good position to see that God is perfect. That this is so should not simply be assumed or taken for granted. In ancient Greek myths, the gods were often to be found fighting, committing adultery, tricking one another. Such "gods" are fun to read about, but hardly perfect in any sense you or I would recognize.

That's not the only point. Even if it is somehow obvious that God is perfect, it is not obvious what perfection means. "Perfect" comes from a Latin word meaning "thoroughly made" and, by extension, "complete." Something is perfect if it is complete, if it "has it all." But an important distinction needs to be made.

In one way, "perfect" means having everything that is required for your kind. Think of bowling. If you roll twelve strikes in a row, the game is over. You have scored 300 points, a "perfect game." Not even God could get a higher score. If you get that score, you have completely maxed out the potentialities in bowling. This is fullness, perfection, for the kind of game that bowling is.

If you were to bowl a perfect game, that would be fantastic. But think of all the other things you would not have accomplished in the course of doing so. You would not have hit any home runs or stolen any bases. You would not have proven any mathematical theorems. You would not have changed any diapers. Even if you changed a diaper while the game was in progress, you would not have done so as part of rolling the perfect game. So, while a perfect game is a game that has everything, the word "everything" here really means *everything that bowling has to offer*. It doesn't mean *everything there could possibly be*. Something that had everything there could possibly be would be perfect in a stronger and deeper sense.

What this means is that there are two senses of "perfect." One is this: having everything good that belongs to your nature. In this sense, a perfect dog has four legs, a tail, a good sense of smell, and so on; a perfect book has a sound binding, all its pages, and so on; a perfect game in bowling has 300 points. But the other sense is this: having every possible goodness, period. Aquinas calls this "universal perfection."

With this distinction in hand, we can say not merely that God is perfect, but that he is universally perfect. The argument relies on something we saw in the previous section—namely, that God's essence and existence are identical. To be God is to be—not in the sense of just barely being there, but in the sense of having unlimited existence. God has every possible form of being and goodness, to the maximum possible extent. And that is precisely what universal perfection is.

8.7 God's Uniqueness

Once we have established that a divine being is universally perfect, we can explain quite quickly why there can be only one divine being. In any situation in which we have two things that really are distinct from each other, it must be that one of them has something that the other lacks. But a divine being lacks nothing; this follows from universal perfection. Therefore, there cannot be two of them: if there were, then there would be beings that lacked something while also lacking nothing, and that's a contradiction.

8.8 God's Perfections and How Creatures Participate in Them

God is universally perfect, meaning that he has every possible kind of perfection. If he has every possible kind of perfection, then he has every perfection that creatures can have.[13] That's what makes it possible for him to create things with those perfections. He gives what he himself has. There is an important objection to this claim, however, and replying to it will lead us to make a refinement. Think of Mickey. Mickey has a tail, and indeed it belongs to the perfection of a cat that it have one. If having a tail is a perfection, and if God has all perfections, does that mean that God has a tail? Presumably the answer is "no," but then what has happened to the idea that God has all perfections?

The way forward is to realize that there's a difference between how perfections exist in God and how they exist in creatures. God has all modes of being, but he has them in a superior or "eminent" way.

Let me try to explain this using the example of God's knowledge. When we say that God knows all things, we don't mean that he knows things in the same way we do, except that he knows all of them. It's not

---

13. In philosophy, a *creature* is not something scary from a black lagoon, but instead anything that's been *created*.

as if God's knowledge consists in the fact that if you ask him questions, he can recall the answers, and that what makes him special is that he can do this instantly, and for all possible questions. Rather, God has knowledge of all things all at once, in one simple gaze. He has, you might say, one big thought, a thought that contains all truths in one big conception.

When we say that God has a certain perfection, then, we need to think of that perfection as existing in him in a higher way. One might well wonder how this could apply to a perfection like having a tail. It cannot apply in any straightforward way, of course. Perhaps the following is on the right track: whatever makes tails good for cats, God has *that*, and he has it to the maximal degree. Maybe tails are there to help you balance, and balance is part of being an effective agent. Well, although God doesn't literally have a tail, he is an effective agent, and indeed a maximally effective agent. (This is what you would expect of the unsourced source of all things.) Literally having a tail is a perfection for a cat because it contributes to the cat's resembling, in a secondary and imperfect way, the perfect effectiveness of God.

The relationship between God's infinite way of possessing perfections and creatures' finite way of possessing them can be viewed differently—namely, from the side of the creatures. Each thing that exists imitates God's infinite and universally perfect reality. Further, each thing that exists receives its reality from God as the ultimate source. But this imitative reception always involves the creature's falling short of the source it receives from and imitates.

One way to put this is to say that creatures have *partial* versions of what God has. They take their features from him, but they take them only partially—they take part in, or "participate in," what he has *not* by participation but essentially and maximally.

God is the source of everything else: he is upstream from everything else, and everything else is downstream from him. He is what explains everything else, and nothing explains him. He is responsible for everything else being the way it is, and nothing is responsible for him being the way he is. Nothing is before him, or prior to him, in any way, which means (among other things) that he does not fit into any larger context or find his place in any larger setting. He could have been the only thing that ever existed, and the only reason that's not the case is that he freely chose for other things to exist. Everything depends on

God in a completely radical way, and he is extremely different from everything other than himself.[14]

God is so very different from everything else that he doesn't belong to the categories. If you had to choose, of course, you would assign him to the category of substance, but really you shouldn't choose. He exists beyond all categories. Categories are for creatures.[15]

Looking at this from the side of creation, every creature is downstream from God, receptive rather than an unsourced source, explained rather than an unexplained explainer, and posterior rather than prior, in every possible way. Creatures exist, and exist as they exist, only because God grants this to them, and what he grants is inevitably only a participated version of what he himself already is. Creatures are like God, then, but only partially, and the difference is always greater than the similarity.

Traditionally, these points have been discussed under the heading of the *triplex via*, the "threefold road" or "threefold way."[16] The three ways are these: causation, negation, and eminence. First, by considering things that God has caused, we infer that he must in some way have the features or perfections found in those things. For example, if God has caused elephants, then, since elephants are powerful, God must in some way be powerful. Second, we deny or negate all imperfection in the content that we attribute to God. For example, power in created things involves overcoming obstacles. But nothing can be an obstacle for God, who is the source of everything other than himself, including those very things that one might have thought of as being obstacles to him. For

---

14. For discussion of how God is not part of the world, but instead outside the world, and of how that paradoxically makes it possible for God to be radically close to creatures, see Robert Sokolowski, *The God of Faith and Reason: Foundations of Christian Theology* (Washington, DC: The Catholic University of America Press, 1995).

15. Categories were discussed in §7.2.

16. The classic presentation of the *triplex via* is in works from the fifth or sixth century AD by an author known as Pseudo-Dionysius the Areopagite.

What kind of a name is that? Here's the story. A Syrian Christian author who died in the early sixth century wrote a number of works and put down, as their author, Dionysius the Areopagite, a pagan converted by St. Paul (see Acts 17). Whether he did this for literary purposes, or to dishonestly acquire more influence than he would have had otherwise, is not entirely clear, but anyway his works were indeed very influential. It's long been suspected that these works weren't truly written by St. Paul's Dionysius, and nowadays it's standard to refer to their author not as "Dionysius" but as "Pseudo-Dionysius."

this reason, we should exclude the notion of overcoming opposition from our understanding of divine power. Third, we include, as best we can, a higher or eminent mode in the perfections we attribute to him.

We can now revisit points discussed earlier. In §5.6, I acknowledged that even readers sympathetic to moderate nominalism might feel that universals—instantiables, kinds—are somehow *there*, above and beyond their individual instances. Well, maybe we can think of "universals" as really being something like possible ways to imitate the infinite being of God. When we are tempted to say that the universal Felinity exists above and beyond Mickey and Rusty, and is shared in by them, maybe we should say instead that God exists, in his infinite perfection, and that Mickey and Rusty imitate his perfection in a certain particular and limited way, the way that we call "feline."

Of course, it is not merely that God can be imitated in many ways. It's also that he *knows* all of those ways; and that he knows them precisely as ways in which creatures can exist as imitations of himself; and finally, that he is the agent who knowingly brings it about that such imitations actually exist. This has led philosophers to talk about "divine ideas," God's conceptions of how he can be, and is, imitated.[17]

Now let us revisit a thought from §§6.3–6.4—namely, that possibility can be grounded in the powers of agents, and even in the power of an omnipotent agent. Talking about possible worlds is talking about ways that all things might be. But instead of thinking of possible worlds as entities somehow existing on their own, we can say that talk about possible worlds is best interpreted as talk about how God could have chosen to exercise his creative power. And the question of creaturely imitation of the divine is still entirely relevant: talk of how God could have exercised his creative power lines up with talk of how God can be imitated, this time not by just one entity but by the entire totality of creatures.

A last word about possible worlds and God. To say that a possible world is a total way that *everything* might be seems to imply that even God exists in possible worlds—in all of them, of course, because God

---

17. For a good general account of Aquinas's approach, see Gregory Doolan, *Aquinas on the Divine Ideas as Exemplar Causes* (Washington, DC: The Catholic University of America Press, 2014); for something provocative, see James Ross, "Aquinas's Exemplarism; Aquinas's Voluntarism," *American Catholic Philosophical Quarterly* 64, no. 2 (1990): 171–98.

exists necessarily. However, there is something not quite right about this. Thinking of God as part of the possible worlds can suggest that they—the possible worlds—are somehow prior to God. It can suggest that the possible worlds are the most basic element of reality, with God being one of the lucky beings that finds its place in each of them.[18] This is another reason for thinking of possible worlds talk as metaphorical, or of reducing it to language about what God can do.[19]

Let's also revisit a point made in §7.2. There we saw that reality is diverse from bottom to top, with the result that whatever holds reality together is not commonality of kind. Now we are in a position to see that what holds reality together, apart from the fact that all of it exists, and that all of it is either substance or related to substance, is that it all has a common source. All things other than God have it in common that they come from God. Whatever is, apart from God, is from God, and it imitates God in some way. That brings everything together.

8.9 God's Ubiquity

The next topic to deal with is God's "ubiquity," his being everywhere. A good English word for "being everywhere" is "omnipresent," but this word can create confusion in a Thomistic context, for the following reason. As we will see below, Aquinas distinguishes different ways in which God is everywhere, and one of them is God's being everywhere "by his presence." Given that, it can be confusing to use "omnipresent" to mean "everywhere" because then we would have to express Aquinas's view by saying that God is "omnipresent by his presence."

Anyway, let's stop worrying about the terminology and look at the idea that God is everywhere. It is familiar to speak like this, and yet its meaning is not obvious. If being everywhere means being in all the places that there are, then it's hard to see how God could be everywhere: being in a place requires being physical, and God is not physical.

---

18. This is related to the third Rossian worry about possible worlds mentioned in §6.3.

19. On the importance of divine transcendence, see again Sokolowski, *The God of Faith and Reason*. For discussion and some recent literature on the topic of God and necessary entities, see Matthew Davidson, "God and Other Necessary Beings," *The Stanford Encyclopedia of Philosophy* (Summer 2023 Edition), Edward N. Zalta & Uri Nodelman https://plato.stanford.edu/archives/sum2023/entries/god-necessary-being/.

God is not in any of the places—not, to be sure, because he doesn't exist, but because his mode of existence doesn't involve being here or there at all.

And yet, we do say that God is everywhere, and also that he is omnipresent. Why? One reason has to do with a funny fact about the word "presence." Sometimes that word has to do not with location, but with attention: if someone has gotten distracted, we might say that he is "absent," and someone who is like that habitually is said to be "absent-minded." Being "ushered into the king's presence" doesn't mean only that you are now near him, but also and perhaps primarily that he is paying attention to you. Using the language of presence with these overtones, the fact that God knows everything and is aware of everything can lead us to say that "everything is present to him" and that "everything is in his presence."

Another reason why we speak of God's being everywhere has to do with causation. "You can take the boy out of the country, but you can't take the country out of the boy." Why do people say that? Why is "the country" still always present in the boy, even when he's gone off to the big city? The answer is that "the country"—rural ways of living, or whatever this means exactly—had a big causal influence on him, an influence that stays with him, is present to him, everywhere he goes. In other words, God is present in all things not only in the sense that he knows them, but also in the sense that he has causal influence over them.

God plays a crucial role in metaphysics not only because all creatures are imitations of him, but also because he causes all creatures: they are partial and limited imitations of him because he creates them that way. And his causation is complete: he doesn't just create some creatures, nor does he create them only in certain ways or in certain respects. Everything that exists, other than God, exists because God has caused it to exist. In this causal way, God is in everything. He is everywhere.[20]

---

20. God's universal causation raises interesting and difficult questions. For example, if God is the cause of everything, does that mean that created things have nothing left to do, with the result that they have no causal powers of their own? Does it mean that humans have no free will because, apparently, it's God who causes their actions, not them? Does it mean that God is the creator of evil? The answer to all three of these questions is "no," but discussion of why is not included in this book. For a book that does explore such topics in a Thomistically-inspired way, see W. Matthews Grant, *Free Will and God's Universal Causality: The Dual Sources Account* (New York: Bloomsbury Academic, 2019).

8.10 Relations between God and the World

If God is the cause of all creatures, then there's a causal relation between God and creatures. But relations are accidents, and that gives rise to a problem, inasmuch as we said earlier that God has no accidents. If God is related to creatures, then it seems he has accidents; if he has no accidents, then it seems he is unrelated to creatures. Neither option seems right.

The solution is to recall that in certain special cases, one thing can have a relational accident pointing to another thing without that other thing having a relational accident pointing to it. If Luke is thinking of Rusty, Luke has a relational accident "thinking" that points him to Rusty, but Rusty has no relational accident "being thought about" that points back to Luke. Similarly, creatures have a relation of dependence that points them to God, but God does not have a relational accident of being-depended-on that points him to creatures. All the relational machinery is on the side of the creatures. They have an accident of dependence on God, but he doesn't have an accident of being depended on by them.

Thomists sometimes describe this situation by saying that creatures have relations to God, but God has no relations to creatures. This strikes me as a very bad way of putting things. It's almost as if you are going out of your way to make it seem as if God is cold, distant, and unconcerned. We should be happy to say that God is related to creatures! But what makes this true, its truth-maker, is something that exists in the creatures themselves.[21]

8.11 Talking and Thinking about God

As discussed in §8.8, God and creatures are both alike and unalike. Creatures have some of the same perfections that he has, but in an imperfect way. This raises important questions for how we talk about God and, relatedly, for how we think about God. What I wish to say about this will be based, to a significant extent, on what Aquinas says in *Summa Theologiae* I, q. 13. But I'll put things in my own way, and I'll add things he doesn't say.

---

21. For this general approach to relations, see §7.2.4. For the idea that dependence on God is an accident, see §3.5.

First, there's an important distinction between metaphorical language about God and literal language about God. Both are good, in their place, but they are different, and mixing them up can lead to a lot of trouble. In Isaiah 66:1, it says that the earth is God's footstool. Does this mean that God has feet, and that if we knew where to travel, we could go to the place where they can be seen, sticking down out of the sky? I hope it's clear that the answer is "no." This passage probably means that God is ruler of the earth; it's there to serve him, not the other way around. Or maybe it means something else, but surely it doesn't mean that God literally rests literal feet on the earth.[22]

It is worth asking how we know that the metaphorical interpretation is correct. In theory, one could interpret the passage about the footstool literally and say that the Bible teaches us that God has feet.

A partial answer is that in *other* places in the Bible, it's made pretty clear that God isn't physical. But also, and more relevant from a philosophical perspective, we can figure out by reasoning that there's just no way that the first being has feet or any other bodily parts. If God had bodily parts, then he would have various kinds of potentiality, and also, he would be moveable by other things, both of which are inconsistent with his being the uncaused cause and first being.

Is there danger in using philosophy to interpret divine revelation? Yes, there is. We might be imposing human concepts on revelation. On the other hand, you do have to think when you are attending to revelation. When Jesus says, "I am the good shepherd" and "My sheep know my voice," it would be unintelligible to respond by being disappointed that Jesus is interested in sheep, and not in us humans. Thinking is dangerous, but not thinking is even more dangerous. How to proceed is a complicated question, to be sure, but if you admit that much, then you are admitting that we have to start thinking.

How can the dividing line between literal and metaphorical speech be rigorously explained? The answer has to do with the idea of "pure perfections." Consider, as an example, the statement "God is a rock," and ask yourself whether something could be a rock while having all

---

22. But isn't Jesus God? And doesn't Jesus have feet? Yes, but that's something else. Here, we're just discussing things that hold true of God *qua* God (remember that word *qua*, from §0.3?). Jesus is divine and human both; he has feet, yes, but he has them *qua* human, not *qua* divine.

other perfections. The answer is no; nothing can be a rock and also be intelligent, for example. To be a rock is to have certain modes of being and not others. So being a rock is *a* perfection—a good and actualized way to be—but it's not a "pure perfection": it's not "pure" but instead "impure" because rockiness is bound up with certain lacks or imperfections (such as not being intelligent). Whatever has an impure perfection will necessarily fail to be universally perfect. Now contrast this with "God is powerful," which is a very different kind of statement. Being powerful is a pure perfection. It is not, in and of itself, bound up with imperfections. Something powerful could be universally perfect.

This difference is the key to understanding which predications about God are metaphorical and which are literal. Predications of impure perfections are metaphorical, and predications of pure perfections are literal. Being a rock is not a pure perfection, so when we say that God is a rock, we mean it metaphorically. But being powerful is a pure perfection, so when we say that God is powerful, we mean it literally.

Why does it matter whether we predicate something of God literally or metaphorically? In a nutshell, if a predication is literal, you can use it to infer something about God's nature, but if it's metaphorical, you can't. Take "God is powerful" as an example. This is a case of literal predication, and we can reason from it as follows: "whatever is powerful can do many things; God is powerful; therefore, God can do many things." That's perfectly fine. By contrast, think of "God is a rock," which is a case of metaphorical predication. We don't want to reason as follows: "God is a rock; rocks are either igneous, metamorphic, or sedimentary; therefore, God is either igneous, metamorphic, or sedimentary." Something has gone badly wrong here, and it's gone wrong from the very start. Since "rock" is predicated only metaphorically of God, we can't legitimately use "God is a rock" as the premise of an argument about what God is like. Metaphorical predication is fine in its place, but theological reasoning is not that place.

What is its place? Roughly, we humans are rational, but we are rational *animals*. Unlike the bodiless angels, it's our nature to approach things through sensation and imagination. Talk about God with no sensory or imaginative content would be incredibly hard for us to understand, and furthermore, let's face it, it would leave most of us emotionally cold. A judicious use of metaphorical language takes the extremely spiritual and rational truths about God's transcendent nature and adapts them to the human mind. In philosophy and theology, yes, we push against our limitations and attempt to understand God in a more purely intellectual way, but it's probably not possible for anyone to do this 24/7. There's more to life than philosophy and theology.

So much for the distinction between metaphorical and literal predication about God. From now on, we will talk only about literal predication, and we will distinguish three sorts: univocal, equivocal, and analogical predication. This distinction comes from Aristotle, and Aquinas and others make heavy use of it.[23]

The first thing to say about the trio of univocal, equivocal, and analogical is this: these terms apply only when we have at least two uses of a single word or concept.[24] If I just take a word and use it one time, there's no meaning to the question of whether I used it univocally, equivocally, or analogically. That question arises only when I use a word two or more times. Only then can you ask: were these two uses univocal, were they equivocal, or were they analogical?

Two uses of a word are univocal if the same word is used twice with the same sense. If you say that Socrates is human and also that Plato is human, then the word "human" is getting used univocally.

Two uses of a word are equivocal if the word is used twice with entirely different and unrelated meanings. "Bat" can mean a certain kind of winged mammal, or it can mean a thing used for hitting a baseball. These uses are completely unrelated. If you have ever heard someone accuse someone else of "equivocating," that's what we're talking about here: the accusation is that someone has switched from one meaning of a word to another.

Two uses of a word are analogous if the meanings are different but related. Here's a classic example from Aristotle. We can say that a dog is healthy, and we can also say that the dog's food is healthy, and we can say that the dog's urine is healthy. We don't mean "healthy" in the same exact way throughout. To say that the dog is healthy is, roughly, to say that the dog is in good physiological condition, but to say that the dog's food is healthy is not to say that the food is in good physio-

---

23. It was introduced earlier, in §1.7.

24. There's actually a tricky question about whether what's primary here is words, or concepts, or the realities that these words and concepts point to. I'm going to leave it aside, but if you find you keep wondering about it, well, that's good.

logical condition, and the same holds for the urine. The meanings are not the same, so it's not a case of univocity, but on the other hand, it's not a case of equivocity either. The meanings are clearly related. It's not like "bat" and "bat." We call a dog's food "healthy" when that food *promotes* health, the health of the dog. We call a dog's urine "healthy" when it's a *sign* of health, the health of the dog.

Analogous language is not metaphorical language. It's not a metaphor to say that the dog's food is healthy. The food is literally healthy, "healthy" in a different (but related) sense.

Now let's distinguish two sorts of analogy. First, there is the "analogy of many to one." The health of a dog's food and the health of a dog's urine are analogous in this way. That's because explaining how they are related to each other requires reference to some third thing: the health of the dog itself. The health of the food and the urine are the many, and the health of the dog is the one. The many are related to each other only through their relation to the one. That "one" is the primary meaning of healthy, and the "many" are secondary meanings.

When we come to the health of the food and the health of the dog, things are different. This is also a case of analogy, but here, there's no third thing that each of them is related to. "Healthy" as applied to food is secondary, and it makes no sense apart from its relation to "healthy" as applied to the dog. But "healthy" as applied to the dog is primary: it isn't related to anything beyond itself. This sort of case is called "analogy of one to another"—in this case, analogy of "healthy" as said of food to "healthy" as said of a dog.

Enough about dog food. Let's talk about God. We say things about God that are meant literally; for example, we say that God is powerful or intelligent or loving. But obviously we use these words for created things too. These words can be applied to ordinary humans. If the meanings were equivocal, it would follow that when we say these things about God, there would be no relation at all to what we mean when we say them about humans. And that is clearly not correct. When we say that God is intelligent and that humans are intelligent, the meanings are not wholly different.

If the meanings were univocal, on the other hand, it would follow that when we say these things about God, they would mean exactly the same thing as they mean when applied to humans. When saying that God is intelligent, we would mean that he thinks hard, generalizes from experience, reasons from one proposition to another, and so forth. But that doesn't sound right either; none of that should apply to a non-physical, unchanging, and altogether simple being.

What's left is analogy. When we say that God is intelligent, we mean something related to, but not exactly the same as, what we mean when we say that humans are intelligent. God understands the way things are, but on the other hand he does it in a way that is different from the way in which we do it. He doesn't start from ignorance, he doesn't move from topic to topic, and so on.

Speaking generally now: when we predicate anything of God, the content of what we predicate has to be stripped clean—purified—of any lack or imperfection. We must try to figure out the pure version of the pure perfection. And this pure version will be very different from the "impure" version that applies to us—very different, but not altogether different, or else it would be a case of equivocation.

All this should remind you of the *triplex via* of causation, negation, and eminence. But it's important not to get carried away with the negation idea. Aquinas rejects two approaches that go too far in removing content from predication about God. First, he rejects the view that all our statements about God are negative in the strong sense that we know only what God is not (for example, that he is not material). Beyond knowing what God isn't like, we also know what he is like. Second, Aquinas rejects the view that our statements about God tell us only what God's effects are. For Aquinas, we know not only that God is "the cause of rocks" or "the cause of angels" or whatever; we also know something about what he is like in himself. In short, we don't speak only negatively of God, but also *affirmatively*; and we don't speak only relationally of God, but also *absolutely*.

Perhaps you've noticed that when we talk about God, the analogy is one-to-another. For example, when we say that God is intelligent and also that Aristotle is intelligent, we aren't to suppose that there is some third thing, Intelligence, that God and Aristotle both share in, as if they were both instances of a shared universal. If there were, then God wouldn't be the first being. And this leads me to my final point. Just as "healthy" as applied to dogs is the primary sense of "healthy," while "healthy" as applied to food is a secondary sense, so too "intelligent" as applied to God is the primary sense, and "intelligent" as applied to humans (or angels, or Martians) is a secondary sense. The same applies to everything else we can predicate literally of God. What God has is the real deal, and what we have is an imitation of what he has, a participation in it. What we have is the caused copy; what he has is the uncaused original. This is part of what it means when we say that God has the perfections of all created things, but in a higher and maximally eminent way.

On the other hand, no one starts out with a concept of divine intelligence or power (or whatever) and then only later develops a notion of created intelligence or power (or whatever). We start out with a notion of how these things exist in creatures, and then, with much effort and strain, we try to develop a purified version that can apply to God. So, while God's version of everything is first in being—in existence and causality—it's last in our knowledge. What we know first is creatures, and later (if we're lucky) we know God. Thought travels from creature to creator, but causation and sourcing travel the other way.

An idea of Aristotle's is relevant here. He makes a distinction between what's more knowable to us and what's more knowable in itself. Think of a slightly iffy circle drawn on a blackboard. Now think of the equation that expresses a circle in a Cartesian coordinate system: $r^2 = x^2 + y^2$. The latter is highly intelligible—if you can understand it. The former has less intelligibility in itself, but it's pretty easy to understand.

Created things are better known to us; they are more familiar, and better adapted to our natural form of thought. The creator is less knowable to us; he's very, very, very hard to understand. On the other hand, the creator is more knowable in himself inasmuch as there's more to know, indeed infinitely more. So, we start with what's more knowable to us, and we move to what's more knowable in itself—to the first principle. Arriving at the first principle is the ultimate goal in the activity of asking and answering ultimate questions. Because God is infinite, we can't ever finish, at least not in this life. But we can start.

8.12 A Few Final Thoughts on God and Metaphysics

I would now like to sum up some of the main points that have been made, and to do so in a way that indicates how our philosophical reflections on God as the infinite source of finite being cohere well with biblical religion.

God contains every mode or kind of being that there can possibly be. He contains not just every kind that has been actualized in creation, but also those that never have been and never will be. "Though we could say more, we would never finish, and the sum of our words is: 'He is the all'" (Sir 43:27).

He contains all these kinds of being in their fullness, free of every imperfection, meaning that his version of them is higher and different from the versions that appear in creation. God is very, very different from creatures. One way you sometimes see the point expressed is this: creatures are like God, but each likeness is matched with a greater unlikeness. "For as the heavens are higher than the earth, so are my ways higher than your ways" (Is 55:9).

God is also the source of everything else, in every respect. Whatever exists is caused by God to exist, in every respect, both substantially and accidentally. "In wisdom have you made them all" (Ps 104:24).

Everything that God creates is an imperfect imitation of God's infinite perfection. Maybe, as noted before, people who believe in universals really ought to say this: universals are ways in which individual entities can imitate God. Somewhat similarly, bringing God into the picture can replace serious endorsement of possible worlds. If God exists, with the fullness of being already existing actually in himself and with the power to bring about all possible ways of imitating his being, then we can explain possibilities in terms of what God can do. "Possible worlds," ways that the entirety of things might be, can be understood as ways that the entirety of creatures can, by God's creative power, imitate God. Such ways are grounded not in strange entities (possible worlds taken seriously as things that somehow exist) but in God's own simple infinite reality and power.

To gather these threads together, we can say that God relates to metaphysics, the study of being, as the source of the being that metaphysics studies. He is the ultimate actuality in virtue of which everything else is possible and actual: the possibilities are "there" on account of his own being and power, and he is the one who causes those possibilities to be actualized. Here's St. Paul, quoting pagans in a speech to pagans: "'In him we live and move and have our being'; as even some of your own poets have said, 'For we are indeed his offspring'" (Acts 17:28).

I have included a few biblical quotations to give some sense of how revelation and metaphysics link up. This brings out the way in which revelation is rational, and the way in which philosophy gestures beyond itself. But, for the record, here philosophy gestures beyond itself to something it cannot entirely reach, and it does so without providing the resources for getting further. As Augustine says at the end of *Confessions* VII: "It is one thing to behold from a wooded mountain peak the land of peace, but to find no way to it, and to strive in vain towards it by unpassable ways, ambushed and beset by fugitives and deserters, under their leader, the lion and the dragon. It is a different thing to keep to the way that leads to that land, guarded by the protection of the heavenly commander . . ."[25]

▹ To get started on reading Aquinas himself on the ideas developed in this chapter, begin with *Compendium of Theology* I, chapters 1–35. More detailed are the accounts in *Summa Contra Gentiles* I and *Summa Theologiae* I, qq. 2–26.

---

25. Augustine, *The Confessions of St. Augustine*, trans. John K. Ryan (Garden City, NY: Image Books, 1960), 180.

CHAPTER 9

Metaphysics outside Normal Operating Conditions

9.1 Initial Thoughts on Metaphysics and Theology

METAPHYSICS CAN BE EXPLORED for its own sake, and in the preceding chapters, we have seen what that looks like. Now we are going to explore two theological topics in which metaphysics plays an important but supporting role. We will keep a close eye on two things: first, how metaphysical ideas fit into and support theology; second, how metaphysical ideas get modified under theological pressure.

The two topics are the Incarnation and Transubstantiation. The Incarnation is the idea that the Son of God became human to save humans from sin. There are many aspects to this theological doctrine, most of which are not relevant for a metaphysics book. What we will be focusing on is the following. As Christians understand it, the Incarnation involves a person who is already divine—the Son of God—becoming human as well. As we shall see below, a person is a special kind of *substance*; and being divine and being human are ways of having *natures* or *essences*. The doctrine of the Incarnation, then, deploys important metaphysical ideas. But how are they deployed? And what difference does it make that they are getting deployed outside their normal philosophical context?

Transubstantiation, as understood by Catholics and some other Christians, is the idea that, in the celebration of the Lord's Supper (the "mass," as Catholics usually call it), what was bread and wine comes to be Christ's body and blood, even while retaining the outward appearances of bread and wine. Those outward appearances are *accidents* of bread and wine. The doctrine of Transubstantiation, then, deploys the metaphysical concept of *accident*. How does it get deployed there? And what difference does it make that this deployment is theological?

Before going on, however, we really ought to think more about the difference between philosophy and theology. This was touched upon very briefly in the introduction to this book, when I explained that philosophy involves the use of reason alone, without reliance on revelation. Let me now say a bit more.

Theology, like philosophy, is a form of rational investigation. Anyone who says that philosophers use reason, while theologians rely on faith instead, should be rebuked. A lot of theology is extremely rational and extremely sophisticated, but even sloppy and naive theology is still a work of reason; it's just an unimpressive work of reason. What makes theology special, then, is not that it doesn't use reason—it does!—but instead that it also relies on a special form of authority—namely, divine revelation.

Divine revelation, of course, is a highly contested idea. It's highly contested whether God has ever revealed himself. On the assumption that he has, it's highly contested where that revelation is to be found. In the Hebrew Scriptures? In the Christian Bible (but which version?)? In the Koran? In the Book of Mormon? For the purposes of this introduction to Thomistic metaphysics, I'm going to take as my starting point what Thomas Aquinas would have taken as his starting point—namely, that the Christian Bible, as interpreted in Catholic Christianity, is the fullest source of divine revelation. If you're thinking that this is a rather large assumption, and that at some point it might be reasonable to ask whether it's warranted, then of course you are right! But this isn't the place for exploring all that.

Divine revelation, on the Christian understanding, tells us that certain things are true: that there is a God; that there is only one God; that God has an intellect and a will; that God is perfect; that God is the creator of everything other than himself; that God exists in three persons, Father, Son, and Spirit; that the Son and the Spirit have been sent for the sake of our salvation; and on and on. When we accept this revelation by the divinely-given virtue of faith, we have assurance, indeed certainty, that these things are true.

Let me comment further on the idea that divine revelation tells us that certain things are true. You might have noticed that the list of revealed truths I gave in the previous paragraph included some points that came up in chapter eight, but also some points that did not. That's not merely because chapter eight fell far short of being a complete discussion of God (although it certainly did). It's also, and primarily, because chapter eight was a *philosophical* investigation of God, while some of the things taught to us by divine revelation are beyond the ability of philosophy to discover. Some truths about God—for example, that God is a Trinity of persons, Father, Son, and Spirit—are inaccessible to unaided human reason, and knowable only by divine revelation. If God doesn't tell us these things himself, we will never figure them out on our own.

Once that's noted, it's worth asking why God reveals not only truths that are beyond philosophy, but also truths that philosophy is capable of discovering on its own, truths such as those we looked at in chapter eight. Aquinas's answer here is a good one: Without revelation, knowledge of God would be had only by a few people, and only after an enormous amount of inquiry, and only mixed in with errors due to the fallibility of human reason. God wants us to be saved, and he doesn't want our knowledge of him to depend on how much intelligence and free time we have. For that reason, he reveals things to us.

It might seem that the gift of faith is the death of metaphysics. Precisely because faith gives us assurance that certain things are true, it might seem to rule out questioning and end in dogmatism. But experience proves that this is not so. A standard definition of theology is "faith seeking understanding," and many people have used faith as a starting point for serious intellectual inquiry. It's not as if revelation answers all questions or does so in detail. It is necessary to ask hard and tricky questions about what divine revelation really says, and what it really means, and what it really implies, and how it could be true. If there is no divine revelation, then obviously this is all a mistake, but it's certainly not complacency or laziness. Revealed truths need not put an end to inquiry; instead, they can serve as one of its starting points. Revelation can even make inquiry bolder, by giving it assurance that its starting point is solid.

So far, I have distinguished philosophy from theology by focusing on whether or not revelation gets used, and that is indeed the crucial difference. But there is an additional way of thinking about the difference between them. It doesn't make for a hard-and-fast distinction, but it is still helpful. Philosophy focuses mostly on creation, rather than on God.

To be sure, as we've already seen, there can be philosophical study of God, but even there, it's a study of God that takes creation as its starting point, and it often returns to creation by examining God not so much in himself, but instead as cause of creation. Theology, by contrast, tends to focus mostly on God, rather than on creation. It does, to be sure, discuss creation, but mostly in light of how it relates to God—how God serves as its creator and sustainer, how God saves humans, and so on. As mentioned, this doesn't give us a completely sharp distinction between philosophy and theology, but it does point to a difference between them: one is more God-focused, and the other is more creation-focused.

One last point before this section is over. Theology and philosophy are different, but they are related in the following very important ways. First, theology makes use of philosophy. The traditional way of putting it is to say that philosophy is *ancilla theologiae*, handmaiden of theology. Second, even prior and deeper to getting help from philosophy, theology presupposes that philosophy is there in the first place, or anyway it presupposes some knowledge of created reality. Revelation does tell us some things that unaided reason could have found out for itself, but it doesn't come close to telling us everything we need to know about creation. To give a very simple example, the Bible tells us that Moses and the Israelites crossed the Red Sea, but it doesn't tell us what a sea is, or exactly where the Red Sea is located. If we started with complete ignorance of creation, we couldn't get started with the task of understanding revelation.

To conclude this section, then, let me sum up by saying that our goal in this chapter will be to get a kind of "sample pack" of metaphysics in theology, in the form of two case studies. We will examine a pair of claims that are made on the basis of revelation, with an eye on how the attempt to understand them ends up requiring metaphysical ideas.[1]

9.2 Incarnation

One good way to introduce the Christian doctrine ("teaching") of the Incarnation is this. There was a Jewish rabbi, Jesus, who had a significant following but who also came into conflict with religious and secular authorities. This conflict came to the point that he was crucified by

---

1. I discuss Aquinas's approach to these issues in my *Aquinas on the Metaphysics of the Hypostatic Union*, chapter four.

the Roman government, but afterwards some of his followers said he had risen from the dead. They came to hold that the divine offer of salvation was somehow especially channeled through him: that he not only preached about this salvation but was somehow personally bound up with its arrival. He was the anointed one, the Messiah, the Christ, and perhaps something even more. This religious movement grew, quickly coming to include not only Palestinian Jews but also pagans throughout the Roman empire. The experiences and reflections of these followers came to be recorded in a number of documents, among them letters and gospels.

Experience prompts reflection, and these followers of Christ, the Christians, discussed and debated among themselves what had really happened, and who this Jesus really was. Over the course of a complicated and sometimes controversy-ridden process, they came to hold, explicitly and articulately, that Jesus was not only human, but also divine. It was not merely that he was especially gifted and inspired by God, but that he was God himself.

This process of making things explicit developed roughly in tandem with a similar process concerning the uniquely Christian understanding of God as Trinitarian: there is indeed only one God, and yet somehow this one God exists as three persons, Father, Son, and Spirit. The doctrine of the Trinity is very interesting in its own right, but for present purposes what matters is simply to situate the doctrine of the Incarnation in its Trinitarian context: the person who became human is the Son. The person those earliest Christians had experienced was not a human being who had become divine; he was a divine person who had become human by "assuming" a human nature—that is, by taking it to himself.

The classic formula that was arrived at by the fourth and fifth centuries looks like this: Jesus is *one person* who exists in *two natures*, divinity and humanity. This is worth walking through in some detail.

First, the notion of "person." A person, as classically understood, is a special kind of substance. A substance (see §1.1) is an independent, unified individual, and therefore, since a person is a special kind of substance, a person is a special kind of independent, unified individual.[2]

---

2. Recalling some points made in §1.1, let me clarify that here substance means "basic being" and not essence or nature.

What makes persons different from substances that aren't persons is this: persons have reason. A cat and a human are both substances, but humans are persons while cats are not.[3]

To say that persons have reason is to suggest something about their natures, so that leads to the second element of the classic formula, namely "nature." This should be familiar from earlier chapters, and especially from §1.2, although we have more often referred to it using the word "essence." A nature is what something is at the most basic level; a thing's nature constitutes that thing as an independently subsisting thing of a certain kind.

To say that Christ is *one* person is to push back against any suspicion that he might actually be a team of persons working closely together. Jesus is not a human person working closely together with a divine person, the Son; rather, he and the Son just are the very same person. To say that Christ has two natures, and that these natures are humanity and divinity, is to say that Christ really is human, and that he really is divine. He is not merely human in outward appearance, he is really and truly human; he is not merely inspired by God, he is literally divine.

The core points can be put in terms of two principles, the "integrity principle" and the "unity principle." The unity principle states that Christ is really one person. The integrity principle states that each of Christ's natures is there in its fullness and integrity.

What has been presented up to this point is the standard Christian view of who and what Christ is: one person existing in two natures, humanity and divinity. This raises questions, of course, indeed dozens of them. For just one example, if Christ has both a human and a divine nature, then it would seem to follow that he has both a human and a divine mind; but if he has two minds, then how can he be one (non-crazy) person?[4]

For present purposes, I will focus on only one of the many questions raised by the doctrine of the Incarnation. It has a rather arcane and metaphysical feel to it, but then, this is a book on metaphysics!

---

3. We speak of Father, Son, and Spirit as persons and even as substances, but this involves stretching those words pretty far—it involves using them analogously. As noted in §8.8, God does not belong to the category of substance.

4. I explore this question in Michael Gorman, "Personal Unity and the Problem of Christ's Knowledge," *Proceedings of the American Catholic Philosophical Association* 74 (2000): 175–86.

As previously discussed (see especially §1.2 and §3.3.3), a substance's essence, unlike any of its accidents, constitutes or establishes it at the most basic level. It explains why that substance is an independently subsisting thing of a particular kind. But if we apply this to the case of the Incarnation, we might have a question. If Christ has two natures, then it seems he has two principles in virtue of which he is an independent existing thing. But that would seem to mean that he is two independent existing things. His divinity, one might think, establishes him as a divine person, and his humanity establishes him as a human person. But this pretty clearly violates the unity principle.

To protect the unity principle, one might argue that Christ is not entirely human; he has the outward appearance of being human, maybe even a body, but ultimately, he does not really have a complete human nature. This maneuver would indeed protect the unity principle, but at the cost of abandoning the integrity principle: out of the frying pan, into the fire. Another, more subtle way of doing the same thing is by thinking of Christ's human nature as being an accident rather than a substantial nature. This isn't really consistent with holding to the idea that Christ has a true human nature.

Faced with all this, someone who was still convinced of the traditional doctrine might be tempted to say: "Well, I don't understand it, but I still believe it, so that's that." I wouldn't want to say that no one should ever believe anything that he can't fully understand; if that were really the rule, then few of us would be entitled to believe that airplanes fly. Accepting the truth of things we can't fully understand can be legitimate. However, in the case at hand, I think that faith can still make progress as it seeks understanding.

Let's go back over the problem more slowly. One could say that the role of a substantial nature is to make something be an independently subsisting thing of a certain kind. But this makes it hard to spot the fact that substantial natures actually play two distinguishable roles: they make something be independently existing, and they make it be of a certain foundational kind. Now simply to note this distinction is not yet to solve anything, because if both of these functions are required for being a substantial nature, then we still have a problem. If Christ's divine nature must perform both functions, and his human nature must perform both functions, then his divine nature must make him an independently existing person, and at the same time his human nature must make him an independently existing person—a second independently existing person.

However, even if distinguishing the functions does not solve anything all by itself, it is still useful; distinguishing them allows us to consider them more carefully and to consider whether we are understanding them rightly. In particular, it allows us to reconsider the function of establishing something as an independently existing substance. As I will argue, there are two ways to think about that function, but only one of them is the one that makes sense for Christology.

Before going on, however, I want to note something important—namely, that the way I'm putting things runs the risk of being misleading. It's pretty reifying to speak of a human nature, or any substantial nature, as something that can "exercise a function"; this is the sort of point I worried over at length in §3.3.3. However, I think it's a risk worth running here. It makes it far less complicated to say what needs saying in this section, and it also makes it simpler to set out some comparisons in §9.4. Just be wary.

Let us focus on the substance-making function. One way to think about it is as follows: any substantial nature must, necessarily, establish something as a substance. So, for example, a cat-nature isn't a cat-nature unless it actually establishes an independently existing cat. If this is the right way to think about it, then the Christological problem we've been discussing cannot be solved, because then Christ's humanity won't be a real human nature unless it actually establishes something as an independently existing human person (making Christ a team of two persons). On this way of understanding the function in question, accepting the integrity principle makes it impossible to accept the unity principle.

But there is another way to think about this function. Instead of saying that a substantial nature is something that *must* establish an independently existing substance, we can say that a substantial nature is something that *can* establish an independently existing substance. On this way of thinking, something could be a substantial nature even if it didn't actually establish a substance, so long as it—the nature—was still the sort of thing that *could* do so. To pick a distant analogy, something doesn't have to actually explode in order to be a bomb, it just has to be the sort of thing that could explode.

How would this reconfigured way of thinking about substantial natures help with the Incarnation? The problem was that, seemingly,

Christ's human nature would not be a real human nature unless it actually established an independently existing person—that is, a *second* person. That would mean that the unity principle would be violated. But if we say instead that Christ's human nature need only be *capable* of establishing an independently existing person, then we could hold that Christ's human nature is a real human nature even if it doesn't actually establish an independently existing person. It would still be a real human nature because it would still have the intrinsic capacity to establish a person.

If the human nature has that capacity, why doesn't it exercise it? The following strikes me as the most promising answer: because that human nature is joined to the Son. Think of it this way. Whatever the Son's human nature does will be something that it does to the Son, or for the Son. If *your* head lacks all hair, that makes *you* bald, not anyone else, and if *my* head lacks all hair, that makes *me* bald, not anyone else. In a roughly parallel way, the Son's human nature, if it makes anyone human, will make *him* human, and if it establishes anyone as an independently existing person, then it will establish *him* as an independently existing person. Now, prior to having a human nature, the Son was not human, so when he assumed the human nature, it had an opportunity to exercise the function of making something human, and it did so. But prior to having a human nature, the Son was already an independently existing person, so when the human nature was joined to him, it did not get an opportunity to make the Son an independently existing person. In and of itself, the human nature had the capacity to make something be a person, but its union with the Son made it unable to exercise that capacity. It arrived too late to make an independent person (but not too late to make an already-existing person human).

The way to preserve the doctrine of the Incarnation, then, is to rethink the substance-making function of substantial natures. However, there still might be a problem. It might seem that taking this approach means we've just given up on philosophical metaphysics. We spent a lot of time coming up with a theory of essence or nature (think back to §1.2), but now we have just ditched it in favor of something derived from theology. Putting it in a relatively non-aggressive way, we could say, "It's a shame that we didn't start with theology; we could have saved a lot of time." Putting it more aggressively, we could say,

"It's rather ridiculous to allow one special case, based on revelation, to substitute for philosophical thinking."

In response, I think we can say that in a very important sense, this theological refinement of the philosophical idea of essence doesn't really undercut the philosophical idea after all. The philosophy-only understanding of essence or nature says that a person's nature makes that person exist independently. The theological refinement of essence or nature says, more cautiously, that a person's nature *can* make that person exist independently. However, as we developed the point just above, the only reason why a nature would not exercise that person-making capacity would be that it was united to an already-existing substance or person, as happens in the Incarnation. This means that even according to the theology-influenced version of the idea of nature, a person's nature *will* establish that person as an independently existing person unless that nature is a *second* nature, a nature added to an already-existing person. In your case, my case, Socrates's case, and everyone's case but Christ's, human nature is not joined to a pre-existing substance or person. In every case but Christ's, a person's human nature is his *only* substantial nature, with the result that it, the substantial nature, most definitely will exercise its person-making capacity. In other words, a substantial nature will refrain from exercising its substance-making capacity only when it belongs to a substance with multiple substantial natures; but the Incarnation is the only case where this happens; therefore, outside of the Incarnation, the philosophy-only understanding of nature gives the same result as the theology-influenced version does.

In brief, then, in all the cases that philosophy deals with, the philosophical account of essence gives us the right answer. What's more, it would be awkward, or worse, to constantly be saying "unless of course we are dealing with the Incarnation" every time you wanted to talk about natures. So, while theological reflection has led us to refine the philosophical account of nature, the refinement it proposes applies only to the theological case that provoked it, leaving the metaphysical cases as they were before, and giving us excellent reason to use the philosophical formulation in philosophical contexts.

I have claimed that our theological refinement of the idea of essence doesn't render the philosophical idea useless. Now I want to consider a different reason for doubting that the theological refinement is legitimate. The worry is that the move is too desperate and costly. If we must modify one of the basic concepts of metaphysics to avoid conflict with Christianity, doesn't that reveal that actually it's Christianity that's the problem? (If my bank account shows that I'm overdrawn, no one will allow me to revise the laws of mathematics to prove that really I'm solvent!)

Here there is no way to avoid the following: it makes a difference, a huge difference, whether or not one actually believes in Christian revelation. If Christian revelation is not true, then this whole discussion has been, at most, an interesting thought-experiment, fun to play around with but not telling us anything about how the world actually is. But if, on the other hand, Christian revelation is true, then the Incarnation is a fact, and there is nothing wrong with adjusting our preconceived philosophical notions to fit the facts.

The worry was that the theological refinement involves modifying a basic concept of metaphysics, and the response to the worry is to admit that this is what is going on, but to deny that it is worrisome. If divine revelation is real, then bringing our thoughts into line with it could hardly be a mistake. On the other hand, it's important not to turn this into an excuse for sloppy thinking. So let me make a few remarks intended to show how theological adjustments to metaphysics can be intellectually respectable.

First, if there really is such a thing as God, then God is going to be very different from us. We saw this point made already in chapter eight on the basis of purely philosophical argumentation. It shouldn't be surprising, then, to find that our ordinary philosophical ideas—ideas we developed for the purpose of thinking about the created world around us—are not adequate for understanding the transcendent creator.

Second, even though the theological version of the concept of nature is different from the philosophical one, it's hardly devoid of content. It took pages to explain it! Rethinking the notion of nature is nothing like "blind faith" or "just repeating slogans that you don't understand." The fact that the rethinking is based on revelation doesn't prevent it from having plenty of intelligible conceptual content.

Third, to repeat a point made already, theological refinements to metaphysics don't mean that the metaphysics we were applying to creation has been completely wrong the whole time. Theology pretty much leaves philosophy as it is, only adding a special twist that allows us to handle a unique case. It enables us to see just a little bit more, while leaving what we used to be able to see fully visible.

9.3 Transubstantiation

Now let us turn to our next case study. This one concerns something that Catholics and some others believe in, often called "Transubstantiation."

The basic idea goes like this: At the Last Supper before he was crucified, Jesus seemed to share bread and wine with his disciples, but, as recounted in the Gospels, when he did so, he said, "Take and eat, this is my body" and likewise "Take and drink, this is my blood," and finally "Do this in memory of me." Catholics and some others take this pretty much at face value, in the following way. Doing what Christ did, in his memory, they engage in a Eucharistic ("thanksgiving") ritual in which the priest says the above words, after which he and the congregation eat and drink what appear to be bread and wine, but what they believe to be Christ's body and blood. But how can something change not at all in appearance—still appearing as bread or wine—and yet change so greatly in what it is essentially?

To keep things simple, we will deal henceforth only with the example of the bread. We will, that is, consider how what once was bread can continue to appear as bread while becoming Christ's body, but without also explaining how what once was wine can continue to appear as wine while becoming Christ's blood. There's no important metaphysical difference between the two cases, so this saves us from saying everything twice.

Let us now begin, remembering all the while that our purpose is to provide a case study of the role of metaphysics in theology. The key metaphysical concepts at work are essence and, especially, accident. We start with something that is bread by nature; afterwards, we have something that is Christ's body by nature. This is not any ordinary transformation, but a transition to a new essence, nature, or substance—in technical terminology, it's transubstantiation.[5] At the same time, the appearances that belonged to the bread before Transubstantiation remain even after Transubstantiation, and these appearances (whiteness,

---

5. As we saw in §1.1, "substance" can mean essence, although that's not how it is used in this book.

roundness, and so on) are accidents. In this case of Transubstantiation, then, the essence is changed while the accidents remain the same.

And now we come to what will, for us, be the crucial question. As we saw in §1.1 and in §3.3.1, accidents by nature *inhere* in substances. Mickey's grayness and agility exist in him, as "metaphysical parts," as modifications or enhancements or specifications of him, as ways for him to be. If the whiteness of the host, after Transubstantiation, is really an accident (and what else could it be?), then it seems it must inhere in something. But in what? Not the bread; according to the doctrine we are investigating, the bread exists no longer. But also, interestingly, not in Christ's body: the doctrine of Transubstantiation does not say that Christ's body comes to be small, round, and white. Instead, as classically understood by theologians like Thomas Aquinas, the accidents do not inhere in any substance at all. And this then is the difficulty: If an accident must inhere in a substance, then isn't the doctrine of Transubstantiation asking us to believe something impossible—namely, that certain accidents, for example, whiteness, exist without inhering in a substance? Either they don't inhere in a substance, in which case they are not truly accidents (but then what are they?) or else they do inhere in a substance—namely Christ—giving us the bizarre result that Christ is a human being who is round, flat, and (let us say) less than two inches in diameter. Can anything be said that would lessen the intellectual pressures here, other than "it's a mystery, try not to think about it"?

A good way forward can be found. It's similar to what we saw in the previous section, inasmuch as it involves revising something we learned in philosophical metaphysics. Instead of saying that an accident is something that *must* inhere in a substance, we can say that an accident is something that *can* inhere in a substance. The accidents of whiteness and so on can still be accidents, even if they do not actually inhere in any substance: they are accidents on the basis of the fact that they *can* so inhere. They no longer inhere in any substance, and yet they are still the sort of thing that can inhere, as is proved by the fact that at one time, they actually did inhere: when the bread was still in existence.

As noted, this move has a kind of parallelism with the move made in the case of the Incarnation: something that (in philosophy) is understood in terms of actually performing a certain function is, in theology, understood only in terms of being able to perform that function. There is another parallelism as well: Just as in the case of the Incarnation, here too it turns out that the new theological understanding does not cause disruption when placed back into the old philosophical contexts. If we say that an accident is something that can inhere, it will still be true to call Mickey's agility an accident because that agility, unlike Mickey himself, can inhere (and also actually does inhere). So, the theological version won't lead to any philosophical errors. Meanwhile, the philosophical version will remain perfectly useful in philosophical contexts: Apart from the case of the Eucharist, accidents that *can* inhere will also always be accidents that *do* inhere. It will be satisfactory, then, for philosophical purposes, simply to say that accidents are what inhere.[6]

9.4 Comparisons between the Assumed Human Nature and the Orphaned Accidents

Further discussion of similarities and differences between our two case studies will shed light on them both.

Human natures standardly establish the independent existence of persons, and accidents standardly add secondary, non-foundational actualizations to already-existing substances. This makes them quite different from each other. Interestingly, however, Christ's human nature has a certain surprising similarity to post-Transubstantiation accidents: neither that human nature nor those accidents perform either of the functions in question. Christ's human nature causes nothing to be a person, and the same is true of the whiteness that used to belong to the bread. The whiteness that used to belong to the bread does not actualize accidental potentialities in any substance, and the same is true of Christ's human nature.

So far, then, and contrary to expectations, the two are alike. But they remain different in the following very important way. Although Christ's human nature actually performs neither of these two functions, it could perform the first, while it is entirely incapable of performing the second. It's the sort of thing that, were it not joined to a pre-existing person, could give rise to an independent person, but it's not the

---

6. I have explained how one might adopt a certain way of thinking about accidents in order to solve a theological problem. Wippel argues that Aquinas himself adopts this way of thinking, or one similar to it, for philosophical reasons, prior to any theological concern; see Wippel, *The Metaphysical Thought*, 229–37.

sort of thing that could, under any circumstances, actualize mere accidental potencies in a subject. By contrast, the accidents in the Eucharist, while also performing neither of the functions we have been talking about, are able to perform the second, but are entirely unable to perform the first. These accidents could never establish something as an independently existing substance, while they could (and indeed at one time did) actualize a substance's accidental potentialities. So, while in one way these two metaphysical principles are alike, in another way they are pretty much opposed to each other.

The differences between the cases are related to the following further difference. In the case of the Incarnation, we have a union where we would not normally expect to have one, inasmuch as we have a substantial nature united to an already-existing person. In the case of the Eucharist, we have no union where we would normally expect to have one—namely, inasmuch as we have an accident not united to a substance.

And here's another contrast. While Christ's human nature doesn't establish a substance as existing, it still makes a substance human: it makes the Son of God human. But the whiteness that formerly belonged to the bread doesn't make anything white.

These comparisons are not meant to prove anything new, but only to make clearer, by contrast, what's going on in these two different cases.

9.5 Summary Thoughts on Metaphysics and Theology

Metaphysics ordinarily thinks about ordinary, finite, created things. God, however, is infinite, and infinitely powerful, which means he can exist and act in ways that go beyond the capacities of the creatures we normally consider. Furthermore, God can exist and act in ways that even the best philosophers could never come to learn about without divine revelation. For reasons like these, when we find metaphysical concepts at work in theology, we will sometimes find them deployed outside of their normal operating conditions.

Revelation is not only the source of this thinking, but also a crucial constraint upon it. Theological inquiry is like all other inquiry inasmuch as the answer is not known until the inquiry is over; in theology, however, certain answers are ruled out in advance—namely, those that contradict revelation. It may seem strange or offensive to say that certain conclusions are ruled out in advance, but remember that without revelation, theology doesn't even exist in the first place. Absent revelation, no one would sit around asking himself whether, by any chance, a divine person has ever been joined with a human nature, and, if so, how many, and in what way. (Four human natures joined to two divine persons? Five human natures joined to three divine persons?) In a philosophical context, such questions don't even arise. Someone will pursue an inquiry about the Incarnation only as a response to revelation. For that reason, it makes perfect sense for theological inquiry to hold itself accountable to what has been revealed: doing so means holding itself responsible to what makes theology theology, to what makes theology possible in the first place. (Of course, maybe there's no such thing as revelation, or maybe we're entirely wrong about what it says, but those are entirely different issues.)

In passing, it's worth remembering that to speak of understanding revelation is, almost always, to speak of a messy process. It would be nice if God revealed himself in a loud voice coming out of the clouds, a voice speaking in unambiguous sentences, but this is not the way things go. Near the beginning of §9.2, I spoke of "a complicated and sometimes controversy-ridden process," but perhaps I should have said *very* complicated and *very* controversy-ridden, spread out literally over centuries. A good slogan to remember is "doctrine is not defined until it is denied." To choose an example from the early fifth century: people are just going along, living their lives as Christians, and then a priest named Eutyches seems to be saying that in Christ, divinity and humanity are merged. Arguments begin, and eventually a consensus emerges that this is wrong, and that what we need is an explicit formulation that few had ever seen a need for before: a formulation asserting that Jesus is one person existing in two natures. But that only sets the stage for a later controversy over whether Jesus's having two natures means that he has two wills. Theology does make progress, in the sense that certain errors get excluded, but further questions and clarifications will always arise.

Because of these questions, and the need to answer them, the proper response to revelation is not to throw up one's hands and say, "It's a mystery." Eventually, of course, our natural reasoning powers will reach their limits, and we will have to admit that we don't fully understand how divine things go. God is indeed a mystery (to us). But prior to that, we can often make a lot of progress in thinking about what has been revealed. And when we do hit our limit, we can do so in an intelligent way, arriving at a good understanding of what it is that we don't understand.

Let us return to our focus on metaphysics outside its normal operating conditions. Revelation presents the believer with certain claims. It is sometimes very difficult to sort out what these claims really mean, and very difficult to sort out how those claims can be made consistent with other claims. In thinking it through, one inevitably makes use of concepts drawn from metaphysics, like person, nature, and accident. But often enough, one finds that success requires coming up with new and creative versions of these concepts. Revelation sets the boundaries for what an acceptable solution would look like, and creative metaphysical reflection finds a solution within those boundaries. As mentioned before, philosophy is sometimes called a "handmaid of theology." This shouldn't be interpreted in too subservient a way. A handmaid is sometimes an advisor, or even a judge. Metaphysics makes a real positive contribution to faith's quest for understanding.

To conclude, let me make clear that the examples we have worked through are only two of many. The doctrine of the Incarnation gives rise to many issues that one could talk about, beyond the one discussed here.[7] The doctrine of the Eucharist gives rise to many issues that one could talk about, beyond the one discussed here. And there are many other theological doctrines to think about: the nature of divinity and the character of God as tri-personal, the question of salvation, the afterlife, the Church, and many others. You could spend a whole life thinking about them and never get bored.

▸ The narrow Christological point discussed this chapter is based on *Summa Theologiae* III, q. 3, art. 1, ad 3. To get started on reading Aquinas himself on the incarnation, begin with *Compendium of Theology* I, chapters 202–11. Next, try his account in *Summa contra gentiles* IV, chapters 27–49. Aquinas's most extended discussion of the hypostatic union is *Summa Theologiae* III, qq. 1–26.

▸ To get started on reading Aquinas on the Eucharist, begin with *Summa Contra Gentiles* IV, chapters 61–68. Aquinas's most important discussion of the Eucharist is *Summa Theologiae* III, qq. 73–83; he focuses on the accidents in q. 77.

---

7. I talk about some of them, and how Thomas Aquinas addresses them, in my *Aquinas on the Metaphysics of the Hypostatic Union*.

CHAPTER 10

Not the Conclusion

THIS BOOK HAS BEEN a presentation of a number of central ideas in metaphysics, understood from a basically Aristotelian-Thomistic point of view. A key theme throughout has been the priority of substances, of basic beings. Another key theme has been that basic beings are not the only beings there are. This second theme has been crucial to my claim that we need to resist excessive reification in metaphysics. We fall into false reification when we fall into thinking that being a substance is, in the end, the only way to be—that's what leads us to treat non-substances as substances, or as quasi-substances.

The fact that there are basic beings and non-basic beings means that an inventory of reality is like the list of guests at a wedding. Some people are, so to speak, the central guests: immediate family and close friends of the bride and groom. Some guests are, so to speak, less central: cousins and less-close friends. Some guests are very peripheral indeed, like annoying spouses of people you have to invite. Everyone is invited, but some are invited for their own sake, while others are riding on the coattails of others.

Toward the end of the book, we started thinking about God. I proposed that thinking about God can allow us to make sense out of certain metaphysical issues that are otherwise very hard to make sense out of. But here, as we near the end, I want to mention a way in which God makes things more puzzling for metaphysics. I have built this presentation of metaphysics around substances, basic beings. But if there is a God, and if everything depends on God, then it turns out that the basic beings we encounter every day—the basic beings that include you and me—are not absolutely basic after all. They are, you might say, only relatively basic. As far as creation goes, basic beings are where the buck stops, but all of creation is received from a source infinitely beyond itself. It's as if everything we thought we owned turned out to be only borrowed.

Every book has to stop somewhere, so in a sense, this is the conclusion. But there's a lot more metaphysics left to do. For one thing, I am confident that this book contains errors. Naturally I don't know where they are, or I would have fixed them. But just because I haven't found them doesn't make me think they aren't there. That's one reason why there's more metaphysics left to do: to fix the errors. But if there were no errors anywhere, there would still be enormous amounts of work remaining. Things I have talked about need further development, and there are many things I haven't talked about at all. As Robert Sokolowski says in his *Husserlian Meditations*, the proper punctuation for a philosophical judgment is not a period but "!?" Whenever a philosophical judgment is made, something big is happening (!), but also there's a need for further questioning (?).[1]

I hope, then, that this is not the conclusion of your metaphysical thinking. If you look to the next page, you will find a list of readings you might want to follow up with. But my final word will be taken from A. G. Sertillanges: "Never read when you can reflect."[2]

---

1. Robert Sokolowski, *Husserlian Meditations* (Evanston, IL: Northwestern University Press, 1974), 249.

2. A. G. Sertillanges, *The Intellectual Life*, trans. Mary Ryan (Washington, DC: The Catholic University of America Press, 1987), 149.

Recommended Readings

Obviously, it would be self-defeating for me to say that no one should ever read introductory philosophy texts! I will, therefore, list a few that you might find helpful. But after that, and more importantly, I will mention some of the original historical sources that you should be digging into. Those sources are harder to understand, but they are richer. In the long run, the payoff is greater. Think of textbooks as an on-ramp to the big highway, and aspire to traveling on the highway.

Some Textbooks

Norris Clarke, *The One and the Many: A Contemporary Thomistic Metaphysics* (Notre Dame: University of Notre Dame Press, 2001).

Edward Feser, *Scholastic Metaphysics: A Contemporary Introduction* (Heusenstamm: Editiones scholasticae, 2014).

Robert C. Koons and Timothy H. Pickavance, *Metaphysics: The Fundamentals* (Chichester: Wiley-Blackwell, 2015).

Michael J. Loux and Thomas M. Crisp, *Metaphysics: A Contemporary Introduction*, Fourth edition (London: Routledge, Taylor & Francis, 2017).

Joseph Owens, *An Elementary Christian Metaphysics* (Houston, TX: Center for Thomistic Studies, 1985).

Original Sources

Aristotle:

- The primal text of metaphysics in the Thomistic tradition is Aristotle's *Metaphysics*.
- Also useful and important are the following works by Aristotle: *Categories* and *Physics*.

Aquinas:

- It's a bit harder to say what to read first as far as Aquinas's metaphysics is concerned, because much of his metaphysics is embedded in theological discussions. At the end of each chapter, I have suggested how you might start on the topics of that chapter. More generally, however, there's a lot to be said for starting with the following two short philosophical works: *On the Principles of Nature* and *On Being and Essence*.

More Recent Works (More or Less in the Analytic Tradition)

D. M. Armstrong, *Universals: An Opinionated Introduction* (Boulder: Westview Press, 1989).

Michael Gorman, "Essentiality as Foundationality," in *Neo-Aristotelian Perspectives in Metaphysics*, ed. Daniel Novotny and Lukas Novak (London; New York: Routledge, 2014), 119–37 and also "The Essential and the Accidental," *Ratio* 18 (2005): 276–89.

Jorge J. E. Gracia, *Individuality: An Essay on the Foundations of Metaphysics* (Albany: State University of New York Press, 1988).

Saul Kripke, *Naming and Necessity* (Cambridge: Harvard University Press, 1980).

David K. Lewis, *On the Plurality of Worlds* (Oxford: Blackwell Publishers, 2001).

E. J. Lowe, *The Four-Category Ontology: A Metaphysical Foundation for Natural Science* (Oxford: Clarendon Press, 2006).

E. J. Lowe, *A Survey of Metaphysics* (Oxford: Oxford University Press, 2002).

Alvin Plantinga, *The Nature of Necessity* (Oxford: Clarendon Press, 1974).

Gilbert Ryle, "Systematically Misleading Expressions," *Proceedings of the Aristotelian Society, New Series* 32, no. 1 (1932): 139–70.

Peter van Inwagen, *Material Beings* (Ithaca, NY: Cornell University Press, 1995).

Bibliography

Aertsen, Jan. *Medieval Philosophy and the Transcendentals: The Case of Thomas Aquinas.* Leiden: E. J. Brill, 1996.

Alston, William P. "Ontological Commitments." *Philosophical Studies* 9, no. 1–2 (1958): 8–17.

Anscombe, G. E. M. "Modern Moral Philosophy." *Philosophy* 33, no. 124 (1958): 1–19.

Armstrong, D. M. "Against Ostrich Nominalism: A Reply to Michael Devitt." *Pacific Philosophical Quarterly* 61, no. 4 (1980): 440–49.

———. *Universals: An Opinionated Introduction.* Boulder: Westview Press, 1989.

———. *A World of States of Affairs.* Cambridge Studies in Philosophy. Cambridge: Cambridge University Press, 1997.

Augustine. *Confessions.* Trans. John K. Ryan. New York: Image Books, 1960.

Azzouni, Jody. *Ontology without Borders.* Oxford: Oxford University Press, 2017.

Berto, Francesco and Mark Jago, "Impossible Worlds," *The Stanford Encyclopedia of Philosophy* (Summer 2023 Edition), Edward N. Zalta & Uri Nodelman (eds.) https://plato.stanford.edu/archives/sum2023/entries/impossible-worlds.

Bobik, Joseph, and Thomas Aquinas. *Aquinas on Matter and Form and the Elements: A Translation and Interpretation of the* De Principiis Naturae *and the* De Mixtione Elementorum *of St. Thomas Aquinas.* Notre Dame: University of Notre Dame Press, 1998.

Brower, Jeffrey E. *Aquinas's Ontology of the Material World: Change, Hylomorphism, and Material Objects.* Oxford: Oxford University Press, 2014.

———. "Aquinas on the Problem of Universals." *Philosophy and Phenomenological Research* 92, no. 3 (2016): 715–35.

Clarke, W. Norris. *The One and the Many: A Contemporary Thomistic Metaphysics.* Notre Dame: University of Notre Dame Press, 2001.

Cory, David. "Agency and Materiality in Aquinas's Soul Theory." PhD diss., The Catholic University of America, 2018.
Davidson, Matthew. "God and Other Necessary Beings," *The Stanford Encyclopedia of Philosophy* (Summer 2023 Edition), Edward N. Zalta & Uri Nodelman (eds.), https://plato.stanford.edu/archives/sum2023/entries/god-necessary-being/.
Decaen, Christopher. "Elemental Virtual Presence in St. Thomas." *The Thomist* 64, no. 2 (2000): 271–300.
Devitt, Michael. "'Ostrich Nominalism' or 'Mirage Realism'?" *Pacific Philosophical Quarterly* 61, no. 4 (1980): 433–39.
Doolan, Gregory T. *Aquinas on the Divine Ideas as Exemplar Causes*. Washington, DC: The Catholic University of America Press, 2008.
Feser, Edward. *Scholastic Metaphysics: A Contemporary Introduction*. Heusenstamm: Editiones Scholasticae, 2014.
———. *Five Proofs of the Existence of God*. San Francisco: Ignatius Press, 2017.
Frost, Gloria. *Aquinas on Efficient Causation and Causal Powers*. Cambridge: Cambridge University Press, 2022.
Garcia, Robert K. "Two Ways to Particularize a Property." *Journal of the American Philosophical Association* 1, no. 4 (2015): 635–52.
———. "Tropes as Character-Grounders." *Australasian Journal of Philosophy* 94, no. 3 (2016): 499–515.
Geisel, Theodor Seuss. *One Fish, Two Fish, Red Fish, Blue Fish* (New York, NY: Random House, 2013).
Goris, Wouter and Jan Aertsen, "Medieval Theories of Transcendentals," *The Stanford Encyclopedia of Philosophy* (Fall 2019 Edition), Edward N. Zalta (ed.), https://plato.stanford.edu/archives/fall2019/entries/transcendentals-medieval/
Gorman, Michael. "Personal Unity and the Problem of Christ's Knowledge." *Proceedings of the American Catholic Philosophical Association* 74 (2000): 175–86.
———. "The Essential and the Accidental." *Ratio* 18, no. 3 (2005): 276–89.
———. "Independence and Substance." *International Philosophical Quarterly* 46, no. 2 (2006): 147–59.
———. "Personhood, Potentiality, and Normativity." *American Catholic Philosophical Quarterly* 85, no. 3 (2011): 483–98.

———. "Categories and Normativity." In *Categories: Historical and Systematic Essays*, edited by Michael Gorman and Jonathan J. Sanford, 151–70. Washington, DC: The Catholic University of America Press, 2012.

———. "Essentiality as Foundationality." In *Neo-Aristotelian Perspectives in Metaphysics*, edited by Daniel Novotný and Lukáš Novák, 119–37. London; New York: Routledge, 2014.

———. "Two Types of Features: An Aristotelian Approach." *Ratio* 27, no. 2 (2014): 140-154.

———. *Aquinas on the Metaphysics of the Hypostatic Union*. Cambridge: Cambridge University Press, 2017.

———. "Intellect and Will: Free Will and Free Choice." In *The New Cambridge Companion to Aquinas*, edited by Eleonore Stump and Thomas Joseph White, 211–30. Cambridge: Cambridge University Press, 2022.

———. "On the Ontological Statuses of Features." In *The Philosophical Legacy of Jorge J. E. Gracia*, edited by Robert A. Delfino, William Irwin, and Jonathan J. Sanford, 133–42. Lanham, MD: Rowman & Littlefield, 2022.

Gracia, Jorge J. E. *Individuality: An Essay on the Foundations of Metaphysics*. Albany: State University of New York Press, 1988.

Grant, W. Matthews. *Free Will and God's Universal Causality: The Dual Sources Account*. New York: Bloomsbury Academic, 2019.

Henninger, Mark Gerald. *Relations: Medieval Theories, 1250–1325*. Oxford: Clarendon Press, 1989.

Hoffman, Joshua, and Gary S. Rosenkrantz. *Substance among Other Categories*. Cambridge: Cambridge University Press, 1994.

Jacobs, Jonathan D. "A Powers Theory of Modality: or, How I Learned to Stop Worrying and Reject Possible Worlds." *Philosophical Studies* 151, no. 2 (2010): 227–48.

Kass, Leon. *The Hungry Soul: Eating and the Perfecting of Our Nature*. Chicago: University of Chicago Press, 1999.

Koons, Robert C. "Forms as Simple and Individual Grounds of Things' Natures." *Metaphysics* 1, no. 1 (2018): 1–11.

———, and Timothy H. Pickavance. *Metaphysics: The Fundamentals*. Chichester; Malden, MA: Wiley-Blackwell, 2015.

Kripke, Saul A. *Naming and Necessity*. Cambridge: Harvard University Press, 1980.

Lewis, David K. *On the Plurality of Worlds.* Oxford; Malden, MA: Blackwell Publishers, 2001.

Loux, Michael J., and Thomas M. Crisp. *Metaphysics: A Contemporary Introduction.* Fourth Edition. London; New York: Routledge, 2017.

Lowe, E. J. *A Survey of Metaphysics.* Oxford; New York: Oxford University Press, 2002.

———. "Identity, Individuality, and Unity." *Philosophy* 78, no. 3 (2003): 321–36.

———. *The Four-Category Ontology: A Metaphysical Foundation for Natural Science.* Oxford: Clarendon Press, 2006.

McMahon, William E. "Reflections on Some Thirteenth- and Fourteenth Century Views of the Categories." In *Categories: Historical and Systematic Essays,* edited by Michael Gorman and Jonathan J. Sanford, 45–57. Washington, DC: The Catholic University of America Press, 2004.

Merricks, Trenton. *Objects and Persons.* Oxford: Clarendon Press, 2006.

Nagel, Thomas. "What Is It Like to Be a Bat?" *The Philosophical Review* 83, no. 4 (1974): 435–50.

Neurath, Otto. "Anti-Spengler." In *Empiricism and Sociology,* edited by Marie Neurath and Robert Cohen, 158–213. Dordrecht: D. Reidel, 1973.

Novák, Lukáš. "Conceptual Atomism, 'Aporia Generis' and a Way Out for Leibniz and the Aristotelians." *Studia Neoaristotelica* 6, no. 1 (2009): 15–49.

O'Connor, Timothy. "Emergent Properties." In *The Stanford Encyclopedia of Philosophy.* Edited by Edward Zalta. Stanford University, 1997–. August 10, 2020. https://plato.stanford.edu/archives/win 2021/entries/properties-emergent/.

Oderberg, David S. *The Metaphysics of Good and Evil.* London: Routledge, 2020.

Owens, Joseph. *An Elementary Christian Metaphysics.* Houston: Center for Thomistic Studies, 1985.

———. *An Interpretation of Existence.* Milwaukee, WI: Bruce Publishing Company, 1968; reprinted, Houston: Center for Thomistic Studies, 1985.

Pasnau, Robert. "On What There Is in Aquinas." In *Aquinas's* Summa Theologiae: *A Critical Guide,* edited by Jeffrey Hause, 10–28. Cambridge: Cambridge University Press, 2018.

Pawl, Timothy. "A Thomistic Account of Truthmakers for Modal Truths." PhD diss., St. Louis University, 2008.
Plantinga, Alvin. *The Nature of Necessity*. Oxford: Clarendon Press, 1974.
———. *Does God Have a Nature?* Milwaukee, WI: Marquette University Press, 1980.
Pruss, Alexander R. "The Actual and the Possible." In *Blackwell Guide to Metaphysics*, edited by R. M. Gale, 313–33. Oxford: Blackwell Publishing, 2002.
———. *Actuality, Possibility and Worlds*. New York: Continuum, 2011.
Quine, Willard Van Orman. "On What There Is." *The Review of Metaphysics* 2, no. 1 (1948): 21–38.
Ross, James. "God, Creator of Kinds and Possibilities." In *Rationality, Religious Belief, and Moral Commitment: New Essays in the Philosophy of Religion*, edited by Robert Audi and William J. Wainwright, 315–34. Ithaca, NY: Cornell University Press, 1986.
———. "Aquinas's Exemplarism; Aquinas's Voluntarism." *American Catholic Philosophical Quarterly* 64, no. 2 (1990): 171–98.
Rota, Michael. "Substance and Artifact in Thomas Aquinas." *History of Philosophy Quarterly* 21, no. 3 (2004): 241–59.
Ryle, Gilbert. "Systematically Misleading Expressions." *Proceedings of the Aristotelian Society, New Series* 32, no. 1 (1932): 139–70.
Searle, John. *Mind, Language, and Society: Philosophy in the Real World*. New York: Basic Books, 1998.
Sertillanges, A. G. *The Intellectual Life: Its Spirit, Conditions, Methods*. Translated by Mary Perkins Ryan. Washington, DC: The Catholic University of America Press, 1998.
Sevier, Christopher Scott. *Aquinas on Beauty*. Lanham, MD: Lexington Books, 2015.
Simons, Peter. "Particulars in Particular Clothing: Three Trope Theories of Substance." *Philosophy and Phenomenological Research* 54, no. 3 (1994): 553–75.
Sokolowski, Robert. *Husserlian Meditations: How Words Present Things*. Evanston, IL: Northwestern University Press, 1989.
———. *The God of Faith and Reason: Foundations of Christian Theology*. Washington, DC: The Catholic University of America Press, 1995.

Spade, Paul Vincent. "The Warp and Woof of Metaphysics: How to Get Started on Some Big Themes." 1999. www.Pvspade.Com/Logic/Docs/WarpWoof.Pdf.

Spencer, Mark K. "The Category of *Habitus*: Accidents, Artifacts, and Human Nature." *The Thomist* 79, no. 1 (2015): 113–54.

Stump, Eleonore. *Aquinas*. New York: Routledge, 2003.

Thornton, Allison Krile. "Disembodied Animals." *American Philosophical Quarterly* 56, no. 2 (2019): 203–17.

Toner, Patrick. "St. Thomas Aquinas on Mixture and the Gappy Existence of the Elements." *History of Philosophy and Logical Analysis* 18, no. 1 (2015): 255–68.

Toner, Patrick. "On Substance." *American Catholic Philosophical Quarterly* 84, no. 1 (2010): 25–48.

van Inwagen, Peter. "The Doctrine of Arbitrary Undetached Parts." *Pacific Philosophical Quarterly* 62, no. 2 (1981): 123–37.

———. *Material Beings*. Ithaca, NY: Cornell University Press, 1995.

———. *Metaphysics*. Fourth Edition. Boulder: Westview Press, 2015.

White, Kevin. "Act and Fact: On a Disputed Question in Recent Thomistic Metaphysics." *The Review of Metaphysics* 68, no. 2 (2014): 287–312.

Williams, Donald C. "On the Elements of Being: I." *The Review of Metaphysics* 7, no. 1 (1953): 3–18.

Wilson, Jessica, "Determinables and Determinates", *The Stanford Encyclopedia of Philosophy* (Spring 2023 Edition), Edward N. Zalta & Uri Nodelman (eds.), https://plato.stanford.edu/archives/spr2023/entries/determinate-determinables/

Wippel, John F. *Metaphysical Themes in Thomas Aquinas*. Washington, DC: The Catholic University of America Press, 1984.

———. *The Metaphysical Thought of Thomas Aquinas: From Finite Being to Uncreated Being*. Washington, DC: The Catholic University of America Press, 2000.

Wittgenstein, Ludwig. *Philosophical investigations*. Edited by P. M. S. Hacker and Joachim Schulte. Translated by G. E. M. Anscombe, P. M. S. Hacker, and Joachim Schulte. Rev. 4th ed. Chichester; Malden, MA: Wiley-Blackwell, 2009.

Index

accidental: arrangement, 67; beings, 184; categories, 170, 173; change, 44–48, 51–52, 55, 60, 89–90, 106–7; features, 15, 24–32, 35–36, 44, 84–85, 88–89, 127, 159, 174, 181; form, 51–52, 55, 90, 109–111; kinds, 176; potentiality, 91, 226–27

accidents, 24–28, 35, 39, 44–45, 50–51, 54, 58, 60, 86, 106, 123, 127, 133, 159, 162–77, 195–96, 204, 229; as non-essential features, 84–85, 88–89; contingent, 26, 58; necessary, 26, 94, 103, 153; in transubstantiation, 213–14, 219, 224–27

action: as category, 171–73, 184

actual world, 145, 149–50. *See also* possible worlds; impossible worlds

actuality, 50, 52–54, 66, 89–96, 103–4, 145, 149, 192, 211; actuality-before-potentiality, 152–55. *See also* potentiality

actualization, 41, 53–54, 89, 93–94, 102–3, 148, 152, 226; as good, 184–85

actus essendi, 93

Aertsen, Jan, 177, 179, 185–86

agent causation, 98. *See also* causation; cause

aliquid: as transcendental, 177, 179–81

Alston, William P., 130

analogy, 38–39; of being, 39, 167; of many to one, 208; of one to another, 208–9; as applied to God, 38–39, 209

analytic: metaphysics, 74, 83; philosophy, 4, 89, 173; tradition, 25

angels, 18, 27, 118, 132–33, 206, 209

Anscombe, Elizabeth, 4; on Hume, 99–100

Anselm, St., 289

Aquinas, St. Thomas, xiv, 2, 4, 36, 39, 50, 52, 54–55, 63, 66, 69, 83, 88, 91–92, 96, 106, 109, 111, 124, 126, 132, 133–35, 158, 161, 163, 166, 171, 173, 177, 179–81, 185–90, 193, 195–97, 201–2, 204, 207, 209, 212, 214–16, 225–26, 229; on five ways (to God's existence), 106, 189–93; on God's ubiquity, 202; on kinds of predication, 207; on final cause, 106; on realism or nominalism, 133–35; on the subject matter of metaphysics, 187

Aristotle, 2–4, 9–10, 12–13, 38, 50, 59, 121, 147, 157, 163, 170–71, 177, 189 192–93, 209; on final cause, 106; on kinds of predication, 207

Aristotelian: categories, 172, 175; realism, 124, 131

Armstrong, D. M., 2, 70, 88, 122, 126

artifacts, 68–69, 102

atoms, 24, 45–46, 57–60, 63–68

Augustine, St., 41, 182, 212

Averroes, 2

Avicenna, 2

Azzouni, Jody, 78

INDEX

beauty: as transcendental, 182, 185
being: analogy of, *see* analogy; as subject of metaphysics, 12–13, 18, 187; as transcendental, 179–82; not a genus, 163, 166, 186; qua being, 12, 18, 187. *See also* existence
Berto, Francesca, 147
Bible, 188, 205, 214, 216
biblical religion, 210
biology, 9, 22, 107
Bobik, Joseph, 66
bonum: as transcendental, 177, 179–81
Brower, Jeffrey E., 89, 124, 126, 135
bundle theory of substance, 92–94, 98–102, 104, 106–7, 110

categories, 13–14, 17, 19, 87, 163, 167–77, 182, 186, 200; metaphysical, 159–61, 164, 166, 168; nine accidental, 170–71; ten Aristotelian categories, 172
causation, 16, 94, 96–110, 188, 200, 203, 209–10; agent, 98; cinematic perspective on, 97–108; counterfactual approach to, 100–101, 104; event, 98; in reproduction, 106; material, 107; snapshot perspective on, 97, 108–10
cause: substance as, 98; efficient, 105–10; final, 105–10; formal, 105–8; four causes, 108, 110; material, 105–10; moving, 105
change: accidental, *see* accidental; as actualization of potentiality, 52–54, 90–91, 97; and causality, 97–111; and identity, 25, 47–50; and Aquinas's First Way, 189–92; and time, 41–44; as an approach to essential and accidental features, 25–26, 44–45; as an objection to some theories of substance, 79–82;
in relation to parts and wholes, 89; in Transubstantiation, 224–25; substantial, *see* substance; as involving succession of forms in matter, 51–52, 54; without succession, 54–55
chemistry, 6, 8–9, 11, 63, 107
Christ. *See* Jesus Christ
Christology, xiv, 216–29
Commentary on Aristotle's Metaphysics, 163, 186
Commentary on Aristotle's Physics, 186
Compendium of Theology, 212, 229
Confessions, 41, 212
conspecificity, 123–27, 133
contingency, 141; modal, 158, 191
Cory, David, 55, 92
counterpart theory, 150–51
creatures: likeness to God, 198–204, 210–11
Crisp, Thomas M., 1, 44, 74, 76,

Davidson, Matthew, 202
Decaen, Christopher, 66
Descartes, René, xiv, 100
Devitt, Michael, 122, 130
differentia, 160–62
Disputed Questions on Truth, 179, 186
divine: ideas, 157–58, 201; omnipotence, 140; power, 158, 201; essence, 195. *See also* God
Doolan, Gregory, xiv, 201

endurantism, 43
ens: as transcendental, 177, 179–82
epistemic questions, 14
equivocal/equivocation, 38, 207–9
esse. *See* existence
essence: as part, *see* parts and wholes; distinct from existence, *see* existence; of God, *see* God; theological refinement of, 222–23. *See also*

essential; features; foundational theory of essence
essential: features, *see* features; kinds, 176
Eucharist, 17, 224, 226–27, 229
evil, 177; as privation, 183, 185; and God's causation, 203
existence: as act and as fact, 92–94; as part, *see* parts and wholes; as common to all beings, 177–82; as distinct from essence, 93–94, 181; of God, *see* God; of non-substances, 36; of possible worlds, *see* possible worlds; of universals, *see* universals. *See also* being

features: accidental, 15, 24, 26–27, 35–36, 44, 84–85, 88, 127, 59, 174, 181; essential, 15, 24, 27–28, 31–33, 44, 84–85, 88–89; necessary, 25–26, 28
Feser, Edward, 192
form, 16, 50–55, 63, 66, 89–92, 95, 103, 105–11, 196; substantial, 51, 66, 89–90, 106, 109. *See also* accidental
foundational theory of essence, 27–33, 84. *See also* features
four-dimensionalism, 42–43, 49
Frankenstein, 59, 61
free will, 14, 193, 203
Frost, Gloria, 173

Garcia, Robert K., 86
genus, 48, 160–66, 171, 176, 178, 186; being not a genus, 163–66, 173, 178, 186; predicated of a difference, 163–64
geometers, 87
God: as studied by metaphysics, 13, 17, 187–212, 231–32; as studied in light of revelation, 213–29; as Trinity, 217–18; as basis for ontological goodness, 182, 185–86; cannot do the impossible, 140–41; as creator, 17, 153, 157, 182, 203, 210, 214–16, 223; essence and existence of, 195–96, 198; proofs for existence of, 188–93; "proof" from possibility, 155–58; relation to the world, *see* relation; ubiquity of, 202–3; uniqueness of, 198–202; universal perfection of, 197–202; as unsourced source, 193–94; as spoken of through causation, negation, and eminence, *see triplex via*. *See also* divine
good: as transcendental, 177, 179–81
Gorman, Michael, 21, 31, 34–35, 173, 218
Gracia, Jorge J. E., 86, 115, 133
Grant, W. Matthews, xiii, 203

habitus: as category, 170–72
Henninger, Mark, 94
Hoffman, Joshua, 167
Hume, David, 18, 194; on causation, 98–101
Humphrey objection to counterpart theory, 151. *See also* possible worlds
Husserlian Meditations, 232

identity, 16, 47–50, 55, 58, 60, 95, 117, 181; in kind, 48–49; numerical, 48–50, 81
impossible worlds, 147. *See also* actual world; possible worlds
Incarnation, 33, 213, 216–29
indexical, 149
individuals, 20, 23, 48, 79, 113–15, 117–21, 123, 125, 131–35, 147, 149, 172, 175; as non-instantiable

instances, 115–17, 132. *See also* instance, instantiability/instantiation, particulars
individuation, 131–33
infima species, 161
instance: of *non-being*, 166; of universals, 20, 72, 78, 115–18, 123, 127, 131–32, 162, 166, 201, 209. *See also* individuals; particulars
instantiability/instantiation, 23, 115–17, 132, 148, 201. *See also* individuals, instance
integrity principle, 218–20
intentio, 179

Jacobs, Jonathan D., 154
Jaeger, Andrew, xiii
Jago, Mark, 147
Jesus Christ, 17, 33, 205, 213, 216–28

Kass, Leon, 63
Koons, Robert C., 86
Kripke, Saul A., 151
Langan, Thomas, 177
language: about God, 38–39, 202, 204–10; analogical, equivocal, metaphorical, univocal, *see* predication; everyday, *see* 130; relationship to reality, 128–30. *See also* systematically misleading language
Leibniz, Gottfried, 50
Lewis, David, 29, 43, 100–110, 148–52, 155, 181; on counterpart theory, 150; on possible worlds, 149–51
Loux, Michael J., 1, 44, 74, 76
Lowe, E. J., 26, 175–76

malum, 183. *See also* evil
Mary, 228
matter, 7, 16, 46–47, 50–55, 63, 66, 89–92, 95, 103, 105–11, 132, 196; prime, 46–47, 52, 66, 89
maximal states of affairs, 146
McMahon, William E., 173
Merricks, Trenton, 22, 69
metaphysics: analytic, *see* analytic; and God, *see* God; metaphysical categories, *see* categories; metaphysical parts, *see* parts; modal, *see* modal; nature of, 8–14, 87; of evil, 185; role in theology, 213–29; subject matter, *see* being
misleading language. *See* systematically misleading language
modal: concepts, 139–46, 150–51, 152; metaphysics, 147, 158, 187; theory of essence and accident, 26, 28, 32, 81
modern philosophy, 14, 107
modern science, 67–68
Moses, 196, 216
Mueller, Anselm, xiv

Nagel, Thomas, 37
natural law, 184
nature, 17, 33, 217–23. *See also* essence
necessity, 16, 26, 140–41, 145–46, 158
Neurath, Otto, 8
nihilism about parts and wholes, 61–62
nominalism, 8, 119–27, 133–35; 176, 201; Dr. Seuss, 121, 124–25, 127, 133–34; extreme, 125; moderate, 127, 133, 135, 176, 201
non-instantiable instances. *See* individuals
normativity, 33–35, 106
Novák, Lukáš, 27, 164

O'Connor, Timothy, 62
Oderberg, David, 185
On Being and Essence, 39, 96, 133–35

On the Mixture of the Elements, 96
On the Principles of Nature, 39, 55, 96, 111, 186
one: as transcendental, 179, 181
one over many problem, 113, 119–21, 127, 130
ontological argument, 188–89
ontology, 12
Owens, Joseph, 1, 3

participation, 199, 210
particulars, 16, 20, 71–73, 77–80, 94, 96, 111, 113–17, 121, 125, 131, 159; as instances of universals, 20, 115; bare, 78–79. *See also* individuals; instance
parts and wholes, 16, 57–96; arbitrary parts, 57–58; beings with parts must be unified into wholes, 180; essence and existence as parts, 92–94, 195; form and matter as parts, 89–92; in substantial unity, 21, 36; metaphysical parts, 70–71, 77, 225; physical parts, 57–69, 96; temporal parts, 41–44; features and substrates as parts, 69–81, 86–89; whole-dependent parts, 59, 61, 64–65, 68–69, 95; whole-independent parts, 59–60, 64–69
Pasnau, Robert, 36, 92
passion: as category, 171–73
Patton, Luke, xiv
Paul, St., 200, 211
Pawl, Timothy, xiii, 154
perception, 98–100
perdurantism. *See* four-dimensionalism
perfection, 34, 194, 197–201, 205–6, 209–11; universal, 197–98; pure, 205–6, 209
person: classical understanding, 217–18; divine, 207, 218–19, 228

phantasms, 100
philosophy: analytic, 4, 89, 173; as *ancilla theologiae* (handmaid of theology), 216, 229; focus on creation, 282; of God, 188; nature of, 5–8; of nature, 14, 16
Physics, 186, 189
physics, 7–9, 63, 192
place where: as category, 170
Plantinga, Alvin, 147–52, 157, 189
Plato, 3, 9, 16, 116, 121, 178, 207; Platonic, 116, 119, 121, 123–26, 131, 133, 147, 151; Platonism, 120
possibility, 16, 80, 142, 146, 152–58, 201
possible states of affairs, 137–39, 144, 147–48
possible worlds, 137–39; 144, 146–58, 201–2, 211; existence of 146–48; obstacle to thinking about God, 152–53. *See also* actual world; impossible worlds
potency: active, 102, 153; passive, 102, 153
potentiality, 16, 41, 46, 50–54, 66, 89–93, 96–97, 103, 107, 152–54, 191–92, 205. *See also* actuality
power: active, 102; passive, 102, 153
predication about God: analogical, 207; equivocal, 207; metaphorical, 206–7; univocal, 207. *See also* language
presence: divine, 202–3; virtual, 65–66
prime matter. *See* matter
privation, 50–53, 103, 167; evil, 183
Proslogion, 189
Pruss, Alexander, 154
Pseudo-Dionysius, 200
pseudo-limbs, 61
psychology, 9

quality: as category, 162, 170–72
quantity: as category, 170–72
quarks, 46, 58, 60, 63–64
Quine, Willard Van Orman, 4, 130

realism, 116, 120–25, 131, 133; Aristotelian, 120; extreme, 124–25, 131; immanent, 121; moderate, 121, 124–26; Platonic, 116, 121; Thomistic, 133
Red Sea, 216
reification, 54, 86, 90, 92–93, 107, 123, 231
relation: between God and creatures, 204; as category, 172–74
res, 36; as transcendental, 177, 179–80
revelation, 5, 188, 205, 211–12, 214–16, 222–23, 227–29
Rosenkrantz, Gary S., 167
Ross, James, 152–53, 157, 201–2; objections to possible worlds, 152–53
Rota, Michael, 69
Russell, Bertrand, 4, 80
Ryle, Gilbert, 29

sacrament, 50
Sanford, Jonathan J., 34, 86, 173
Scholasticism, 3
science, 7–13, 18, 22, 67–68, 75, 107, 187
Scotus, John Duns, 4, 126
Searle, John, 101
Sertillanges, A. G., 232
Sevier, Christopher Scott, 186
Shelley, Mary, 59
Simons, Peter, 78, 81–83
sin of Adam and Eve, 185
sociology, 6, 9
Socrates, 16, 27, 30–32, 54, 123, 145, 148, 150, 171, 173, 207

Sokolowski, Robert, 200, 202, 232
something: as transcendental, 177, 179–81
sophist, 99
Spade, Paul Vincent, 85
species, 20, 48, 71, 123, 127, 132, 160–65
Spencer, Mark K., 173
state of affairs: maximal, 146, 148; impossible, 147; possible, 137–39, 144, 147–48
Strawson, Peter, 4
Stump, Eleonore, 50
Suarez, Francisco, 4
Swift, Taylor, 29, 128
subject, 50, 52, 88, 174, 227
substance: as cause, 98; how related to substantial nature or essence, 84–89, 219–22, 227; substantial change, 44–47, 51–55, 59, 63, 85, 89–90, 106–7; substantial form, 66, 89, 106, 109, 111; substantial potentiality, 91
substrate view of substance, 73, 78–79
Summa Contra Gentiles, 212, 229
Summa Theologiae, 54, 106, 158, 163, 189, 195–96, 204, 212, 229
systematically misleading language, 28–31; "having matter" and "having form," 91–92; "sharing a nature," 122–23, 127; "evil exists," 183

telos, 105, 109
The School of Athens, 121
theology, 5, 9, 13, 17, 50, 207, 213–16, 221–29; Catholic, 17, 50; definition of, 215; giving rise to refinements of philosophy, 222; relation to philosophy, 5, 9, 14, 213–16, 221–29
theory of knowledge, 100

Thomism, 3, 92; Thomist, 105; Thomistic, 2–4, 26, 41, 46, 60, 66–68, 81, 84–85, 89, 92–93, 107–8, 133, 154, 158, 166, 168, 170, 175, 185–86, 202, 214
Thornton, Allison Krile, 35
three-dimensionalism, 42–44
threefold way (causation, negation, and eminence). See *triplex via*
Toner, Patrick, xiii, 21–22, 59, 66, 69
transcendent: divine transcendence, 202, 206, 223; entities, 149, 177; universals, 123–25
transcendentals, 13, 159, 176–82, 185–86; as co-extensional, 181; list in Aquinas, 177, 179
Transubstantiation, 21, 88, 213, 224–26
Trinity, 215, 217
triplex via (causation, negation, and eminence), 200, 209
trope, 72–73, 78, 81–83, 86, 127, 131, 162, 167
true: as transcendental, 177–81
truth: ontic, 180

uncaused cause, 205
unity principle, 218–21
universalism about parts and wholes, 61–62
universals, 20, 23, 71–80, 96, 111, 113–35, 147–48, 159, 175–76, 201, 211; as instantiable, 115, 117, 132, 201; existence of, 78–79, 116–34; Platonic, 147
unmoved mover, 190, 193
unsourced source, 191–94, 199–200
unum: as transcendental, 177, 179–81

van Inwagen, Peter, 14, 22, 58, 61–62, 69, 130
verum: as transcendental, 177–81
virtue, 214
virtutes, 65
virtual presence, 65–66

White, Kevin, 3, 94
whole-dependent parts. *See* parts and wholes
whole-independent parts. *See* parts and wholes
wholes. *See* parts and wholes
Williams, Donald C., 72
Wilson, Jessica, 31
Wippel, John F., 18, 166, 173, 187, 226
wisdom, 9, 10, 187, 211
Wittgenstein, Ludwig, 4, 29

Also from The Catholic University of America Press

The Metaphysical Foundations of Love: Aquinas on Participation, Unity, and Union
by Anthony T. Flood

Aquinas on Transubstantiation: The Real Presence of Christ in the Eucharist
by Reinhard Hütter

Philosophy of Being: A Reconstructive Essay in Metaphysics
by Oliva Blanchette

Intersubjective Existence: A Critical Reflection on the Theory and the Practice of Selfhood
Metaphysics as Mediating Dialogue
by Oliva Blanchette; Edited by Cathal Doherty

The Metaphysical Thought of Thomas Aquinas: From Finite Being to Uncreated Being
Metaphysical Themes in Thomas Aquinas, 3 volumes
by John F. Wippel

Form and Being: Studies in Thomistic Metaphysics
by Lawrence Dewan, OP

Aquinas on the Divine Ideas as Exemplar Causes
by Gregory T. Doolan

Summa metaphysicae ad mentem Sancti Thomae: Essays in Honor of John F. Wippel
Edited by Therese Scarpelli Cory and Gregory T. Doolan

Metaphysical Disputations I, II, and III & V
by Francisco Suárez; Translated and edited by Shane Duarte

The Discovery of Being and Thomas Aquinas: Philosophical and Theological Perspectives
Edited by Christopher M. Cullen and Franklin T. Harkins

Thomas Aquinas on the Immateriality of the Human Intellect
by Adam Wood

Being is Better Than Not Being: The Metaphysics of Goodness and Beauty in Aristotle
by Christopher V. Mirus

Being Unfolded: Edith Stein on the Meaning of Being
by Thomas Gricoski; Foreword by William Desmond

The Voiding of Being: The Doing and Undoing of Metaphysics in Modernity
The Intimate Strangeness of Being: Metaphysics after Dialectic
by William Desmond